Creative Learning, Teaching and Assessment for Arts and Humanities Higher Education

Also Available from Bloomsbury

Reflective Teaching in Higher Education, Paul Ashwin with David Boud,
Susanna Calkins, Kelly Coate, Fiona Hallett, Gregory Light, Kathy Luckett,
Jan McArthur, Iain McLaren, Monica McLean, Velda McCune,
Katarina Mårtensson and Michelle Tooher
Community-Based Transformational Learning, edited by
Christian Winterbottom, Jody S. Nicholson and F. Dan Richard
Dominant Discourses in Higher Education, Ian M. Kinchin and Karen Gravett
Changing Higher Education for a Changing World, edited by Claire Callender,
William Locke and Simon Marginson
Locating Social Justice in Higher Education Research,
edited by Jan McArthur and Paul Ashwin
Subjectivity and Social Change in Higher Education,
Liezl Dick and Marguerite Müller
Social Theory and the Politics of Higher Education, edited by Mark Murphy,
Ciaran Burke, Cristina Costa and Rille Raaper
Leadership in Higher Education from a Transrelational Perspective, Christopher
M. Branson, Maureen Marra, Margaret Franken and Dawn Penney

Creative Learning, Teaching and Assessment for Arts and Humanities Higher Education

Edited by Glenn Fosbraey

BLOOMSBURY ACADEMIC
LONDON • NEW YORK • OXFORD • NEW DELHI • SYDNEY

BLOOMSBURY ACADEMIC

Bloomsbury Publishing Plc, 50 Bedford Square, London, WC1B 3DP, UK
Bloomsbury Publishing Inc, 1359 Broadway, New York, NY 10018, USA
Bloomsbury Publishing Ireland, 29 Earlsfort Terrace, Dublin 2, D02 AY28, Ireland

BLOOMSBURY, BLOOMSBURY ACADEMIC and the Diana logo are
trademarks of Bloomsbury Publishing Plc

First published in Great Britain 2025
This paperback edition first published in 2026

A catalogue record for this book is available from the British Library.

A catalog record for this book is available from the Library of Congress.

Library of Congress Control Number: 2024943640

ISBN: HB: 978-1-3503-3149-5
            PB: 978-1-3503-3148-8
            ePDF: 978-1-3503-3150-1
            eBook: 978-1-3503-3151-8

Typeset by Integra Software Services Pvt. Ltd.

For product safety related questions contact productsafety@bloomsbury.com

To find out more about our authors and books visit www.bloomsbury.com
and sign up for our newsletters.

Contents

List of Figures   vii

List of Tables   viii

List of Contributors   ix

Introduction   *Glenn Fosbraey*   1

Part 1 Inside the Classroom: Collaboration, Environment,
Expectations and Interactivity

1   Creating the Right Learning Environment and Professional
Identity *Amanda Ross*   9

2   'Resources' and 'Sign-Makers': Teaching Identity Construction in
Academic English through Modality and Visuals *Taryn Bernard*   21

3   Students as Collaborators *Jo Trelfa, Claire Ancient, Chris O'Connor
and Josephine Morris*   35

4   The Value of Interactivity: Connections within a Community
*Louise Luff, Elaine Huber, Roel Boomsma, Janine Coupe, Emma Della
Marta, Olga Gouveros, Maria Ishkova, Anya Johnson, Benjamin Lay,
Helena Nguyen, Mesepa Paul and Eagle Zhang*   51

5   Co-Teaching Literature through the Eyes of the Blind Teacher
Chris Mounsey and Stan Booth   71

6   Using Reflection to Cultivate Creativity in Faculty Members
Jonna Myers and Amanda F. Evert   87

Part 2 Outside the Classroom: Module Design, Employability, Well-being
and Post-Uni Care

7   Revisioning and Humanizing Assessment in Teacher
Education *Katherine Bates, John Buchanan, Fiona Dobrijevich,
Sue Lane and Tracey-Ann Palmer*   97

8   Learning from Experience: Creating the Right Online Environment
for Creative Teacher Education *Tony Reeves, Nicholas Houghton and
Ray Martin*   121

9 Embedding Mental Well-being in Modules *Geoff Mills*   137
10 Combining Creativity and Employability in Higher Education
      James Wadsworth   151
11 Enhancing the Post-University Experience via Graduate
      'Writing Weekends' *Glenn Fosbraey*   167

Conclusion: Improving Inclusivity through Creative Approaches
to Learning, Teaching and Assessment *Cassie Violet Lowe*   189

Index   197

Figures

2.1	The identity of the academic writer	26
2.2	Image A (left-hand photo by Leon Wu on Unsplash) and image B (right-hand photo by Derick McKinney on Unsplash)	31
4.1	Roel and Janine recording a business case introduction video	53
4.2	Live collaboration in Microsoft Teams using the co-authoring functionality of Microsoft Excel	54
4.3	Case coach interacting with student groups	55
4.4	H5P activities	58
4.5	Olga's Pencast video	58
4.6	Our team's FACES approach receives its own feedback via the Business School's top teaching award	60
4.7	Louise shares her day in a what's coming up video	63
4.8	Our teaching team photo	64
4.9	A scene from Emma's tutorial	64
4.10	Week 2 Tutorial Padlet	65
7.1	The sixteen Habits of Mind (Images by Dobrijevech, 2022)	99
7.2	HoMs Identified in subject coordinated and taught by Sue Lane	103
7.3	HoMs Identified in subject developed and taught by Dobrijevech	104
7.4	Preparatory drawing exercises and final complex pieces	105
7.5	HoMs Identified in subject developed and taught by Katherine Bates	106
7.6	Multimodal productions (included with permission) in the course designed and taught by Katherine Bates	108
7.7	HoMs Identified in subject developed and taught by John Buchanan	109
7.8	Introduction to example assessment response devised by John Buchanan	109
7.9	Opening lines of example assessment response devised by John Buchanan	110
7.10	HoMs Identified in subject developed and taught by Tracey-Ann Palmer	111
7.11	Emergent framework	116
10.1	A conceptual model of creativity in the employment context	154
10.2	Sequencing of creative thought processing	155

Tables

1.1	Different learning environments for the arts and humanities	12
1.2	Creative learning environments in education (adapted from Davies et al., 2012)	13
1.3	Practical activities for creating the right environment	16
4.1	Our FACES of feedback	61
4.2	A closer look at ongoing behavioural feedback	62
7.1	Mapping across assessment	112
10.1	Plurality of creativity by stakeholder grouping	157
10.2	Plurality of creativity by subject domain	157

Contributors

Claire Ancient is Senior Lecturer in Computer Science in the Department of Digital Technologies at the University of Winchester, UK, having joined the University in 2018. Claire obtained her Fellowship of the Higher Education Academy in December 2017 and completed a Masters in Learning and Teaching in Higher Education in 2023. Claire is interested in researching how she can use technology-enhanced learning to support emancipatory and inclusive education. She is always looking for ways to develop her teaching practice to be more inclusive, with the aim of supporting people to reach their full potential both in their studies and in their future careers.

Katherine Bates is Honorary Fellow at The University of Technology, Sydney, Australia. Katherine has extensive experience coordinating, designing and teaching across a range of English capstone, literacy specializations and educational assessment. Her contributions were acknowledged as a recipient of the 2021 Inaugural FASS Teaching and Learning Award UTS. Her work in tertiary education is informed by extensive teaching experience in elementary and secondary education, various educational leadership roles across systems, and senior education roles regarding national curriculum and assessment. Her research interests include quality teaching, teacher professional learning, and transdisciplinary literacy learning through experiential environmental education.

Taryn Bernard is Senior Lecturer at Stellenbosch University in South Africa and she coordinates the Extended Curriculum Programme (ECP) in the Faculty of Arts and Social Sciences at Stellenbosch University. Taryn was awarded a PhD in applied linguistics in 2015 and she has since developed her expertise in methods of critical applied linguistics such as systemic functional linguistics (SFL) and critical discourse analysis (CDA). These methods of approaching language and textual analysis have not only influenced her approach to research but also her approach to teaching academic English to a culturally and linguistically diverse group of students.

Roel Boomsma is a Senior Lecturer in Accounting at the University of Sydney. His research focuses on the accountability of non-governmental organizations and technological and regulatory change in the accounting profession. His work has been published in leading international journals. Roel's international teaching experience includes the design and delivery of courses in financial accounting, sustainability accounting, accountability & ethics, and qualitative research methods.

Stan Booth is Associate Lecturer in English literature at the University of Winchester, UK. His work explores the less obvious aspects of impairment primarily in the eighteenth century. His other research areas include other world fictions, ethics and bioethics. He is the co-editor of *The Variable Body in History* and a co-parent of two beautiful rescue dogs, May and June.

John Buchanan is Honorary Industry Fellow at the University of Technology Sydney, Australia, where he has taught history and geography method for twenty years. His research interests include teacher quality, recruitment and retention, and social and environmental education, particularly intercultural education. His recent publications include Varadharajan, M. and Buchanan, J. *The Contributions of Career-change Teachers* (2021) and Buchanan, J. *Challenging the Deprofessionalisation of Teachers and Teaching: Claiming and Acclaiming the Teaching Profession* (2020).

Janine Coupe is an Education Focused Senior Lecturer in Accounting at the University of Sydney. Prior to joining academia, she worked for leading Australian and global organizations. Janine is a fellow of the Higher Education Academy and a member of Chartered Accountants Australia and New Zealand. Janine has been the recipient of several awards for her outstanding dedication to supporting and enhancing the student learning experience.

Emma Della Marta is as an assessment specialist in the CA Program for Chartered Accountants Australia and New Zealand (CA ANZ). She has a Masters of Higher Education and is a Fellow of CA ANZ. Emma is an experienced tutor and lecturer in the field of financial reporting with wide commercial experience gained in professional practice and commercial roles prior to becoming an educator.

Fiona Dobrijevich is a practising artist, lecturer and long-time ocean swimmer. Her art practice investigates the relationships between the feminine and the oceanic, the ecological and cultural, the geological and the biological. It refers to her practice of ocean swimming and her sensory bodily encounters with the sea.

Her practice has informed her secondary teaching and lecturing in Creative Arts at the University of Technology Sydney for nearly forty years. Her most recent works can be found at: https://www.fionadob.com/about.

Amanda Faith Evert is a professor who is all heart and bad hair. She is an International ACBSP Teaching Excellence award recipient, Bernhardt Scholar, PTK Distinguished College Administrator, NISOD Master Presenter, Hot Sauce Lover and Coke Zero Addict. She is skilled in experiential teaching/learning methods, marketing, management, motivational speaking, grant writing and accreditation. According to a recent assessment her strengths are ideation, futuristic, strategic, maximizer and competition. Dr Evert loves empowering the people around her to explore their creativity and colour outside the lines.

Glenn Fosbraey is Associate Dean of Humanities and Social Sciences at the University of Winchester, UK, where he has lectured since 2009. Selected publications include *Reading Eminem* (2022), *Exploring Hatred in Popular Music* (2022), *Composing Song Lyrics: Creative and Critical Approaches* (2019) and *Coastal Environments in Popular Song* (2022). Glenn won a national Green Gown Award for Student Engagement in 2017 and has also received a number of Learning and Teaching prizes. He became Senior Fellow of the Higher Education Academy in 2016.

Olga Gouveros is an Education Focused Associate Lecturer in Accounting at the University of Sydney. Before entering education, she worked for leading Australian consulting firms. Olga is a fellow of the Higher Education Academy and a member of Chartered Accountants Australia and New Zealand. Olga has been the co-ordinator of undergraduate core units for several years and is passionate about enhancing the student learning experience.

Nicholas Houghton is an artist based in London and Folkestone, England. His work uses a variety of media, the most common being lens-based accompanied by text, through which he tells stories. He has led teaching and learning programmes for higher education institutions in the UK and internationally and has previously taught at the University of the Arts London, University of Leeds, Cleveland College of Art and Design, Ravensbourne, Université de Quebec and Nova Scotia College of Art and Design. Nicholas has a PhD in assessment practice, and as Director of Research at Ding Learning he supports research into learning design and teaches people how to develop inclusive curricula.

Elaine Huber is Academic Director of the Business Co-design team at the University of Sydney Business School, Australia, who provide academic support to faculty staff wishing to integrate learning technologies into their teaching. She is Director of the Connected Learning at Scale project which guides her current research activities of learning and teaching at scale. Elaine has a PhD in educational evaluation and her other research interests include design and development of blended professional development programs.

Maria Ishkova is a Lecturer in Work and Organizational Studies at the University of Sydney Business School. Maria enjoyed an extended successful career and leadership roles in communication across a variety of industries and advocacy groups. As an education-focused academic she has fine-tuned her multi-award-winning students-as-partners approach and engages in educational research to enhance teaching and learning experience and improve graduates' employability.

Anya Johnson is Associate Professor and Head of Discipline in Work and Organizational Studies at the University of Sydney Business School. Anya is co-director of the Body, Heart and Mind in Business Research Group. She is an Associate Editor of Group and Organization Management journal and has published in leading journals such as the Academy of Management journal on the topic of teams and work design, mental health and wellbeing in the workplace.

Sue Lane works as Music Education Consultant with schools and music organizations, including the Sydney Symphony Orchestra and Musica Viva. She previously coordinated and lectured in Creative Arts Education at the University of Technology Sydney, Australia, focusing on music, movement and dance. Her doctoral thesis is titled, '"We need to put the Arts on the map!" – Exploring the perspectives of primary educators about the teaching of the Arts in Australian primary schools'. Her research continues to investigate the impacts of Music Residency Programs in Sydney and Adelaide.

Benjamin Lay is a tutor in the Accounting discipline at The University of Sydney. Ben was awarded his Doctor of Philosophy at The University of Sydney in 2021. Ben is interested in developing methods of increasing student engagement and understanding, while his research interests include executive remuneration and financial accounting.

Cassie Violet Lowe is Senior Teaching Associate at the University of Cambridge, UK, where she teaches on the Postgraduate Certificate in Teaching and Learning. In the scholarship of teaching and learning, Cassie's research interests are student engagement, students as partners, assessment and curriculum development. Cassie also continues to research and publish in the discipline for which she received her doctorate. In this field Cassie focuses on modern literature, art and visual culture, psychoanalytic theory and aesthetic educational approaches.

Louise Luff is Education Focused Lecturer at the University of Sydney, Australia. Louise has worked in senior professional and commercial financial reporting roles and is a financial reporting specialist. She has a Master of Education, is Fellow of the Higher Education Academy, Member of Chartered Accountants Australia and New Zealand (CA ANZ) and has co-authored several financial reporting textbooks and publications for CA ANZ. Louise's award-winning teaching focuses on enhancing the student experience and business world connection.

Ray Martin is a dyslexia tutor, mainly supporting art and music students. Her expertise in neurodiversity enables her to identify and remove barriers to learning for students with complex learning needs. Ray teaches on postgraduate courses specializing in creative teaching and has published articles on NLP, supporting students, mindfulness and transitioning into university for Autistic Spectrum students. As Inclusivity and Diversity Lead for Ding Learning, Ray promotes the transformative potential of inclusive learning design and teaches people how to develop inclusive and accessible learning experiences.

Geoff Mills has taught across a range of contexts in further and higher education and currently works as a freelance tutor, workshop leader, and course designer in performance and creative writing. As a writer and journalist, he draws on a PGCE in adult education (London), a doctorate in English and Creative Writing teaching methods (Birmingham), and a long-standing research interest in Anglo-American campus culture and literature. Campus-related articles have appeared in *The Guardian*, THES, a BBC exhibition and the Literary Review. Since the Covid-19 pandemic, he has become a vigorous campaigner for well-being issues in higher education.

Josephine Morris is MSc in Rehab, PGDiP/PGCE, BSc, MCSP, PTRP, MA LTHE, and Prof. Doctorate in Education Candidate qualified in 1998 with BSc Hons in Physiotherapy with continuous clinical experience in general rehabilitation. Alongside working full-time as Senior Lecturer at the University of Winchester, UK, she continues to practise her clinical works at Salisbury District Hospital and The Harbour Hospital (CHG Private). She completed her MSc in Rehabilitation at St George's University in London undertaking mixed-method research in healthcare. She continues to progress in her postgraduate studies in higher education and completed PGCE, PGDiP and MA in Learning and Teaching in Higher Education. She is aiming to complete her Professional Doctorate in Education in the next three years with a special interest in transformational education and qualitative studies.

Chris Mounsey worked for several years in theatre before an accident and four months of immobility made reading the only possible occupation, which in turn led to an academic career. Degrees in Philosophy, Comparative Literature and English from the University of Warwick, UK, followed, and a doctorate on William Blake founded an interest in the literature of the eighteenth century. He now teaches at the University of Winchester and is the author of *Christopher Smart: Clown of God* (2001), *Being the Body of Christ* (2012) and *Sight Correction* (2019). He has also edited *Presenting Gender* (2001), *Queer People* (2007), *The Idea of Disability in the Eighteenth Century* (2014), *Developments in the Histories of Sexualities* (2015), *The Variable Body in History* (2016) and *Bodies of Information* (2020).

Jonna Myers is a speaker, author and international award-winning faculty member at Southwestern Oklahoma State University in Weatherford, Oklahoma, USA. Her work centres around creativity, reflection and faculty development as well as assessment and accreditation efforts. She brings a unique voice to an important conversation in the educational space using humour and guided introspection. Ultimately, Myers is passionate about helping colleges and universities cultivate Happy Professors and she is excited for the future of higher education.

Helena Nguyen is Associate Professor in Work and Organizational Studies and Academic Director (Student Development) at University of Sydney. Helena is also co-director of the Body, Heart and Mind in Business Research Group. She is an Associate Editor of the Australian Journal of Management and has published in leading journals on the topic of emotions at work, well-being, safety and performance at work.

Chris O'Connor is an educator at the University of Southampton (WSA), UK, in web technologies and digital design, and is dedicated to supporting educational practices for both undergraduate and postgraduate students. Their research is focused on using online technologies to expand access to higher education opportunities within the creative arts sector for underrepresented groups. Actively exploring virtual reality (VR), mixed reality (MR) and extended reality (XR) technologies aims to contribute to enhancing research, teaching and accessibility in higher education. These immersive technologies serve as tools to foster an enriched educational experience, aligning with a commitment to creating a more inclusive and innovative learning environment.

Tracey-Ann Palmer is Subject Coordinator and Lecturer in Initial Teacher Education at the University of Technology Sydney, Australia. Tracey-Ann Palmer teaches science, adolescent educational psychology and curriculum integration to primary and secondary pre-service teachers. Her research interests focus on encouraging school students to engage with science at school and to choose science for post-compulsory study. Her paper on the factors that students consider when selecting subjects is among the most highly cited in this field.

Mesepa Paul is an Associate Lecturer in the Discipline of Work and Organizational Studies at the University of Sydney Business School. She has a Master of Development Studies (International Development) and Bachelor of Criminology and Criminal Justice. Prior to commencing her academic career, Mesepa has worked in diverse leadership roles in corporate telecommunications industry, community volunteering sector, not-for-profit and government organizations.

Tony Reeves is Managing Director of Ding Learning, a creative learning design agency. Through his work at Ding, Tony works with global businesses and universities to design and develop courses, programmes and learning experiences. He is the co-founder of the Centre for Learning Design and works to promote the transformative potential of learning design in India and South Asia. Tony is also editor of the *Journal for Useful Investigations in Creative Education*, and supports research into creative teaching and learning design. He has a PhD in Technology Enhanced Learning, is a self-confessed learning outcomes nerd and would love to open a jazz club.

Amanda Ross originally trained as a Special Educational Needs teacher in the post 16, Further Education and Skills sector. Amanda moved into teacher education on completion of her Masters in Learning and Teaching in 2011 and is currently Programme Leader for Teacher Education, HE and Professional education at Staffordshire University, UK. Amanda has an interest in professional teacher identity development, mentoring and incidental learning and has recently authored a book on the topic of professional identity development through incidental learning (2021).

Jo Trelfa qualified in the 1980s as a youth and community worker, then worked in that sector for twelve years before taking her deep-rooted practice in social justice, agency and community-building into teaching in higher education in 1999. As Senior Lecturer she led the development of new programmes in the social sciences and then in 2017 moved specifically into education development, leadership and management, focusing on student engagement and the quality of teaching. She is Academic Practice and Enhancement Manager at Queen Mary University London, UK, with particular responsibility for assessment and feedback practices and research expertise in reflection-in-practice.

James Wadworth is currently Head of Quality Improvement at The Lincoln College Group, UK, and has worked in the Higher and Further Education sectors for over twenty-four years. James has a keen interest in learning and teaching, and has supported many students as a lecturer, course leader, teacher trainer and educational developer over more than two decades. Initially lecturing in sports science after completing a Masters' degree and teacher training, James found a passion for educational development and became fascinated with creativity in education, successfully completing a PhD related to creativity in 2021. James is also Fellow of the Higher Education Academy.

Eagle Zhang is a Senior Lecturer in the Accounting Discipline of the University of Sydney. His specialization is in financial accounting and critical accounting research. He has been teaching at both undergraduate and postgraduate levels for financial accounting, management accounting, auditing and accounting theory subjects. His research, teaching and consulting interests revolve around the role of accounting in sustaining dominant socio-political power in the context of globalized capitalism.

Introduction

Glenn Fosbraey

To engage in the scholarship of teaching and
learning requires academic teachers to become learners.

(Brew, 2006: 115)

I teach first and foremost because I enjoy it. I am in this profession because I *want* to be in this profession. Those hours spent in a classroom, away from e-mails, spreadsheets, admin and budgets are the only time when all outside problems fall away and I focus entirely on what's happening there and then. These hours of clarity, no matter what is happening in my life, are vital to me, and I now draw my energy from them. Teaching is my life, and my life is teaching. I wrote in a 2019 paper for the Staff and Educational Development Association that '[w]henever I start planning a lesson, my immediate thoughts turn to an image of myself in the classroom – younger, fitter, more hair, waiting for the class to begin' (Fosbraey, 2018: 13). It's a statement tinged with my customary self-deprecation and a smattering of the tongue-in-cheek, but overall, it's true: whatever I plan to unleash in front of a group of students when I step into that class must first be engaging and entertaining to *me*. After all, if I don't find my own content interesting, why should anyone else? Angela Brew posits that 'when people put themselves in the position of being learners or teachers, they bring all their past experiences of being both a learner or a teacher' (Brew, 2006: 115). Of course, lesson planning is far more nuanced than simply thinking about what we wanted at that age and then pitching it accordingly. For a start, the class isn't filled with clones of my 18–21-year-old self, so what works for me may not work for everyone. There's also the unavoidable fact that it's not 2002 anymore, and the intervening twenty-one years have led to a completely different landscape in what students expect and want, and how students *are*.

When I was at university, 'chalk and talk' still reigned supreme, and with tuition fees still less than £1,000 per year, a number of us (and yes, regrettably, this includes me) didn't mind sitting at the back, hangover, disengaged and counting the seconds until something more interesting came along. Now, as a 2022 *The Guardian* article notes, 26 per cent or young people aged 16–24 are fully teetotal (Ellen, 2022), annual tuition fees, as we all know, often exceed £9,000, and students, in my experience, are significantly more engaged with what they're getting out of their lessons rather than simply concentrating on their social lives out*side* their lessons. Again, there is a much more nuanced and complex discussion here, but the general point is clear: students in 2023 are not going to be the same as we were when *we* were students. And I'm not just talking about those of us who have been in higher education (HE) for a lengthy period of time; even early-career academics would be foolish to assume that the class they are now teaching would have the same needs, ambitions and interests they themselves had a handful of years ago. 'While student engagement is obviously positive for university culture, maybe the main argument for working with student engagement should be that it leads to improved learning outcomes of the students. Arguments have been put forward that engaged students find their learning personally meaningful, they believe the learning tasks are challenging, they find that accomplishing learning tasks is worthy of their time, and they focus on improving their performance and keep on working even when they encounter difficulties' (Bartholomew et al., 2013: 1).

So, what does all this mean for us as educators in HE? For me, it means that we must hang on to that love of what we're teaching, so we must still please ourselves (our first and often worst critic) with our lesson content. But it also means that we need to keep evolving as people and as educators; we must listen to our students, observe our peers – both older and younger than us – and learn from their different styles; we must accept that each class will have a different dynamic with different personalities and be willing and able to be flexible. We must also keep sharing our experiences and our ideas, and never stop trying to innovate – not just for the students' sakes, but for our own, too. Change for change's sake is dangerous, but so is obstinately standing still and refusing to adapt simply because 'this is what we've always done'.

The contemporary university is a contested terrain of strategic needs, as students, teachers and institutions struggle to find their ways through the often-competing needs of national narratives of extended participation, economic stability of institutions and individuals, institutional vision, regulatory constraints and methodological straightjackets. Indeed, there have been a lot of negative words written about HE in recent years, and it's unlikely this trend will change any time soon. Sage's *Encyclopedia of Higher Education* suggests that the sector is in a state of 'ferment', Branch and Christiansen's *The Marketisation of Higher Education* argues that HE has (as we may have gathered from the title) been marketized and Wankel and Ambrose's *Higher Education's Road to Relevance* questioning its existence at all. Others are slightly more neutral in their opinions, with Altbach and McGill Peterson observing that HE 'has been one of the "growth industries" of the twenty-first Century [... with] the existence of high quality and accessible institutions of higher education in any country one of the key predicators of national progress' (Altbach and McGill Peterson, 2007: xii) and Biggs and Tang pointing to 'dramatic changes in the nature of higher education [...] bringing much greater diversity in the student population' (Biggs and Tang, 2011: 3). Embracing such diversity, in terms of both student background and preferred learning styles, is one of many challenges the modern lecturer faces, and they need to be inclusive, adaptable and creative in their thinking if they are to provide a learning experience which allows individuals to flourish and reach their potential. HE should be a place for students to innovate, create and expand their horizons, and in order to create an environment which allows for all these things, tutors need to be able and willing to do the same.

We're not here to 'fix' any of the problems facing the HE sector, nor are we here with any particular political message. This book, which you will hopefully find practical, informative and, most importantly, *readable*, will explore how a diverse range of tutors working in the arts and humanities disciplines have succeeded in 'thinking outside the box' with their teaching, module design and extracurricular activities without losing sight of necessary academic rigour. The book will include (among other things) discussion of experimental learning environments, student and lecturer collaborations, how we can prepare students for the world beyond university with employability and transferable skills, making assessments creative and imaginative, and how we can embed mental well-being techniques into curricula.

Split into two parts which differentiate between Part 1's 'Inside the Classroom' and its ruminations on collaboration, environment, expectations and interactivity, and Part 2's 'Outside the Classroom' which focuses on module design, employability, well-being and post-Uni care, this book will offer discussions, transferable case studies and practical exemplifications on how to navigate and succeed in the sometimes problematic, sometimes joyous terrain of HE, offering solutions to the contextual pushes and pulls of learning and teaching with a focus on enabling a multiplicity processes of learning styles and creative individual expressions, dealing with the need to expand our too often campus and text bound, mono cultural, theory-driven practices.

According to Pokorny, 'the learning environment ... recognises the learners as its core participants, encourages their active engagement and develops in them an understanding of their activity as learners' (Pokorny et al., 2016: 48) and in Part 1, Chapter 1 Amanda Ross examines how different learning environments can be set up and subsequently managed in order to provide creative and dynamic engagement for both the lecturer and the learners. As she points out, '[T]he pandemic has provided an opportunity for educators across the sector to identify good practice that can be maintained moving forwards. This includes a systematically planned approach to classroom practice, incorporating a blended model and innovative approaches.'

In Chapter 2, via a case study on a second-year module for multilingual humanities and social science students at Stellenbosch University, Taryn Bernard seeks to establish why 'identity' should be an anchoring or prominent feature of any course designed to teach an academic variety of a language and academic literacy practices and examines how 'digital technology has radically transformed literacy practices, even within the university system'.

Elkington observes that 'emerging student-centred approaches [in HE] ... emphasize students as "partners", as "producers", as well as independent enquirers, creative thinkers, team workers, self-managers and reflective learners' (Elkington, 2014: 176) and Jo Trelfa, Claire Ancient, Chris O'Connor and Josephine Morris examine collaborations between students and lecturers in Chapter 3, where they examine a practical framework to support implementation of student-as-producer projects, influenced by problem-based learning.

Louisa Luff, Elaine Huber et al. examine the value of interactivity through a collection of vignettes from the Sydney University Business School's Co Design Research Group community in Chapter 4, reflecting upon how their experimental and innovative TEL designs can help the individual, the institution and the sector to continually improve their practice and their educational offerings.

Anwar et al. observe that co-teaching 'is very useful and fruitful for teachers [... giving] them chances to get involved in more philosophical discussions and to learn more about experiences and ways of teaching one to another ...' (Anwar et al., 2021: 329) and in Chapter 5, Stan Booth and Chris Mounsey, often described as the 'Ant and Dec' of The University of Winchester, re-examine the dynamics of co-teaching in their English Literature classes.

In Chapter 6 Jonna Myers and Amanda Evert say that 'it is impossible to fully explore the roles of creativity in higher education without taking an in-depth look at faculty members and the many ways that they promote, discuss, and model creativity'. This chapter discusses the roles professional services staff can play in developing and fostering an atmosphere of collegial creativity.

Neary states that 'learning which is rooted in our doing and our experience … learning to make sound judgements is one of the major tasks for professional education: or of living in modern society … ' (Neary, 2002: 85) and Part 2 begins with Chapter 7 and Katherine Bates, John Buchanan, Fiona Dobrijevich, Sue Lane and Tracey-Ann Palmer looking at authentic learning through assessment. Here they examine why the creativity that teachers customarily apply to their teaching/learning experiences does not routinely transfer to assessment practices before going on to suggest ways this can be remedied.

In Chapter 8, Nicholas Houghton, Ray Martin and Tony Reeves delve into course design, with the process presenting a prime opportunity to overhaul the in-class experience, expounding the benefits of team-based learning activities, and the importance of intercultural awareness through language, resources and learning experiences.

Baik et al. point to course design as one of the key ways to improve student well-being (Baik et al., 2019: 1) and Geoff Mills shares his experience of infusing curricula with mental well-being pedagogy in Chapter 9, arguing that a response strategy to the mental health crises can be addressed with a built-in programme designed to promote mental well-being across the student population as a whole.

In their 2019 paper 'Graduate Employability', Okolie et al. say that 'employability is not just about getting a job [… but] developing critical, reflective abilities, with a view to empowering and enhancing the learner' (Okolie et al., 2019: 623). James Wadworth begins the first of two chapters which focus on post-university care, with his discussion of Employability in Chapter 10 illustrating what HE institutions can do to arm graduates with those skills.

Finally, in Chapter 11, I speak about the value of postgraduate socialization through the implementation of bespoke writing weekends. This chapter presents a case study of the most recent event and takes a broader look at how universities can stay in touch with and assist their graduates with alumni groups and events after they have finished their studies.

Paul and Elder observe that criticality and creativity are mutually beneficial, and that 'when engaged in high-quality thought, the mind must simultaneously produce and assess, both generate and judge the products it fabricates' (Paul and Elder, 2019: 5). This book is a labour of love from a group of HE educators, separated by their geography, but united in their desire to enhance the student experience through imaginative and creative education that never loses sight of the criticality that is necessary for a complete and rigorous HE student experience.

Sources

Altbach, P.G. and Peterson, M. (eds.) (2007). *Higher Education in the New Century*. Rotterdam: Sense Publishers.

Amey, M.J. and David, M.E. (2020). *The SAGE*. California: Sage.

Anwar, K., Asari, S., Husniah, R. and Asmara, C.H. (2021). 'Students' perceptions of collaborative team teaching and student achievement motivation', *International Journal of Instruction January 2021*, 14 (1): 244–326.

Baik, C., Larcombe, W. and Brooker, A. (2019). 'How universities can enhance student mental wellbeing: The student perspective', *Higher Education Research & Development*, 38 (4): 674–87.

Bartholomew, P., Brand, S. Millard, L. and Nygaard, C. (2013). *Student Engagement: Identity, Motivation, and Community*. Faringdon: Libri Publishing.

Biggs, J. and Tang, C. (2011). *Teaching for Quality Learning at University*. 4th ed. Maidenhead: Open University Press.

Brew, A. (2006). *Research and Teaching: Beyond the Divide*. Basingstoke: Palgrave Macmillan.

Elkington, S. (2014). 'Academic engagement: Engaging who and to what end?', in C. Bryson (ed.), *Understanding and Developing Student Engagement*. Oxon: Routledge: 176–90.

Ellen, B. (2022). 'Gen Z for zero tolerance: Why British youth are turning off booze'. https://www.theguardian.com/society/2022/jul/24/gen-z-for-zero-tolerance-why-british-youth-are-turning-off-booze (accessed 18 June 2023).

Fosbraey, G. (2018). 'Engagement, partnership, and collaboration in Higher Education', *Staff and Educational Development Association Magazine Educational Developments Issue*, 19 (4): 13–15.

Neary, M. (2002). *Curriculum Studies in Post-compulsory and Adult Education*. Cheltenham: Nelson Thornes.

Okolie, U.C., Nwosu, H.E. and Mlanga, S. (2019). 'Graduate employability: How the higher education institutions can meet the demand of the labour market', *Higher Education, Skills and Work-based Learning*, 9 (4): 620–36.

Paul, R. and Elder, L. (2019). *The Nature and Functions of Critical & Creative Thinking*. Santa Barbara: Foundation for Critical Thinking.

Pokorny, H. and Warren, D. (eds.) (2016). *Enhancing Teaching Practice in Higher Education*. London: Sage.

Race, P. (ed.) (2001). 2000 *Tips for Lecturers*. London: Kogan Page.

Part One

Inside the Classroom: Collaboration, Environment, Expectations and Interactivity

Creating the Right Learning Environment and Professional Identity

Amanda Ross

Introduction

The word 'creativity' conjures up many ideas, which revolve all too often around artistic practice. For far too long, creativity has been defined in terms related to the arts, having been somewhat 'hi-jacked' by this sector (Parrish, 2012). Labels such as artistic creativity can serve as a limiting factor for individuals who avoid trying to 'be creative' because of the pre-conceived idea of their own artistic ability. Creativity is much more than solely about artistic creativity. According to the manifesto compiled by Kleiman, creativity and imagination 'enable you to sustain yourself through the challenges and opportunities you will encounter throughout your life' (2019).

When applying the concept of creativity to education, it is important to view it in a wider sense and the more general meaning which revolves around problem-solving, innovation and ingenuity. According to Philip (2015), theorists have described the processes of creativity as 'iterative and dynamic' (p. 14). Sternberg, Kaufman and Pretz (2002) define creativity as 'the ability to produce work that is novel (i.e. original, unexpected), high in quality, and appropriate (i.e. useful, meets task constraints)' (p. 1). Sternberg (2007) also argues that 'creative people are creative largely not by any particular inborn trait, but rather, because of an attitude toward life: they habitually respond to problems in fresh and novel ways, rather than allowing themselves to respond mindlessly and automatically' (p. 3).

By viewing creativity from this stance, it provides equity of opportunity as more people begin to feel able to engage with the creative process, regardless of artistic talent. Through imaginative activities and contexts, learning can be both enriching and a stimulating experience for both learners and lecturers alike (Wright, 2019). It is from this viewpoint that this chapter is written with a particular focus on the professional identity of the lecturer, in relation to the impact this has on the learning environment. Different learning environments found within the HE sector and how these can be set up and subsequently managed, in order to provide creative and dynamic engagement, will also be explored.

This chapter will be of interest to anyone who is responsible for delivering learning within a HE environment and has a particular focus for those working within the Arts and Humanities. The challenges facing this sector are explored, and the way technology impacts on teaching and learning are key areas which will be discussed. Some particular issues that face the Arts and Humanities are addressed throughout the key topics in this chapter, with an emphasis on the development of identity, reflective approaches to teaching and incidental learning. This chapter provides some practical examples that can be used to encourage creativity for both the learner and the teacher.

The changing face of the higher education (HE) learning environment

The HE sector has historically become reliant on established and somewhat stagnant pedagogical approaches. In recent years the sector has come under scrutiny and pressure to perform against quality measures, driven through the Teaching Excellence and Student Outcomes Framework agenda (Gov, 2016) and regulation of the sector by the Office For Students (2018). Although these measures open up a conversation about challenging practice, the recent pandemic forced the situation, as rapid change was needed. This provided an opportunity for the sector to adapt, challenge convention and try innovative approaches to pedagogical practice (Carolan, 2020).

This swift move to delivery of learning online, termed as 'emergency remote teaching' by Hodges et al. (2020), occurred with little time to plan different approaches in advance. This was unavoidable, but in the aftermath of Covid-19 and as education returns to traditional conventions with the lifting of restrictions, there has been a call for a 'commitment to experiential education, instead of the staid, tired and valueless traditional approaches to higher education' (Sutton and Bitencourt Jorge, 2020: 124).

Online learning is not a new concept, and there has been a drive towards embedding online learning to improve creativity and engagement for the past twenty years (Rossman, 1999; Stott and Mozer, 2016). However, the pandemic provided an opportunity for educators across the sector to identify good practices that can be maintained moving forward. This includes a systematically planned approach to classroom practice, incorporating a blended model and innovative approaches (Morin, 2020; Pokhrel and Chhetri, 2021).

As the way in which knowledge can be produced and shared, many former barriers begin to disappear, as boundaries between online and offline, on-campus and asynchronous learning are blurred. Within HE, content creation, communication and dissemination become possible through the use of technology, not seen before to this extent, enabling a more creative approach to pedagogy and learning environments. This approach can prove challenging within the more practical aspects of delivering learning within the arts and humanities; however, this does not mean that these subject areas do not benefit from this, as tutorials and portfolio-building sessions move online which can have a positive impact on the engagement of learners.

The impact of professional identity on the learning environment

Creating the right learning environment is dependent upon several things. Major considerations are the professional identity of the lecturer, the professional culture of the team and organization where they work. Due to the unpredictable nature of teaching, it is critical for lecturers to develop a strong professional identity alongside their specialist knowledge, which will enable them to act with autonomy and to make their own judgements (Sachs, 2005).

Rogers and Scott (2008) further develop this idea by arguing that lecturers should work towards an awareness of their identity and the relationships, emotions and contexts that shape them. This provides the opportunity for lecturers to (re)claim the authority of their own voice and make a psychological shift in how they think about themselves in their role. Awareness and voice represent the 'contested' place where the normative demands of the external encounter the internal meaning-making and desires of the teacher (p. 739).

According to Jarvis (2010), new experiences are interpreted in relation to past experiences and in a personal way, leading to 'a greater understanding of how we, as individuals, can behave and learn' (p. 7). Philip (2015) argues that employees need sufficient room to be creative and imaginative, but also sufficient restrictions to enable process and results. 'Creativity emerges where management is not about command and control, but rather where diversity is encouraged, and an "emergent" paradigm is followed and there is sufficient organisational support and reward for employees to remain motivated to take risks' (p. 35).

Individuals need to be able to move between groups and communities, operating in these networks and spaces throughout the development of the task or process, as required (Lave and Wenger, 2008). This results in self-managing teams of people, or students working together towards a collective creative outcome, for a period of time. It is within this type of culture that lecturers have the confidence to create the right learning environment for the demographic of their learners and in context of their subject specialism. The next section of this chapter will consider and present different key factors which need to be considered when planning for both online and more traditional learning environments.

Different learning environments in the HE context

A number of different types of learning environments exist for the Arts and Humanities within the HE sector and it is important to acknowledge this (Table 1.1). This is not a definitive list.

When creating the right learning environment, it is important to reflect on the different types of environments where learning is delivered within these subject areas and contexts.

Table 1.1 Different learning environments for the arts and humanities

Different learning environments within the HE sector
Traditional classroom space (seating for up to 30 learners)
Formal lecture theatre (seating up to 200 learners)
Practical workshops (individual spaces within a large area)
Learning online (through a platform such as MS Teams or Zoom). This includes Virtual Learning Environments (such as Blackboard or Moodle)
Informal learning spaces (such as café's, field trips or social learning zones)
Outside space (this is suitable for up to 15 students and is based on 'walking lectures')
External placements (particularly used for professional programmes)

Key factors for creative learning environments

In order for learners to become immersed within the learning, an enabling environment needs to be developed and fostered, built on mutual respect and free from expectations, or time restraints. This allows for flexibility, freedom and open-ended possibility. This flexibility enables the learning to take on new directions in an informal and less-structured manner. This level of spontaneity can also foster opportunities for incidental learning through the engagement of disjuncture as it occurs (Turner, 2021).

Davies et al. (2012) argue that the way the physical space is set up and utilized can directly impact upon how creative learners are when working within the space. It is important to ensure that there is 'a general sense of openness and spaciousness' and that learners are encouraged to make 'use of general areas to support the growth of ideas' (p. 84). They argue that learners should be given some control over their learning and supported to develop these independent skills. It is important that a balance is sought between students having freedom to explore and a structured approach to the sessions. A creative approach should 'lead teachers away from planning a lesson and towards searching for systems that organise and prepare adults and children to think together' (Gandini et al., 2005). This is particularly relevant and important for learners and lecturers within the Arts and Humanities due to the practical, creative process of these subjects.

Davies et al. (2012) present eight key factors needed when creating innovative learning environments (Table 1.2).

Table 1.2 Creative learning environments in education (adapted from Davies et al., 2012)

1.	Respectful relationships
2.	Peer collaboration
3.	Awareness of learner needs
4.	Availability of appropriate materials and engaging resources
5.	Playful/games-based approach with learner autonomy
6.	Working outside of the classroom (the use of different learning environments)
7.	Flexible use of space and time
8.	Non-prescriptive planning

They discovered that through visual displays of work-in-progress, learners continue to be engaged within the task and future tasks. Additionally, access to 'enhanced or specialist resources appear to stimulate creativity' (p. 84). This can include technology or subject-specific resources.

Collaboration with peers is seen as a significant feature of a creative environment, which can be further encouraged through the use of creative resources and learner-led tasks. The use of partnerships, external agencies and informal spaces can also increase engagement and is viewed as crucial to the sharing of practice and the creation of knowledge and skills for long-term impact.

Finally, engagement is stimulated through the introduction of new and exciting activities and set tasks. These could include some element of novelty, but should also be authentic, or in other words, as close to the real-world context as possible. This type of simulated and authentic learning is a central element of learning within the Arts and Humanities in the HE sector.

Key factors for successful online learning environments

As education embraced online learning throughout the pandemic, it is important to draw attention to some of the key factors that need to be considered when designing and managing this type of learning environment. Providing an inclusive learning environment remains a central consideration, and delivery needs to offer opportunities for all learners to access the learning, regardless of any barriers they may encounter, including access to technology. It is important when looking at learning environments to consider the needs of all students, offering both synchronous and asynchronous methods, enabling introverted, or students who could be defined as internal processors, to reflect on flexible content before attending a synchronous discussion forum. Importantly, Hall (2020) also describes the issue of 'Zoom' fatigue that some learners and lecturers alike can experience during synchronous sessions, highlighting the importance of built-in breaks from the screen.

Findings during the pandemic discovered that online, live discussion forums held within synchronous classes provide a positive psychological effect for students, improve student motivation and reduce a sense of isolation (De Gagne et al., 2021; Junod Perron et al., 2020). However, according to the research and findings from Hall (2020), this does not suit all students. Introverted students would 'hide behind the screen', needing time to respond and reflect, compared to students who can respond quickly. Research carried out by Sumuer (2018) also discovered that the online learning environment should be supported with scaffolding techniques so that learners develop effective study skills, particularly in terms of their technological and online communication.

Asynchronous activities designed and accessed prior to synchronous learning during face-to-face sessions can have mixed success; therefore, these need careful consideration at the planning and managing stage of implementation. Research carried out by Yang (2008) discovered that asynchronous online discussion forums provide students with more opportunities to think freely using reflection, resulting in deeper critical thinking compared to the restrictive nature of the traditional classroom. However, this asynchronous approach is most successful when supported by the lecturer, ensuring that collaborative discussions take place and are effective.

Wallace et al. (2021) argue that students preferred the flexibility that asynchronous learning provided as they were able to watch the recorded lectures in their own time and at their own pace. Although this was particularly relevant during the pandemic, when a number of different and unpredictable demands were made on all aspects of life, causing an even greater need for flexibility (Rafi et al., 2020), an expectation for increased flexibility has remained, and this is of particular significance for the Arts and Humanities due to the reflexive nature of the subjects.

Practical approaches

This section of the chapter provides suggestions for practical activities for use within the Arts and Humanities subject areas, but which can also be transferred to different situations and applied within other contexts (Table 1.3).

Informal and incidental learning in practice

Not all learning takes place in a formal learning environment. Informal learning is unplanned and does not require formal instructions, resulting in a learning experience which is dynamic, individual and responsive, self-directed by the learner (Jarvis, 2010). Incidental learning occurs in an unstructured way, as a derivative of another activity, and is never intentional. It always takes place as part of another activity and is therefore buried within other tasks, most effective when situated and social (Turner, 2021).

Table 1.3 Practical activities for creating the right environment

Practical approaches used to create the right learning environment	Sample of activities
Induction to the programme or module	Set clear ground rules to help establish and maintain a safe working space. This includes building an expectation of mutual respect. Learn the names of the students. This will enable you to manage individuals in future sessions. Learn about individual needs and act on this in a supportive and discrete way. Ice-breaker activities will build rapport within the group and encourage inclusion. Move students around to encourage active participation and reduce physical barriers.
Active learning strategies	Problem-solving activities Small group discussions which are semi-structured Student-led tasks which are self-directed Creative resources to encourage and stimulate motivation, including interactive presentations which provide opportunities for discussions and learner participation. The walking lecture which enables learners to learn whilst on the move; taking learning (and learners) into a different dimension.
Consolidation of content	The effective use of demonstrations The use of anecdotal stories and examples from practice to stimulate interest. Using alternative venues as learning spaces and authentic learning opportunities.
Formative assessment	The use of individual questions to encourage engagement and check knowledge Quizzes to stimulate motivation Self and peer assessment to encourage reflection and engagement with the material being taught Mock tests to prepare students for summative assessment and build confidence
Communication strategies	Clear and concise communication, allowing time for learners to process information. This includes written and oral communication. Mindful use of language, and where technical jargon is used, a definition is provided. The use of images to support language and stimulate interest. Being aware of body language and picking up on visual cues. Presenting information to the whole room through the use of eye contact and being mindful about where you are positioned.

Some form of disjuncture, often a by-product of another activity, occurs which acts as an initial trigger, forcing the individual to examine their knowledge so they are able to interpret the experience. Turner (2021) argues that professional identity 'determines the disjuncture that an individual chooses to recognise and respond to. The individuals' professional identity is shaped through prior experience and the context they operate within, and as such can limit what they are able to "notice"' (p. 44).

This type of learning can result in providing individuals with opportunities to find very personalized, creative solutions and innovations. Incidental learning also supports learners to move towards a learner-centred and autonomous style of learning, which is personally significant. It is important for lecturers to provide this type of opportunity and support for learners as they navigate through this process, thus enabling transferability to other aspects of their learning experiences. This is of particular relevance for Arts and Humanities learners due to the individual nature of the construction of artefacts and knowledge creation.

One of the ways to do this is through reflection. In order for reflection to be successful, an opportunity to revisit the experience will enable the learner to recall important details, consider feelings and evaluate the experience. Reflection is central to developing understanding about the way one works and provides the basis for developing professional judgement. This should be supported with critical feedback and is particularly useful for learners within the Arts and Humanities sector (Molloy and Boud, 2013).

Conclusion

It is important to strike a balance between too many demands which can cause stress, and too few demands which can result in boredom (Csikszentmilhalyi, 1997). Since the pandemic, lecturers find themselves in a somewhat fragile situation, as they walk the fine line between reinvention of established practice and ever-evolving digital learning environments. However, this presents a unique opportunity to embrace an exciting opportunity to adopt a more creative approach to practise, rather than rely on more traditional methods. This is not to suggest that tried-and-tested pedagogy is no longer valid, but rather that there are options which can be utilized to engage and motivate learners and stimulate learning in a fresh and creative way. However, we need to be mindful that being creative as a lecturer may not always result in learners engaging in their own creative practice. A re-packaged resource may actually limit the creativity of the learners, where 'those who created the materials had the opportunity to be creative' (Starko, 2018: 20), but the learners' creativity may be restricted. The learning environment should be set up to provide opportunities for all to flourish with new and original ideas.

The Arts and Humanities within the HE sector should be a place where education inspires and where innovation flourishes, and fresh, novel ideas are born. This chapter has provided some ideas and suggestions that can be adapted for use in a variety of different situations and for a range of subjects and levels. I hope that you enjoy adopting new ideas within your learning environments and that your learners respond in a dynamic way. It is important to remember that creative teachers need to 'develop a full repertoire of skills, which they can adapt and apply to different situations' (Craft et al., 2007: 21). Becoming a creative teacher is about an approach and attitude to teaching and not being afraid to try new ideas.

Sources

Carolan, C. (2020). 'COVID 19: Disruptive impacts and transformative opportunities in undergraduate nurse education', *Nurse Education in Practice* [Online], 46. https://doi.org/10.1016/j.nepr.2020.102807 (accessed 11 March 2021).

Cochraine, T. and Antonczak, L. (2015). 'Designing creative learning environments', *Interaction Design and Architecture(s) Journal*, 24: 125–44.

Craft, A., Jeffrey, B. and Leibling, M. (2007). *Creativity in Education*. London: Continuum.

Cropley, D. and Cropley, A. (2009). *Fostering Creativity: A Diagnostic Approach for Higher Education and Organisations*. New York: Hampton Press.

Csikszentmihalyi, M. (1997). *Creativity: Flow and the Psychology of Discovery and Invention*. London: Harper Collins.

Davies, D., Jindal-Snape, D., Collier, C., Digby, R., Hay, P. and Howe, A. (2012). 'Creative learning environments in education – A systematic literature review', *Thinking Skills and Creativity*, 8 (2013): 80–91.

De Gagne, J.C., Cho, E., Park, H.K., Nam, J.D. and Jung, D. (2021). 'A qualitative analysis of nursing students' tweets during the COVID-19 pandemic', *Nursing & Health Sciences* [Online], 23 (1): 273–8. https://doi.org/10.1111/nhs.12809 (accessed 9 April 2021).

Gandini, L., Hill, L., Cadwell, L. and Schwall, C. (eds.) (2005). *In the Spirit of the Studio: Learning from the Atelier of Reggio Emilia*. New York: Teachers' College Press.

Gov (2016). *The Teaching Excellence Framework*. https://www.gov.uk/government/collections/teaching-excellence-framework (accessed on 12 November 2020).

Hall, C.L. (2020). 'From zoom fatigue to belly breaths: Teaching away from the screen', *Teaching Theology & Religion* [Online], 23 (4): 294. https://doi.org/10.1111/teth.12565 (accessed 9 April 2021).

Hodges, C., Moore, S., Lockee, B., Trust, T. and Bond, A. (2020). *The Difference between Emergency Remote Teaching and Online Learning* [Online]. https://er.educause.edu/articles/2020/3/the-difference-between-emergency-remote-teaching-and-online-learning#fn7 (accessed 9 April 2021).

James, M. and Pollard, A. (2011). *TLRP's Ten Principles for Effective Pedagogy: Rationale, Development, Evidence, Argument and Impact.* https://research-information.bris.ac.uk/en/publications/tlrps-ten-principles-for-effective-pedagogy-rationale-development (accessed 11 February 2022).

Jarvis, P. (2010). *Adult Education and Lifelong Learning. Theory and Practice.* 4th ed. London: Routledge.

Junod Perron, N., Dominice Dao, M., Rieder, A., Sommer, J. and Audetat, M.C. (2020). 'Online synchronous clinical communication training during the Covid-19 pandemic', *Advances in Medical Education and Practice* [Online], 11: 1029–36. https://doi.org/10.2147/AMEP.S286552 (accessed 9 April 2021).

Kleiman, P. (2019). *Steps to a Manifesto for Creativity and Imagination in Higher Education.* manifesto_for_creativity_in_he.pdf (creativeacademic.uk) (accessed 4 November 202).

Lave, J. and Wenger, E. (2008). *Situated Learning. Legitimate Peripheral Participation.* Cambridge: Cambridge university press.

Molloy, E.K. and Boud, D. (2013). 'Seeking a different angle on feedback in clinical education. The learner as seeker, judge and user of performance information', *Medical Education,* 47: 227–9.

Morin, K. (2020). 'Nursing education after COVID-19: Same or different?', *Journal of Clinical Nursing* [Online], 29 (17–18): 3117–19. https://doi-org.ezproxy.bolton.ac.uk/10.1111/jocn.15322 (accessed 11 March 2021).

Office for Students (2018). *A New Approach to Regulating Access and Participation in English Higher Education.* https://www.officeforstudents.org.uk/ (accessed 12 November 2020).

Parrish, D. (2012). *Two Kinds of Creativity: A-creativity and i-creativity.* https://www.davidparrish.com/a-creativity-i-creativity/ (accessed 4 November 2020).

Philip, R. (2015). *Caught in the Headlights: Designing for Creative Learning and Teaching in Higher Education.* Robyn_Philip_Thesis.pdf (accessed 11 February 2022).

Pokhrel, S. and Chhetri, R. (2021). 'A literature review on impact of COVID-19 pandemic on teaching and learning', *Higher Education for the Future,* 8 (1): 133–41. Available from A Literature Review on Impact of COVID-19 Pandemic on Teaching and Learning (sagepub.com) (accessed 12 March 2022).

Rafi, A.B., Varghese, P.R. and Kuttichira, P. (2020). 'The pedagogical shift during COVID 19 pandemic: Online medical education, barriers and perceptions in central Kerala', *Journal of Medical Education and Curricular Development* [Online], 7: 1–4. https://doi.org/10.1177/2382120520951795 (accessed 9 April 2021).

Rodgers, C.R. and Scott, K.H. (2008). 'The development of the personal self and professional identity in learning to teach', in M. Cochran-Smith, S. Feiman-Nernser,

J. Mcintyre and K. Demers (eds.), *Handbook of Research on Teacher Education*, 3rd ed., 11. New York and London: Routledge.

Rossman, M.H. (1999). 'Successful online teaching using an asynchronous learner discussion forum', *Online Learning* [Online], 3 (2): 91–7. https://doi.org/10.24059/olj.v3i2.1919 (accessed 9 April 2021).

Sachs, J. (2005). 'Teacher education and the development of professional identity: Learning to be a teacher', in P. Denicolo and M. Kompf (eds.), *Connecting Policy and Practice. Challenges for Teaching and Learning in Schools and Universities*, 5–21. Oxford: Routledge.

Starko, A.J. (2018). *Creativity in the Classroom. Schools of Curious Delight*. 6th ed. London: Routledge.

Sternberg, R.J. (2007). 'Creativity as a habit', in A.-G. Tan (ed.), *Creativity: A Handbook for Teachers*, 3–25. Singapore: World Scientific Publishing.

Sternberg, R.J., Kaufman, J.C. and Pretz, J.E. (2002). *The Creativity Conundrum: A Propulsion Model of Kinds of Creative Contributions*. New York: Psychology Press.

Stott, A. and Mozer, M. (2016). 'Connecting learners online: Challenges and issues for nurse education – Is there a way forward?', *Nurse Education Today* [Online], 39: 152–4. https://doi.org/10.1016/j.nedt.2016.02.002 (accessed 9 April 2021).

Sumuer, E. (2018). 'Factors related to college students' self-directed learning with technology', *Australasian Journal of Educational Technology* [Online], 34 (4): 29–43. https://doi.org/10.14742/ajet.3142 (accessed 9 April 2021).

Sutton, M.J.D. and Bitencourt Jorge, C.F. (2020). 'Potential for radical change in Higher Education learning spaces after the pandemic', *Journal of Applied Learning and Teaching*, 3 (1): 124–8. 245-Article Text-943-4-10-20200622.pdf (accessed 12 March 2022).

Turner, A. (2021). *Professional Identity Development through Incidental Learning*. Switzerland: Palgrave Macmillan.

Wallace, S., Schuler, M.S. and Kaulback, M. (2021). 'Nursing student experiences of remote learning during the COVID-19 pandemic', *Nursing Forum* [Online]: 1–7. https://doi.org/10.1111/nuf.12568 (accessed 9 April 2021).

Wright, K. (2019). 'Sparking creativity', *Advance HE*. https://www.advance-he.ac.uk/news-and-views/Sparking-creativity (accessed 4 November 2020).

Yang, Y.T.C. (2008). 'A catalyst for teaching critical thinking in a large university class in Taiwan: Asynchronous online discussions with the facilitation of teaching assistants', *Educational Technology, Research and Development* [Online], 56 (3): 241–64. https://doi.org/10.1007/s11423-007-9054-5 (accessed 9 April 2021).

2

'Resources' and 'Sign-Makers': Teaching Identity Construction in Academic English through Modality and Visuals

Taryn Bernard

Introduction

This chapter is written for those of us who teach academic writing in arts and humanities faculties across the globe by offering an illustrative example from the Global South. I begin this chapter by highlighting that the complex and multifaceted concept of 'identity' is an important component of any sociolinguistic understanding of language and language use, including academic writing. I draw on literature from social science and humanities disciplines in order to establish why 'identity' should be an anchoring or prominent feature of any course designed to teach an academic variety of a language and academic literacy practices. After I have established this, I present an overview of the key components of a curriculum that was designed with this principle in mind, with particular attention to the component designed to teach 'modality'. From an applied linguistic perspective, modality refers to the linguistic resources that allow speakers to express attitudes and judgements. An understanding of modality encourages people to pay closer attention to how communicators represent themselves and others in the text, but it also equips students with the metalanguage to discuss how this takes place and it enables them to consciously select the language resources to construct their own identities. While this may seem complex, I illustrate how one can teach modality through *visuals* and why, in contemporary society, it is important to do so. Since we are all social beings with our own identities, the focus on identity and modality in the curriculum also encourages a reflective approach to teaching, while the use of images in teaching academic writing encourages creative learning, teaching and assessment practices.

Contextualizing academic literacy: Views from the Global South

Academic literacy, and the development of academic literacy skills in English in particular, has become an important feature of higher education (HE) institutions across the globe. This is, in part, due to processes of globalization and migration which have resulted in more people from diverse backgrounds, cultures and languages entering a system which has historically been structured according to Western, white and English cultural and linguistic norms. Initiatives aimed at the development of English academic literacy skills are often viewed as a mechanism to increase access and participation in university life and to the discourses and disciplinary knowledge of the university. For this reason, academic literacy is viewed as an important component of 'foundational provision' in South Africa, an umbrella term for academic support programmes that aim to widen access and participation in HE to 'non-traditional students', which typically includes first-generation students, students who speak English as a second language as well as students from lower socio-economic-status backgrounds (see Leibowitz and Bozalek, 2015).

Across the globe, dominant approaches to the development of academic literacy skills have changed over time. In an effort to achieve social justice, many practitioners have moved away from prescriptive approaches that value English monolingualism to approaches that recognize the perspectives, knowledge and languages that the students bring with them to university. Such approaches are typically rooted in models of applied and sociolinguistics, specifically the sub-disciplines of systemic functional linguistics (SFL) as well as new literacy studies (NLS), and critical discourse analysis (CDA). NLS, and many approaches to CDA, are rooted in SFL and they all share the view that literacy is a social and cultural practice (see Coffin and Donohue, 2012; Gee and Green, 1998; Rogers, 2004). This means that even academic literacy practices are conceptualized as 'socially regulated ways of doing things' (van Leeuwen, 2008: 6), where regulation takes place to different degrees and in different ways – through strict prescription, tradition, the influence of experts or the constraints of technological resources (e.g., van Leeuwen, 2008: 7). This also highlights the ideological nature of literacy practices, where ideologies are understood as a system of beliefs that influence practices (including language practices). As an illustrative example of this, Mills (2016: 15) points out that Western or colonizing powers have historically used an autonomous model of literacy to oppress cultures and communities whose literacy practices are considered marginal. Any pedagogical or analytical approach rooted in SFL, NLS or CDA aims to make the ideological nature of texts and textual practices explicit.

In defining ideologies as a system of beliefs that influence practices, I am also highlighting how the complex and multifaceted concept 'identity' is an important component of language and language use, since ideologies and identities are closely intertwined. In fact, as far back as 1998, Ivanič claimed that writing (as a form of language *use*) is an act of identity in which people align themselves with socio-culturally shaped subject positions (i.e. ideologies), and thereby play their part in reproducing or challenging dominant practices and discourses, and the values, beliefs and interests which they embody. Therefore, language use and writing are not just about conveying 'content' but also about the representation of *self* (see also Burgess and Ivanič, 2010; Clark and Ivanič, 2013 as well as Hyland, 2018). Ivanič (1998) and Clark and Ivanič (2013) have also been influential in highlighting that writing is often difficult because people do not feel comfortable with the self that they are required to portray in writing, a self which is dictated and limited by the conventions of the genre. For students, academic writing can pose a conflict of identity because the self that is required from them feels alien to them (Ivanič, 1998). This is particularly important for students who speak the languages and operate within knowledge systems that are not traditionally valued in HE contexts, and so I return to this point in the section 'Case study'.

The digital and multimodal turn

David Howes, a sensory anthropologist, succinctly claims that 'the digital revolution has put an end to literacy as we know it' (Howes in Mills, 2016: xiii). While we know that humans have always learned to communicate through multiple sign systems or *modes,* each of which offers a distinctive way of meaning-making, digital technologies have enabled us 'to capture, create, modify, combine and disseminate image on a much broader scale than in the past' (Mills, 2016: 66). This can be referred to as the 'digital turn' in academic literacy practice and research, a term used to succinctly refer to a differently constituted technological world, a world which 'throws up its different problems' (Kress, 2011: 139).

While it is true that universities have traditionally placed more value on the spoken and written word than other modes of communication, the university has always been a place of symbols, images, signs and signifiers. Subsequent to the digital turn, lecturers incorporate visuals in their lectures, have increased their use of PowerPoint, create videos or embed videos, images and audio into PowerPoints and they require students to be able to interpret these texts in context. In other words, digital technology has radically transformed literacy practices, even within the university system.

The theory of multimodality, positioned within the applied linguistic and theoretical framework of social semiotics (which is also rooted in SFL; see Andersen, Boeriis, Maagerø and Tonnessen, 2015), is useful for understanding the role that non-linguistic modes of communication (still and moving images, colour, sound, space, gestures, gaze and posture) play in the creation of meaning. Multimodality refers to the existence of multiple modes in the process of textual meaning-making. Scholars within social semiotics, scholars who work with multimodality, recognize that there are always several semiotic modes in the design of a semiotic product or event, even in the case of an academic essay. These scholars also realize that meaning-making in the digital era requires more than just the production of knowledge but also a process of knowledge transformation between two or more different symbolic forms. In the classroom, theories of social semiotics and multimodality urge practitioners to recognize, rather than ignore, the prevalence, cultural-situatedness and importance of non-linguistic modes of communication.

In South Africa, Thesen (2001, 2007) and Archer (2006) have explored the use of multimodality in foundational classrooms at the University of Cape Town (UCT). Thesen (2001) highlights that humanities and social science students are required to engage with four 'layers' of language: the English language system, academic discourse, mode-specific language associated with the analysis of the visual and a metalanguage of critical analysis. Drawing on this, Archer (2006) argues for the need to make conventionalized multimodal practices in HE explicit in order to enable students to access them. In designing a pedagogy for social justice, Archer argues that six features are important: Questioning boundaries between domains, exchanging cultural practices, harnessing students' representational resources, developing metalanguages of reflection, creating less regulated curriculum spaces and, finally, interrogating the relation between text and context in a social justice agenda. In the design of my own curriculum, I have tried to ensure that the curriculum harnesses students' representational resources, that it develops students' metalanguage of reflection and that the course is able to create less regulated spaces. In the following section, I discuss how this was achieved.

Case study

Texts in the Humanities 123 is a semester English academic literacy module for second-year, multilingual humanities and social science students at Stellenbosch University. The students have already been introduced to the fundamentals of academic writing, including paragraph writing, referencing and argumentation in their first years. The module aims to: (1) introduce students to the idea that language and identity are related, and that identity is (re)constructed through language, (2) create awareness of the types of devices and resources that are used to (re)construct identity and, in the process, (3) equip students with the metalanguage to identify these devices and resources in text, and (4) enable students to consciously draw on these devices and resources when using language and creating their own texts. The curriculum takes an explicit multimodal approach to pedagogy, which means it goes beyond written and spoken language to include a range of modes in both the lectures and formal assessment practices. In the subsections below, I discuss the components of the curriculum: the topics that are discussed in each component, the way in which they are discussed (their theoretical basis) and the types of assessments that students are required to complete.

Component 1: Identity

In the first component of the module, students are introduced to the complex notion of 'identity'. The concept is first tackled from an essentialist perspective before moving onto poststructuralist, constructionist and intersectional perspectives of identity (see Norton and De Costa, 2018 for an overview of these theories of identity as they relate to language teaching). Students are encouraged to adopt a poststructuralist idea of identity – or the idea that identity is multifaceted, performed, fluid and (re)constituted through language. As prescribed readings, students are given journal articles by Makubalo (2007) and Bornman and Potgieter (2017), both of which adopt poststructuralist perspectives of identity and speak to language and identity in the South African context. Makubalo (2007) reports on the use of English in South African schools after the fall of apartheid and touches on ideologies related to the use of English in South Africa, while Bornman and Potgieter (2011) investigate the language tensions in South African universities, with a particular focus on Afrikaans-speaking students.

Classroom discussions about the Makubalo (2007) and Bornman and Potgieter (2011) readings, in conjunction with YouTube videos that tackle similar topics, encourage students to understand the notion of standard and non-standard varieties of languages as well as the concept of 'language ideologies', and to reflect on how these concepts are evident in their own lives, in rural and urban parts of South Africa. As part of this component, students are also taught about reflective thinking and reflective writing, and asked to draw comparisons between reflective writing and traditional academic writing (see Ryan, 2011 for a social semiotic perspective on how to improve reflective writing in HE). For their first summative assessment, students are asked to submit an assessment in which they are asked to reflect on the way in which language constitutes their own identities. Students are assessed on whether they have understood how identity and language are related and on their ability to adopt a reflective style of writing.

In the final section of this component, students are asked to engage with the following question in class: 'What is the identity of an academic writer?' Students are asked to return to the Makubalo (2007) and Bornman and Potgieter (2011) readings in order to comment on how these authors construct themselves in the texts. Figure 2.1 presents some of the most common answers to this question, which are utilized in the Components 2 and 3 of the curriculum.

In our discussion about the identity of an academic writer, it is explicitly acknowledged that language use and writing are not just about conveying 'content' but also about the representation of *self* (see Burgess and Ivanič, 2010; Clark and Ivanič, 2013 as well as Hyland, 2018). It is also acknowledged that novice writers and students are required to present themselves as confident, assertive and knowledgeable before they have authentically adopted those

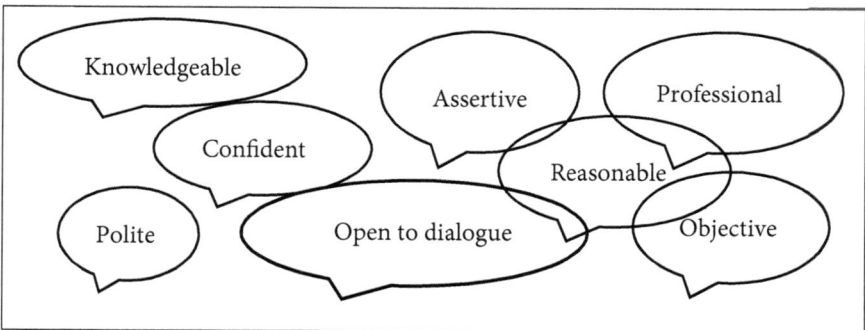

Figure 2.1 The identity of the academic writer.

subject-positions. This second component of the curriculum aims to equip students with the resources in English to do this.

Component 2: 'Resources', 'range of choices' and writers as 'sign-makers'

In Component 2 of the module, students are taught that, apart from conveying information and constituting identities, language offers us the *resources* to be able to *represent* people, objects and situations. Students are taught that this too is an identity issue. In other words, the naming and the textual representation of *people* (including the self) is an important aspect of many texts, including academic texts. From the perspective of SFL, when it comes to representing people, the communicator has *a range of choices* available to them when deciding how to represent individuals or groups of individuals. These choices may be unconscious or conscious, and they are also limited by genre, ideologies and discourses.

While some of these choices are unpacked in Component 3, for now, how choices are limited by ideologies and discourses can be illustrated by engaging in a class discussion about gendered pronouns. Students in this module are able to recognize that selecting pronouns in English to indicate a multitude of gender identities is a relatively new, global phenomenon that has taken place due to shifting ideologies about gender in society. Students are also asked to compare contemporary choices in pronouns to the archaic and patriarchal use of 'he' to refer to all humankind (or 'mankind!') or pronouns in their own mother tongues. Gendered pronouns are a good example of how ideologies around gender impact on (language) practice and have, in this case, increased the *range of choices* available to communicators in English when representing identities, including their own. In CDA, the choices that communicators have to represent people in the social world are called 'representational strategies'. Even though these choices may be unconscious or conscious, and they are also limited by genre, ideologies and discourses, they also allow us to *highlight* certain aspects of identity we wish to draw attention to or *omit* those we do not.

Finally, in Component 2, students are also urged to recognize themselves not just as writers or communicators but as meaning-makers and *sign-makers*. The switch to 'sign-makers' pays homage to the work done in multimodality and social semiotics and pre-empts the work we will do later with visual texts, but it also encourages students to recognize the range of resources they have at their disposal, as speakers of multiple South African languages.

Component 3: The 'resources' and 'range of choices' that (academic) 'sign-makers' have to represent identity

In Component 3, students are introduced to some of the linguistic resources in English that are used by writers to represent the identities of others as well as their own. These resources include naming strategies, transitivity, intertextuality and modality.[1] In the following section, I present a brief overview of naming strategies (or referentials), tense and intertextuality, before focusing on modality.

In CDA, 'naming strategies' refers to nouns, pronouns and noun phrases that are used to *refer* to people. Hence, naming strategies are also called 'referentials'. Van Leeuwen (2008) developed a complex framework for identifying how people can be represented or 'hidden' in a text, with ideological implications. For example, people can be represented on a spectrum from being highly individualized and personalized (where they are named), to being represented in terms of being part of a group and/or depersonalized (referring to people as 'stakeholders', for example). In discussions about naming strategies that include visual texts, audios and videos, students are urged to reflect on the referentials most valued in academic texts and what choices are appropriate for naming when writing academic texts in English.

In SFL, identity construction in texts can be understood or analysed through transitivity analysis. Although transitivity is a method of analysis that focuses on the verb in the sentence (as representative of 'processes' in the real world), attention to 'the agent' and the 'affected entity' as it is done in transitivity analysis is useful in helping students to understand the representational and ideological nature of language. Specific attention is paid to active and passive tenses in this module, specifically passive-agent deletion. Numerous examples from various modes are used to illustrate how identities can be represented differently in active and passive tenses, but students are also urged to reflect on this in terms of academic writing (which often favours passive construction).

In CDA, intertextuality refers to the way in which writers weave other voices into their texts. This can be done in implicit or explicit ways, as is the case with referencing. In this component of the module, attention is paid to reporting clauses and how speakers and writers reveal their own attitudes and judgements of the people they are citing, the voices they are including, through variations in reporting clauses (in spoken and written English), or in the use of direct speech or indirect speech. This shifts the focus from referencing as a textual practice to referencing as an issue of identity construction and representation.

Finally, in traditional grammar, a modal or a modal auxiliary is a word such as 'can' or 'would' that shows possibility, intention, necessity, probability, obligations, factuality, certainty and doubt, among other aspects of opinion, attitude, judgement and commitment. For this reason, modals and modal auxiliaries are an important aspect of identity construction in English academic texts. Applied linguists distinguish two main types of modality: deontic modality and epistemic modality. Deontic modality relates to obligation or permission and includes modal verbs, such as 'must' and 'may' as well as modal auxiliaries, such as 'can', 'could', 'may', 'would' and 'might'. Epistemic modality expresses the writers' commitment to their propositions. The two main categories of epistemic modality are *hedging* and *boosting*. While the use of hedges emphasizes the need for caution when interpreting the meaning of the text, boosters allow writers to express confidence and conviction and make strong claims about the state of affairs. Boosters are also viewed as the markers of involvement and solidarity with an audience, stressing shared information, group membership and direct engagement with readers (Bureković and Zolota, 2019). The difference between hedges and boosters is represented in (a) and (b) below:

(a) Hedge: The evidence *might suggest* that …
(b) Booster: The evidence *clearly* indicates that …

Bureković and Zolota (2019) argue that hedges or cautious language is one of the most essential stylistic aspect of academic writing since it helps authors to mitigate the force of their statements. It thus enables them to express their opinions while avoiding absolute certainty or overgeneralization. It is clear that hedges are the devices of tentative language in academic communication. By adopting this communicative strategy the authors apparently project an image of a polite person, a person who takes the views of others into consideration Additionally, these pragmatic markers provide an opportunity for readers to contest the author's ideas and opinions in a respectful way. Consequently, hedges make sentences more acceptable to the reader by increasing their chances of acceptance. This helps to achieve the balance needed in academic writing – the need to provide objective and accurate information while persuading readers of reliability of the knowledge (Bureković and Zolota, 2019).

Before beginning an exercise that requires them to incorporate modals, students are asked to revisit their description of the identity of an academic writer before deciding on the type of modals and modal auxiliaries that are appropriate in an academic context, or the type of modals that suit the type of identity they wish to construct for themselves and others in their texts. Before completing an exercise where students are asked to use modals, students are asked to consider what their stances (attitudes and judgements) are towards the literature and visual texts they are engaging with. Once they have completed their exercise, they are asked to reflect on their choice of modals and whether they have expressed their attitudes and judgements accurately. This component not only helps students to find their voice, but also leads to interesting discussions about objectivity in academic writing, thus making academic writing more accessible.

Teaching modality choices in writing through visuals

In the previous section, I focused on representational nature of modals and modal auxiliaries in spoken and written English. In this section, I illustrate how these representation features can be considered and taught in the classroom using visuals. Kress and van Leeuwen (2006), working within a socio-semiotic framework, have identified visual resources or 'visual modals' that can be used to present the sign-maker in particular ways and to highlight or conceal levels of truth or commitment to reality. In social semiotics, 'modality' is understood as referring to the degree to which a sign or image claims to be something true or real.

In order to illustrate these ideas in class, I draw on stock images and the work of Machin (2004), who highlights the generic nature of stock images, which also means that stock images represent the ideologies and practices of the dominant social class. When analysing the way meaning is created through visuals, I compare photographs to written texts in order to highlight how each mode has different affordances for the sign-maker but that the sign-maker can use either mode to represent their own identity as well as the identity of others. In this section, I cover a few useful tools for drawing students' attention to the meaning potential of features of images. These tools are limited to 'angle' and 'degrees of articulation'. As with attention to modality is writing, knowledge of these features also increases the students' ability to describe what they see.

Photographers as sign-makers can choose to represent their participants from various angles: straight on, from below, or from above. Each angle has a number of effects. Shooting from above may cause a participant to seem vulnerable while the photographer is represented as having power or agency. Similarly, shooting from below might assign power or agency to the photographic participants while the meaning is created that the photographer is less powerful. Class discussions take place regarding the angle that is used to capture the people in Image A and Image B below, for example (Figure 2.2).

In addition to angle, students are taught that degrees of articulation in relation to detail, light and shadow, tone and colour saturation call all work to represent identities in various ways. Degrees of the articulation of detail refer to 'the scale from the simplest line drawing to the sharpest and most finely grained photograph' (Machin and Mayr, 2012: 202). Although Image B is sharp and finely grained, the detail of the woman's face has been diffused slightly by the lighting. In this sense, modality has been lowered. In other words, as is typical of stock images, the woman is not represented as a specific person but as a generic person, a type. Her identification with this type is specified by her clothes, hairstyle and posture. The same is true for the people represented in Image A, where they are clearly characterized as 'students': light and shadow are also used to represent identities in Image B. In the image of students above, the light is coming from above, shining on the word 'academics' and filtering down onto the students, who are simultaneously represented in shadow. In conjunction with the students raised arms, Image A works to perpetuate ideologies around the importance of HE.

Figure 2.2 Image A (left-hand photo by Leon Wu on Unsplash) and image B (right-hand photo by Derick McKinney on Unsplash).

Component 6: Final assessment and reflection

For their final assignment, students are asked to write an essay on language in HE by drawing on the information in the Bornman and Potgieter (2011) reading and relating this information to their own experiences. Students are requested to illustrate their experiences through photographs, and some students choose to do a workshop with a professional photographer and borrow a professional camera. Students are explicitly asked to focus on modality and on their use of modals both in writing and in their images and to present themselves in ways that are appropriate for an academic 'sign-maker'. In asking students to create images along with academic written texts, academic literacy practices become less regulated (see Section 'Contextualizing academic literacy'), and the classroom itself becomes an 'unregulated space' that permits 'a range of student resources to emerge' while enabling 'access to dominant forms' (Archer, 2014: 191). Finally, students are asked to reflect on their choice of modals in the written component as well as modality in their photographs, and reflect on the identity that they constructed for themselves through this. This reflection is attached as an appendix to their final assignments.

Conclusion

This chapter offers a practical example of how to teach advanced English academic literacy skills by incorporating the concept of 'identity' as well as ideas developed within SFL, NLS, CDA and social semiotics. In the process, the students are encouraged to see themselves as 'sign-makers' rather than simply as novice or deficit academic writers. This approach also encourages students to *recognize* the multilingual and multimodal resources that they already carry with them and which enable them to interpret and create complex meanings in contemporary society. In addition to this, the curriculum develops students' metalanguages of reflection and creates less regulated curriculum spaces, which urges students to interrogate the relationship between text and context (Archer, 2014). Ultimately, the design of the academic literacy curriculum, which includes various modes of teaching and assessment, aims to contribute to the repositioning of English academic literacy curricula and pedagogical practice in South Africa, a context where literacy and literacy practices are heavily loaded and where the linguistic practices of HE institutions are continually called into question (Thesen, 2007).

Note

1   The term 'modality', which refers to elements of grammar such as modal verbs and modal auxiliaries is different to the term 'mode' or 'modes' as it is used in the field of multimodality.

Sources

Andersen, T.H., Boeriis, M., Maagerø, E. and Tonnessen, E.S. (2015). *Social Semiotics: Key Figures, New Directions*. London: Routledge.

Archer, A. (2006). 'A multimodal approach to academic "literacies": Problematizing the visual/verbal divide', *Language and Education*, 20 (6): 449–62.

Archer, A. (2014). 'Power, social justice and multimodal pedagogies', in C.E. Jewitt (ed.), *The Routledge Handbook of Multimodal Analysis*, 189–97. London: Routledge.

Bornman, E. and Potgieter, P.E. (2017). 'Language choices and identity in higher education: Afrikaans-speaking students at Unisa', *Studies in Higher Education*, 42 (8): 1474–87.

Bureković, M. and Zolota, S. (2019). *Modality, Hedges, and Boosters in Postgraduate Academic Writing*. Proceedings of the International Symposium on Active Learning, 6–8 September, Adana, Turkey.

Burgess, A. and Ivanič, R. (2010). 'Writing and being written: Issues of identity across timescales', *Written Communication*, 27 (2): 228–55.

Clark, R. and Ivanic, R. (2013). *The Politics of Writing*. London: Routledge.

Clark, U. (2013). *Language and Identity in Englishes*. London: Routledge.

Coffin, C. and Donohue, J.P. (2012). 'Academic literacies and systemic functional linguistics: How do they relate?', *Journal of English for Academic Purposes*, 11 (1): 64–75.

Fairclough, N. (2014). *Critical Language Awareness*. London: Routledge.

Gee, J.P. and Green, J.L. (1998). 'Chapter 4: Discourse analysis, learning, and social practice: A methodological study', *Review of Research in Education*, 23 (1): 119–69.

Holmes, J. (1997). 'Women, language and identity', *Journal of Sociolinguistics*, 1: 195–223.

Hornberger, N.H. and McKay, S. (eds.) (2010). *Sociolinguistics and Language Education* (Vol. 18). Bristol: Multilingual Matters.

Hyland, K. (2018). *Metadiscourse: Exploring Interaction in Writing*. London: Bloomsbury Publishing.

Ivanič, R. (1998). *Writing and Identity: The Discoursal Construction of Identity in Academic Writing*. London: John Benjamins.

Kress, G. (2011). '"Partnerships in research": Multimodality and ethnography', *Qualitative Research*, 11 (3): 239–60. https://doi.org/10.1177/1468794111399836.

Kress, G. and Van Leeuwen, T. (2006). *Reading Images: The Grammar of Visual Design*. London: Routledge.

Leibowitz, B. and Bozalek, V. (2015). 'Foundational provision – A social justice perspective', *South African Journal of Higher Education*, 29 (1): 8–25.

Machin, D. (2004). 'Building the world's visual language: The increasing global importance of image banks in corporate media', *Visual Communication*, 3 (3): 316–36. https://doi.org/10.1177/1470357204045785.

Machin, D. and Mayr, A. (2012). *How to Do Critical Discourse Analysis*. London: Sage.

Makubalo, M. (2007). '"I don't know … it contradicts": Identity construction and the use of English by high school learners in a desegregated school space', *English Academy Review*, 24 (2): 25–41.

Mills, K.A. (2016). *Literacy Theories for the Digital Age: Social, Critical, Multimodal, Spatial, Material and Sensory Lenses*. Toronto: Multilingual Matters.

Norton, B. and De Costa, P. (2018). 'Research tasks on identity in language learning and teaching', *Language Teaching*, 51 (1): 90–112. https://doi.org/10.1017/S0261444817000325.

Rogers, R. (2004). *An Introduction to Critical Discourse Analysis in Education*. London: Routledge.

Ryan, M. (2011). 'Improving reflective writing in higher education: A social semiotic perspective', *Teaching in Higher Education*, 16 (1): 99–111.

Thesen, L. (2001). 'Modes, literacies and power: A university case study', *Language and Education*, 14 (3): 132–45.

Thesen, L. (2007). 'Breaking the frame: Lectures, ritual and academic literacies', *Journal of Applied Linguistics and Professional Practice*, 4 (10): 33–53.

Van Leeuwen, T. (2008). *Discourse and Practice: New Tools for Critical Discourse Analysis*. Oxford: Oxford University Press.

3

Students as Collaborators

Jo Trelfa, Claire Ancient, Chris O'Connor and Josephine Morris

Introduction

According to Dianati and Oberhollenzer (Dianati and Oberhollenzer, 2020: 1–15), 'methods of teaching and learning have remained relatively unchanged, with teachers bestowing knowledge to their students in a one-way hierarchical approach to learning'. This being the case was of interest to us, the authors of this chapter. As educators, we wanted to challenge this approach and consider how students can be included as active partners in the creation of knowledge rather than passive recipients. Specifically, we wanted to explore the role and purpose of the higher education (HE) lecturers/teachers in that space. In this chapter, we discuss and reflect on our experiences of integrating student-as-producer to support co-creation within a module on an MA Learning and Teaching in Higher Education (LTHE) programme. We propose a novel framework which we found supported student–staff collaboration, built on the use of student-led problem-based learning. Named 'the Triple P Framework', this model encourages creative problem-solving through student–staff collaboration using three steps: Pinpointing the problem, Probing the challenges and then Presenting the solution. Throughout this process, students are encouraged to actively engage in reflective practice using Action Learning Sets, a model we also used as part of our own journey of discovery in relation to our educator roles.

Background and context

We are three students who are also lecturers (ranging from early career to established) exploring pedagogy in theory and practice, plus the Course Lead who had introduced a new module to the MA LTHE programme they were taking, entitled 'Constructing Knowledge in Higher Education'. The module aimed to push at and explore the boundaries of those 'unchanged' teaching and learning dynamics. Each of us had dual roles, of collaborators during the module whilst also implementing and reflecting on our learning as we applied it in our own teaching contexts as educators. Whilst our contexts and backgrounds are diverse, our practice is underpinned with theory and the practical nature of our subjects: software engineering, digital design, physiotherapy and pedagogy.

Changing 'one-way hierarchical approaches' is of course not new. It was Brian Simon's (1981) critical comparison of the English 'instrumental approach to teaching' with 'pedagogic through and practice in Europe' that informed the work (2000–12) of the Teaching and Learning Research Programme (TLRP) to effect teaching approaches to improve outcomes. In fact, interest in 'active learning', methods that put the student at the centre of their learning, has been a focus in post-war HE (James and Pollard, 2011: 276). With roots in citizenship building and constructivism of Piaget and Vygotsky (Alanazi, 2016: 1–8), active learning countered traditional notions of 'there is a best way in doing everything, and that [...] best way can always be formulated into certain rules' (Taylor, 1912: 36). Instead of passive students being instructed, the aim is one of design and facilitation that enables them to engage 'in any way that can promote active thought' (Gifkins, 2015). Integrating new knowledge into an existing base whilst at the same time building on it is a process of meaning-making in the development of understanding, competency and autonomy as learners.

Yet even within this arena, our concern was that despite re-locating the student as active rather than passive, focus still remains on the teacher who designs and facilitates the learning environment, underpinned as it is by the assumption that without lecturer choreography of their learning, students will become 'lost and frustrated' (Kirschner, Sweller and Clark, 2006: 75–86). Our interest, therefore, was how we might *fully* take on 'traditional assumptions about the identities of, and relationships between, learners and teachers' (Matthews, 2017) in our teaching practices.

Indeed, earlier in the course to explore pedagogy in theory and practice, one of the themes was 'student engagement', this being a more recent focus in HE institutions. Student engagement is defined as

> [T]he energy and effort that students employ within their learning community
> [...] shaped by a range of structural and internal influences, including the

complex interplay of relationships, learning activities and the learning environment.

(Bond et al., 2020: 3)

It is a focus based on the premise that

The more students are engaged and empowered within their learning community, the more likely they are to channel that energy back into their learning, leading to a range of short- and long-term outcomes, that can likewise further fuel engagement.

(Bond et al., 2020: 3)

Even so, a rich curriculum plus provision of extra-curricular activities in which students can engage as consumers is different to students-as-partners where 'all participants are actively engaged in and stand to gain from the process of learning and working together' (Healey, Flint and Harrington, 2014: 7). Moreover, students-as-partners is different to students-as-producers, the latter recognizing the variety of experiences and knowledge that students bring to the learning table and, crucially, encouraging them to drive their *own* learning.

Imagining the above as a continuum of student–lecturer relations, we conceived this as 'master-apprentice' of instructivism (Ranciere, 1991), at the one end, to collaborators in the egalitarian pursuit of knowledge of students-as-producers at the other (Neary, 2020).

But what would students and lecturers collaborating together to push at and explore the boundaries of traditional 'unchanged' teaching and learning dynamics actually involve? What would be the challenges and how would they unfold? We knew the arguments for changing our approaches to teaching and learning but what would it involve in experience?

Immersed in practices of and in the module as well as in our own teaching, in this chapter we discuss what student-as-producers *can* mean, what it involves, and the challenges for 'us-as-lecturers-and-students'. At the same time, by creating this chapter together, we reflect on our own learning *and* model ourselves as co-producers along the way. Already readers will be spotting complexities, including

- the creation of a 'module' collaboratively, which essentially requires discrete knowledge that must fit regulatory framework requirements of pre-stated Learning Outcomes; and
- explaining a collaborative approach and reassuring students who need to pass 'it' in order to be able to complete their qualification.

Values, roles and interaction

On a cognitive level, it is apparent that collaborative learning is approached as a process of active co-construction of knowledge. But further, this is not an individual endeavour, but a social process based in interpersonal interaction, that is located in history and culture, space and place. Furthermore, to ensure that teaching and meaning are not 'done to' others through the power of one, the collaborative process is accompanied by commentary and reflection. As Damsa puts it, an awareness of '*how* the epistemic aspects of the interaction unfold, *how* it is regarded and discussed, and *how* it is materialised into knowledge objects through collaborative work' [emphasis added] (Damsa, 2013: 5). As a consequence, students and teachers are more likely to 'invest fully into the work, use their skills to the fullest potential, create something with the utmost care, strive for perfection, and recognise their responsibility to the craft itself and the community it is serving' (Baer and Shaw, 2017: 1213–17). This sits within the arena of heutagogy. The 'essence of heutagogy' is focused 'on what and how the learners want to learn, not on what is to be taught' (Hase and Kenyon, 2013). This does not mean that the lecturer is not present. Instead, their role becomes one 'facilitator or guide' (Hase and Kenyon, 2013).

Risks and challenges

The risks and challenges we experience, as well as expressed by our students as we attempted to take a collaborative approach into practice emerged and unfolded from the outset and onward. These concerns broadly encompassed:

1. Students not 'getting' the approach and feeling cheated by not being fed information, expressed as, for instance 'What am I getting for my money?'
2. Lecturers feeling disempowered and disavowed of their knowledge, for example expressed as 'I am paid for my knowledge and expertise, so what is my purpose if I am not communicating it to students?'
3. Lecturers and students engaging at the outset with good intention but becoming disillusioned, or lose their confidence (because, after all, a choreographed path through a wood of trees is clear to all parties!). This was expressed, for example, as 'It's a nice idea but at the end of the day, its better we stick to what we know best.'

4. High-risk stakes of engagement, expressed variously, such as for the lecturers, 'My students have to pass the relevant National Occupational Standards if they are to be able to qualify and practice in the professions, they can't make it up as they go along', and similarly for the students 'It's fun but I need to know what I have to pass in so I can get on and pass.'

Students not 'getting' the approach and feeling cheated by not being fed information

This is not surprising. As Stoszkowski and McCarthy explain:

> Most students are products of a teacher-centred, outcome-based educational system, where the environment is 'more for grades and degrees than for developing curious, self-directing, lovers of learning.
>
> (Stoszkowski and McCarthy, 2019: 4)

This is the case even whilst it is acknowledged that such systems 'are ill suited to equip people to work and live in a knowledge economy' (Linden and Patrinos, 2003: 28) and self-determined learning would be more effective. Indeed, 'changing the way people learn' is one of The World Bank directives pointed up to better support society in its 'demands' for 'teamwork, problem solving, motivation for lifelong learning' (Linden and Patrinos, 2003: 28).

Further, the OECD put the case for

> a personalised learning environment that supports and motivates each student to nurture his or her passions, make connections between different learning experiences and opportunities, and design their own learning projects and processes in collaboration with others.
>
> (OECD, 2018: 4)

But in the UK this is paralleled by a more recent and stronger requirement to train teachers in ways that 'presents teaching as general, easily replicated sequences of activities' (Institute of Education, Faculty of Education Society, 2021). Added to this, focus by the Office for Students on 'regulatory "sandbox" activity for providers wishing to experiment in innovative and flexible approaches *in a way that continues to satisfy our requirements*' [emphasis added] (OfS, 2021: 15). It does not augur well for lecturers or students who wish to radically change their teaching and learning approaches.

On the other hand, however, is the epistemological risk for student, lecturer and professions that being left to design their own learning creates the potential to evolve a 'warped perspective' (Barnett, 2007: 143) of their chosen subject. Similarly, if not engaging with a pre-determined curriculum, the risk ontologically is of students not gaining the required 'personal qualities and dispositions' (Barnett, 2007).

Indeed, these are reasons why Subject Benchmarks and National Occupational Standards exist in the first place. Moreover, the disciplines in focus for us as we explored collaborative approaches were fields with skilled worker shortages and so methods that might be perceived as putting graduation into jeopardy were a risky business. Therefore, for all these reasons there is always a significant focus on graduate outcomes and the need to ensure that students understand the core requirements of their field.

But we contend there is a balance to be had. Of course, students are not just graduates, they are graduates of their chosen study/professional qualification, yet there is value too in collaborating in the class as well as working on their own to explore, create and produce the subject for themselves. Here, then, is space for 'curiosity, open mindedness, imagination, and problem solving', the core higher-order, transferable skills of creativity (General Teaching Council for Scotland, 2022: 2). In the UK this has a history in early and primary education but not at a tertiary level. Creativity, indeed, play, is just as critical in HE (Sinfield, Burns and Abegglen, 2019: 24).

In sum, collaborative approaches challenge power dynamics, the assumed hierarchies of who holds knowledge, what knowledge is, who gets to speak and who controls the 'play' in the room.

Even so, some students were troubled about not understanding the approach or by feeling cheated at not being fed information. We found a way forward by providing a suggested schedule for the module that was designed to scaffold progress without tying them to specific milestones. At the same time, we used the first session to describe and explore collaboration and partnership in learning and its value to their specific discipline. The schedule was enabling students to take increasing amounts of responsibility for their own learning. After all, as Blaschke emphasizes, we need to develop as

> lifelong learners who can survive and thrive in a global knowledge economy – 'learners who have the capability to effectively and creatively apply skills and competencies to new situations in an ever-changing, complex world'.
>
> (Blaschke, 2012: 57)

Lecturers feeling disempowered and disavowed of their knowledge

Thus, it is now clear that an important aspect of a collaborative approach to teaching and learning is that students discover learning for themselves. It led to a dilemma for some of us in relation to what, then, should we do in the classroom. Specifically, if lecturers are employed for their expertise, how were they meant to apply it? Indeed, a key application of the affordances of heutagogy has been its 'net-centricity' (Anderson, 2010: 33), bringing in to question the need for teachers at all.

The role of facilitator rather than guardian of, in Ranciere's terms, 'choreographer' of learning (Ranciere, 1991), was, we felt, an experience that had resonance with Schön's work on the significance of 'coaches' (Schön, 2001: 204). In his writing, coaches demonstrate their *capacity* for professional artistry and in doing so 'help' students develop it too.

'Professional artistry' is a complex concept for which a detailed exploration lies beyond the exegesis of this chapter and can be found in Trelfa (Trelfa, 2020). To summarize sufficient to understand it in relation to coaches, it concerns more than mere competence, comprised as it is of, as Trelfa posits, 'Identity-Of, Identity-As' through 'The Trappings, Connection, Being Prepared, Performance, Qualities of Me and Reflective Practice' of professional practice (Trelfa, 2020: 49–74), 'in the texture of the everyday' (Trelfa, 2020: 60).

'Capacity' involves subject and discipline-based expertise, creative and analytical thinking, social skills of application, and contextual understanding. We can surmise that 'helping students' to develop those same attributes requires capability, that is, 'coaches' (in Schon's terms) who have 'the ability to identify and define problems and handle complex contexts, the ability to adapt to change, generate new knowledge and continuously improve' (Hartviksen, Aspfors and Uhrenfeldt, 2019: 1–19). Applied to teaching, this takes skilful praxis, working with individuals and groups of a range of sizes, at different levels and with differing learning needs and preferences. Regardless of whether the topic of student/s focus fell within our direct specialist knowledge, we found that we drew on our research experience to signpost how they could discover information for themselves whilst also building our own learning about the topic with them simultaneously. In turn, this enables students to engage authentically in ways that suit their personal needs.

But importantly for us, students are collaborators in this process and not merely receivers of coaching, the risk with Schon's recommendation; and to that matter, and where collaborative approaches can differ to heutagogy, it is a shared process. 'Collaboration' requires interpersonal, group and teamwork, and thus the development of associated attributes, dispositions and skills (Barkley, Major and Cross, 2014).

This does not mean it was easy! We found that we needed to give ourselves time and space to generate momentum and ownership of this different relationship and way of working together, matched similarly by students as they too strived to build their understanding and confidence. Here we found our skilful facilitation had fit with Amabile and Kramer's research in motivating teams in organizations (Amabile and Kramer, 2012: 131–3). Underpinned by the values highlighted above, our practice comprised of:

- respect, by deeply hearing the frustrations, and concerns (own and students!) whilst continuing to take the process forward;
- encouragement, holding a foundation of belief in capacity and capability to engage in collaborative learning and to trust the unfolding process;
- emotional support, a key aspect of the facilitation role, requiring confidence to be able to encompass this skilful area of interaction; and
- facilitating affiliation, through a range of activities and the underpinning structuring and support of reflective Action Learning Circles, the approach was taken forward.

Thus, lecturers' practice in these skills was essential, albeit a different, and for some new, 'knowledge' to just their subject discipline.

Lecturers and students engaging at the outset with good intention but becoming disillusioned, or losing their confidence

We found that throwing lecturers with little experience of working in such demanding ways, or confronting lecturers set in comfortable ways of how they teach and now asking them to do something different, risked them becoming disillusioned or losing confidence. Recognizing the essential nature of practice in, and application of, such skills, and the need for time to build up confidence and momentum, led to the creation of 'The Triple P Learning Framework'.

This Framework assists in promoting a collaborative approach to learning and developing those critically important (so-called) soft skills. Indeed, skills linked to respect, encouragement, emotional support and facilitating affiliation are highlighted in the TLRP, OECD and World Bank reports as being vital in supporting lifelong learning.

The Triple P Learning Framework

Pinpoint – Discover the problem or issue.
Probe – Work together to research the issue and form possible solutions.
Present – Demonstrate to the class promoting presentation skills and facilitate peer to peer learning.

The Triple P Learning Framework builds from Barell's 'Directed Inquiry' model from problem-based learning (Barell, 2007). It does so by being distinctive in its simplicity, important for staff given the range of their subject disciplines, teaching experience and confidence, and given the range of potential classroom/ student topic areas that might be stimulated. Moreover, it is distinctive in its application. Students identify the issues that they need and want to research. Through the approach, the lecturer supports the students working on their own and in groups in relation to what they need to consider for carrying out their enquiry, such as the validity of different knowledge, the significance of argument and evidence, and the importance of creativity. Finally, the presentation element enables students to reflect on what they have learnt, demonstrate their findings and also facilitate shared learning, both about the topic itself and *how* the learning process they were engaged in enabled that insight. In other words, not just what they learned about the topic, but what they learned about learning, themselves and each other.

Whilst working with The Triple P Learning Framework to support the adoption of collaborative approaches to learning and teaching, it was clear to us in our endeavours together as well as in our own teaching and classrooms that 'students' of course are not homogeneous! Although supporting a particular classroom approach, it remained critical within it to recognize that each person has their own learning histories, preferences, needs, traits and qualities. This includes the fact that whilst *we* were working in such a way that appreciated the significance of collaborative approaches, not everyone does. As Stoszkowski and McCarthy note, 'Although some students may thrive in an environment that affords them greater freedom and autonomy, others may not' (Stoszkowski and McCarthy, 2019). Of course, the nature of mass education means, even in adult education where choice plays a part, that entirely individualized approaches cannot be put into practice by teachers, ironic in the context of self-directed learning. But we found that such tensions could be alleviated through The Triple P Learning Framework.

Interestingly it is for this reason that Stoszkowski and McCarthy recommend *not* 'deploying [collaborative approaches] over shorter periods (a single semester or academic year, for example)' (Stoszkowski and McCarthy, 2019). Yet we found doing so to be an extremely useful and important way forward, that is, to incrementally build collaborative approaches through The Triple P Learning Framework. From our experience, the Framework enabled individuals to encounter, reflect on and build or hone the 'requisite attributes' (Stoszkowski and McCarthy, 2019; Ibid) to understand and engage.

It was also clear to us that collaborating in teaching and learning would not become the approach of choice by all lecturers, even whilst the value of doing so was understood. Yet our finding was that by engaging in the experiment at all impacted on our pedagogy. Not all of us would go on to fully immerse ourselves and our classrooms in a heutagogical end of the instructivist-students-as-producers continuum, but experiencing the skills and practices broadened our scope and understanding of what was possible. In our case we were already lecturers with an interest in exploring pedagogy and so arguably open to this anyway. But in an educative epoch where featured focus is on student engagement and active learning, the model enabled engagement which piqued curiosity and the development of skills that can only help towards such ends even if not fully embracing students-as-producers.

High-risk stakes of engagement

The Triple P Learning Framework takes inspiration from design thinking (Lewrick, Link and Leifer, 2020) and software 'hackathons', both of which are based on the facilitation of agency, focus, ownership and collaboration in building ideas. However, where contexts for design thinking and hackathons are (typically) low risk, students in HE are assessed on their knowledge and are, for the most part, anxious to at least pass, or indeed do extremely well. Moreover, the performance and practice quality of teaching staff is, to an extent, explicitly or implicitly, judged on student grades, whether through mechanisms such as the National Student Survey and the Teaching Excellence Framework, both delivered through the Office for Students, a government office in the UK, or exam boards and informal staff – and student – departmental comparisons. As Stoszkowski and McCarthy posit:

> [I]f our education system typically rewards specific quantities of knowledge rather than qualities of behaviour, why would a student *[and in our case, lecturers]* want to be more heutagogical?
>
> (Stoszkowski and McCarthy, 2019; Ibid)

This was particularly an issue for highly prescribed subject areas such as physiotherapy and we can assume the same for other equally necessary managed knowledge and practice bases for qualification in heightened interventionist fields.

Indeed, we found that where all four risks and challenges collide was the pressure to perform, whether student or staff, wrapped around variously with expectations about teacher–student dynamic, concerns about training standards, the 'TEDTalk' influence of sharp, edited, super-lit and choreographed teaching, concerns about best value for money, and finally, best teaching for internal and external evaluation purposes.

The essential significance of meta-commentary and reflection about the collaborative process itself was found to be a critical anchor here. In the form of Action Learning Sets run by the students, the module schedule signposted how often they should meet and how some of the time should always be spent on reminding and discussing why they were involved in exploring collaborative approaches. It also affords space to reflect on how the particular source of frustration or concern at any point could be considered part of this overarching endeavour. The facilitator joined these Action Learning Sets at regular intervals and took part in those same conversations, reflecting with them from their perspective. Doing this brought us back to the underpinning principles and creative ground of why we were doing what we were doing. It was a process of 'unlearning' whilst also learning (Neary, 2020; ibid).

Conclusion

This chapter is, at heart, a case study on challenging the 'enforced stultification of students' with lecturer as 'master explicator' by engaging in collaborative teaching and learning and allowing a shared, creative process to unfold (Ranciere, 1991; ibid: 7). If nothing else, it required courage to embrace precarity, the lived felt and emotional experience of precariousness. Precariousness can be exhausting and destructive; precarity can be painful and paralysing. But precarity can also be a source for creativity, of acceptance of uncertainty and doubt, that means mistakes are inevitable but so is learning from them. It reveals something of Choonara's '*beautiful* precarity' [emphasis added], of 'escape' (Choonara, 2020: 430) from externalized control and a lack of agency. Barnett highlights the need to recognize risks but points out if we are risk-averse we limit the growth potential for our students (Barnett, 2007; Ibid: 144); we are not providing the 'requisite space' for them to 'grow intellectually' (Ibid: 145). This is particularly important in a world where lifelong learning is becoming increasingly vital.

Our case study reveals the benefits of:

- incrementally building collaboration within modules through The Triple P Framework to support student-led inquiry;
- a suggested module/course schedule to scaffold that engagement that involves Action Learning Sets to enable reflection on their topic as well as learning itself;
- explaining the collaborative approach and its value to learning in the first session; and
- the skilful praxis of facilitation highlighted above.

These inform, but do not control or choreograph, the teaching and learning, and in this our experience matches those of Peters and Mathias's endeavours in this area, that is 'It forges connections and collaborations that would otherwise lie undiscovered, demonstrating the real possibility of achieving a "radical collegiality"' (Peters and Mathias, 2021: 71). Whilst active learning has its roots in citizenship, collaborative teaching and learning focuses on the nature of that 'citizenship'.

Our experience additionally reveals the importance of opportunity and need for lecturers to train in collaborative approaches to teaching and learning. 'Constructing Knowledge in Higher Education' both mirrored and modelled the values, principles, roles and interactions of collaborative, student-driven teaching and learning in HE, even into writing this chapter itself. Engaging in its precarity and creativity is a vastly different, important and revealing experience than simply being taught about it can ever be. Indeed, our contention is that this is the only way it can evolve to actuate TRLP's principles for effective teaching and learning. Specifically, that effective teaching and learning 'depends on the research and learning of all those involved'; 'recognises the significance of informal learning'; 'fosters individual and social processes and outcomes'; 'promotes the active engagement of the student as learner'; and 'equips learners for life in its broadest sense'.

Sources

Alanazi, A. (2016). 'A critical review of constructivist theory and the emergence of constructionism', *American Research Journal of Humanities and Social Sciences*, 2 (1): 1–8.

Amabile, T. and Kramer, S. (2012). *The Progress Principle: Using Small Wins to Ignite Joy, Engagement, and Creativity at Work*. Boston: Harvard Business Review Press.

Anderson, T. (2010). 'Theories for learning with emerging technologies', in G. Veletsianos (ed.), *Emerging Technologies in Distance Education*, 23–39. Edmonton: Athabasca University Press.

Baer, M. and Shaw, J. (2017). 'Falling in love again with what we do: Academic craftsmanship in the management sciences', *The Academy of Management Journal*, 60 (4): 1213–17.

Barell, J. (2007). *Problem-based Learning: An Inquiry Approach*. Thousand Oaks, CA: Corwin Press.

Barkley, E., Major, C.H. and Cross, P. (2014). *Collaborative Learning Techniques: A Handbook for College Faculty*. 2nd ed. San Francisco: Jossey-Bass Wiley.

Barnett, R. (2007). *A Will to Learn: Being a Student in an Age of Uncertainty*. Maidenhead: Society for Research into Higher Education and Open University Press.

Blaschke, L.M. (2012). 'Heutagogy and lifelong learning: A review of heutagogical practice and self-determined learning', *International Review of Research in Open and Distance Learning*, 13 (1): 56–71.

Bond, M., Buntins, K., Bedenlier, S., Zawacki-Richter, O. and Kerres, M. (2020). 'Mapping research in student engagement and educational technology in higher education: A systematic evidence map', *International Journal of Educational Technology in Higher Education*, 17 (2): 3.

Choonara, J. (2020). 'The precarious concept of precarity', *Review of Radical Political Economics*, 52 (3): 427–46.

Damsa, C. (2013). 'Knowledge co-construction and object-oriented collaboration. A study of learning through collaborative construction of knowledge objects in higher education'. PhD diss., Department of Education Faculty of Educational Sciences, University of Oslo, 5.

Dianati, S. and Oberhollenzer, Y. (2020). 'Reflections of students and staff in a project-led partnership: Contextualised experiences of students-as-partners', *International Journal for Students as Partners*, 4 (1): 1–15.

General Teaching Council for Scotland (2022). 'Creativity in learning and teaching: A professional guide for teachers', *GTC Scotland*: 2.

Gifkins, J. (2015). 'What is active learning and why is it important?' *E-International Relations*, Blog (Posted 8 October): ISSN 2053–8626.

Hartviksen, T.A., Aspfors, J. and Uhrenfeldt, L.L.(2019). 'Healthcare middle managers' experiences of developing capacity and capability: A systematic review and meta-synthesis', *BMC Health Services Research*, 19 (546): 1–19.

Hase, S. and Kenyon, C. (2013). *Self-determined Learning: Heutagogy in Action*. London: Bloomsbury Publishing.

'Healey, M., Flint, A. and Harrington, K. (2014). 'Engagement through partnership: Students as partners in learning and teaching in higher education', *Yorks: The Higher Education Academy*: 7.

Institute of Education, Faculty of Education Society (2021). 'IOE responds to the ITT market review consultation', *University College London,* 18 August.

James, M. and Pollard, A. (2011). 'TLRPs ten principles for effective pedagogy: rationale, development, evidence, argument and impact', *Research Papers in Education*, 26 (3): 276.

Kirschner, P., Sweller, J. and Clark, R. (2006). 'Why minimal guidance during instruction does not work: An analysis of the failure of constructivist, discovery, problem-based, experiential, and inquiry-based teaching', *Educational Psychologist*, 41 (2): 75–86.

Lewrick, M., Link, P. and Leifer, L. (2020). *The Design Thinking Toolbox: A Guide to Mastering the Most Popular and Valuable Innovation Methods*. New Jersey: John Wiley and Sons Inc.

Linden, T. and Patrinos, H. (2003). 'Lifelong learning in the global knowledge economy: Challenges for developing countries'. *A World Bank Report*. Washington DC: The International Bank for Reconstruction and Development, May 28.

Matthews, K. (2017). 'Five propositions for genuine students as partners practice', *International Journal for Students as Partner*, 1 (2): 1.

Neary, M. (2020). *Student as Producer: How Do Revolutionary Teachers Teach?*. Hampshire: Zero Books, John Hunt Publishing.

OECD (2018). 'The future of education and skills: Education 2030', *Paris: OECD*: 4.

OfS (2021). 'Consultation on our strategy for 2022–25'. *Office for Students*, London, 11 November, 15.

Peters, J. and Mathias, L. (2021). 'The pedagogy of partnership', in M. Seal (ed.), *Hopeful Pedagogies in Higher Education*, 59–74. London: Bloomsbury Publishing.

Ranciere, J. (1991). *The Ignorant Schoolmaster: Five Lessons in Intellectual Emancipation*. Stanford, CA: Stanford University Press.

Schön, D. (2001). 'The crisis of professional knowledge and the pursuit of an epistemology of practice', in J. Raven and J. Stephenson (eds.), *Competence in the Learning Society*, 185–207. New York: Peter Lang.

Simon, B. (1981). 'Why no pedagogy in England?' in B. Simon and W. Taylor (eds.), *Education in the Eighties: The Central Issues*, 124–45. London: Batsford.

Sinfield, S., Burns, T. and Abegglen, S. (2019). 'Exploration: Becoming playful – The power of a ludic model', in A James and C. Nerantzi (eds.), *The Power of Play in Higher Education: Creativity in Tertiary Learning*, 23–32. Switzerland: Palgrave Macmillan Cham.

Stoszkowski, J. and McCarthy, L. (2019). 'Heutagogy: Panacea or predicament in higher education?' *BERA Blog* (Posted 16 January 2019).

Taylor, F. (1912). 'The principles of scientific management', Addresses and Discussions at the Conference on Scientific Management, Dartmouth College Conferences. First Tuck School Conference October 12–14, 1911, Norwood, MA: The Plimpton Press, 36.

Trelfa, J. (2020). 'Facilitating reflective practice in higher education professional programmes: Reclaiming and redefining the practices of reflective practice'. PhD diss., Faculty of Education, University of Winchester UK.

4

The Value of Interactivity: Connections within a Community

Louise Luff, Elaine Huber, Roel Boomsma, Janine Coupe, Emma Della Marta, Olga Gouveros, Maria Ishkova, Anya Johnson, Benjamin Lay, Helena Nguyen, Mesepa Paul and Eagle Zhang

Introduction

Creativity in learning and teaching comes in many shapes and sizes. One channel of wide-scale interest is the use of technology-enhanced learning (TEL) approaches to promote interactivity. We have seen the role of online and blended learning grow in prominence due to the recent Covid-19 pandemic along with growth in the use of online collaboration and communication tools and sophisticated learning-management systems.

What do we mean by interactivity? Gleason and Lane (2009) define interaction as 'the act or process of interacting – the process of communicating itself' (p. 5). A growing body of evidence has shown that interactivity is the key to human learning and intelligence (Churchill et al., 2013). Interactivity has also been described as a multidimensional construct (Gleason and Daws, 2012), with each element contributing to online student learning in different ways and to different degrees. Providing students with opportunities to interact through purposefully designed activities and messaging is the first step. For this interactivity to be meaningful for learning, students need to build connections with each other and the content through active learning (Bryant, 2022).

While it is widely acknowledged that technology should never lead pedagogy (Anderson, 2009; Bower, 2017), many of our innovative teaching practices are grounded in learning technologies that enhance the student experience and improve learning outcomes. An additional driver of the growth of TEL is the need to improve the digital literacies of both the learner and the teacher (Huber and Shalavin, 2018). Integration of technology into all aspects of teaching and learning is paramount, and an effective way to do this is to deliver education in interactive ways. The teacher can scaffold students' literacies through provision of opportunities for them to select and use their own technologies for learning (Bryant, 2022).

Developing a community of practice (CoP) (Wenger, 2000) in TEL is an effective method for teaching academics to reflect upon and share their experimental and innovative TEL designs. It can help the individual, the institution and the sector to continually improve their practice and their educational offerings (Reilly et al., 2012).

Set in the context of the rapid move to online learning during the Covid-19 pandemic, we know that students felt isolated, experienced high cognitive load and anxiety, and were searching for support and direction that went beyond current learning in preparation for an uncertain post-university world ahead (Hamza et al., 2021). Through a collection of vignettes, the University of Sydney Business School Co-Design Research Group community will showcase its TEL stories of interactivity and their impact on the student experience so the broader community can also learn from our practices. In this chapter we reflect on our practice of developing learning opportunities that are technology infused and support creative approaches. We discovered the approaches that worked and those that didn't, and through collaborative practices, we tell our stories, synthesize these lessons and share our practice.

Business is about people, and these four stories highlight the human side of business. In today's fast-paced, digital world, underlying concerns such as (lack of) interaction, connection and development of lifelong learning skills are key issues. *How* we interact and connect is of relevance to all disciplines including arts and humanities, and as we model such behaviours for our students, they embed these skills into their learning futures. This chapter speaks to our teaching community, educational designers and practitioners, providing evidence of innovative practice and our joy of sharing.

A group context: Emulating the workplace

Roel Boomsma and Janine Coupe

The sudden shift to a fully online learning environment during the Covid-19 pandemic prompted us to rethink student assessment in our postgraduate financial accounting unit. Most of our students were located outside Australia with limited opportunities to immerse themselves in Australian culture or to interact with other students or teaching staff. We decided to restructure and redesign our assessments to create a sense of belonging (McEwen, 2019) and to make students feel part of a learning community (see Figure 4.1). We utilized the communication platform Microsoft Teams (MS Teams) to run a series of interactive and collaborative business case assignments. Each business case assignment was completed in a small group of three to four students. Utilizing MS Teams provided students with the opportunity to connect with their peers, helped students to develop relevant business skills and enhanced their online teamwork skills. By using MS Teams we were also able to better prepare students for the contemporary workplace where remote work and online collaboration have become the norm. Furthermore, our business case assignments exposed students to one of the most popular online communication and information sharing platforms with millions of daily users (Warren, 2021).

Our group assignments required students to complete a business case in weeks 4, 9 and 12 of a 13-week semester. The three assignments, supplemented with team-building and practice activities, increased the opportunities for teams to bond with each other and allowed us to scaffold the increasing difficulty of the assignments (Hesterman, 2016). To evoke feelings of studying in Australia for our predominantly international cohort, each business case took its inspiration from real-life Australian businesses and exposed students to Australian history and culture. Our cases also integrated aspects of modern finance (cryptocurrencies) and were designed to address relevant business challenges, including shifts in operating models to cope with the consequences of Covid-19.

Figure 4.1 Roel and Janine recording a business case introduction video.

The small student groups completed each business case during a three-hour timetabled session in a private channel meeting in MS Teams. As MS Teams was used for all lectures and online tutorials, students were comfortable with its use before the first business case assignment. Timetabling the assessment reduced the tendency for students to work separately on group assignments and removed the problem of scheduling their own meetings, something they reported became increasingly difficult due to their physical isolation and dispersed locations.

Our business cases required students to use MS Teams to work together in international teams in a virtual environment. We encouraged peer interaction by giving student groups their own private channel in MS Teams – a focused space for collaboration that allowed students to chat, organize video meetings and work on the case material. The seamless integration of Microsoft Excel (MS Excel) into MS Teams made it possible for students to view, edit and collaborate on the case material without leaving their private channel video meeting. We provided students with an Excel workbook file that contained the case material, the questions and an answer template. The collaboration and co-authoring functionality of MS Excel and MS Teams made it possible for student groups to share the Excel workbook file in their private channel and work on it together during the case session. When collaborating on the Excel workbook file, students were able to see each other's edits in a matter of seconds regardless of whether they were sitting next to each other or on opposite sides of the world (see Figure 4.2).

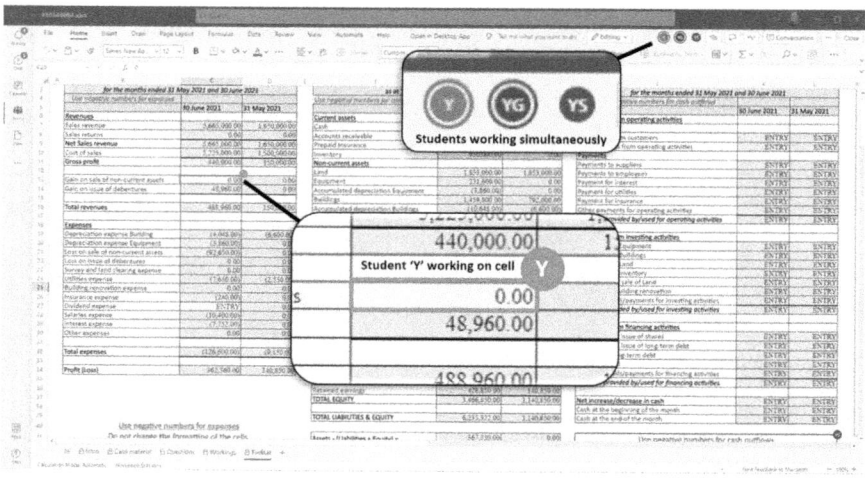

Figure 4.2 Live collaboration in Microsoft Teams using the co-authoring functionality of Microsoft Excel.

Our decision to use MS Excel and MS Teams for the group assignment was influenced by calls from academics, practitioners and professional bodies to better integrate current and emerging technologies into the accounting curriculum (Al-Htaybat, von Alberti-Alhtaybat and Alhatabat, 2018; Jackson, Michelson and Munir, 2020). Our business cases required students to use basic MS Excel functionality to analyse information, record financial transactions and prepare and interpret financial statements. Student feedback expressed appreciation for both the connections made and the realistic nature of the assignments.

To foster teacher–student interaction, an influential factor in students' learning performance (Sun et al., 2022), we asked members of the teaching team to act as 'case coach'. During the three-hour timetabled session, all student groups had the opportunity to invite a case coach to their private channel meeting to seek advice and guidance (see Figure 4.3). This approach simulated the professional workplace where junior staff can call on a senior for guidance and support. It also helped to build rapport among students and staff.

Our use of MS Teams is a vignette of collaboration and active learning in a series of business case assignments. It helped to build a sense of belonging among students new to the University of Sydney Business School. As educators, we benefited from the process of rethinking assessment tasks and opened our minds to the possibilities of technology-enhanced active learning adaptable to both on-campus and remote learning environments.

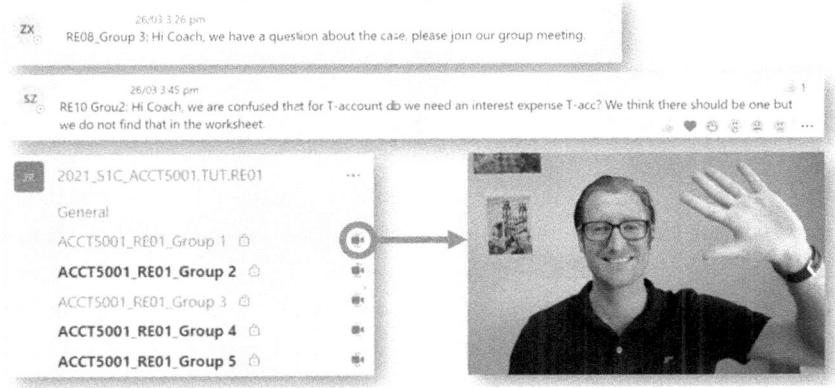

Figure 4.3 Case coach interacting with student groups.

A modular, interactive approach

Olga Gouveros

This epic journey leaves behind didactic lectures and static lecture notes and moves to an interactive, modular approach to teaching and learning. Through a range of educational technologies such as Pencasts, Genially and HTML5 Package (H5P), the lecture experience has been reshaped into a series of modules with short videos interspersed with interactive activities for students to check their understanding through instant feedback, helping them connect with their discipline knowledge.

Most of our students in a core undergraduate first-year accounting unit find it challenging to move from their high school learning environment to the more independent, student-driven university learning environment. After working on this unit for over a decade, it was decided that the unit needed a deep review to make it more engaging for students and to assist them in grasping the key business concepts at the first-year, first-semester level. Our first-year core unit underwent a complete curriculum review and redesign to redevelop the unit using a hybrid teaching style and set weekly interactive modules. Students often found it difficult to grasp key accounting concepts and found the ninety-minute didactic lectures 'boring' and 'too long', and attendance dropped half-way through the semester. Our goal was to re-engage the students, whilst still teaching them the core accounting and business concepts as well as equipping them with desired graduate qualities, such as improved communication and critical thinking skills.

A modular approach to teaching enables the learner to have more control over their learning and accept greater responsibility for their learning (Adesope and Ahiakwo, 2016). Adopting a modular approach provides flexibility to students as they could choose *when* they would attempt the module and whether they would complete the module in one or multiple sittings. We still set a ninety-minute session in each student's timetable as 'lecture time' and built these ninety-minute modules in the unit's Canvas learning management site. Every student also attends a ninety-minute tutorial focusing on the content in the previous week's module. This enables students to practise the key concepts taught in the modules and discuss these concepts in small groups.

By taking a student-centred approach to learning, we engaged the students right from the first week, by asking for submissions throughout the module on short learning activities (interactives) and monitoring the completion of the modules and associated activities through analytics (Nicol and Macfarlane-Dick, 2006).

During the unit design and build we used a collaborative process that involved input from educational developers, unit coordinators, learning designers and media producers. This ensured the modules were of high quality and efficiently used different forms of educational technology to engage, convey and assess learning. Each module started with an overview checklist so that students could check off each section of the module once they understood that learning outcome. In the unit feedback surveys, students commented that this simple tool enabled them '*to monitor what they understood*' and '*where they should seek further assistance*'.

Instead of one ninety-minute lecture, I worked with the production and media teams to produce short, chunk-style concept videos which ranged in time from five to fifteen minutes. After each concept video, I utilized a form of educational technology such as Genially, H5P or Padlet to create interactives that tested the students' understanding of the concepts taught in the videos. These were inserted under a 'Check your understanding' header to clarify that students needed to master these concepts before moving on (see Figure 4.4).

The inbuilt activities and quizzes enabled immediate feedback to students on their learning. Students were able to test themselves and review their own progress. This helped improve students' knowledge retention of the unit content and to master the key accounting concepts. These interactives assisted and motivated students to become more independent learners, and we observed the impact this type of learning had in the tutorials. Students were engaging with the learning materials, were more prepared to answer tutorial questions and demonstrated a higher level of knowledge of the learning materials than in past semesters. The learning activities in the modules also acted as a conduit for feedback at more regular intervals, rather than just after the main assessments. The continuous informal assessment enhanced the students' deeper learning (Biggs and Tang, 2011).

For topics that required calculations, I created Pencasts and spoke through each step of the calculation process. The Pencast technology allowed me to break down the question in smaller sections and explain each part in detail as if I was working directly with the student in class (see Figure 4.5). This was especially useful due to the move to fully online learning as it provided the students with a connection to the lecturer and helped to lessen the isolation the students were feeling during their first semester. We also used background images of the

Try this poll question now: Which statement do you think reflects a positive psychological perspective of failure in a business:

Which statement do you think reflects a positive psychological perspective of failure in a business?

Time for practice now, answer the following question that tests how you can classify the most common forms of business organisations.

Drag the words into the correct boxes for each sentence.

1. _____ are businesses owned by one person who is the sole investor of capital into the business.

2. For a sole proprietorship, _____ means the owner's personal assets may be at risk if things go wrong in the business.

3. _____ are businesses owned by two or more individuals who each invest capital, time and/or talent into the business and share in its profits and losses.

4. Within a partnership, each partner is an _____ of the partnership, meaning each partner has the authority to act for the other partners.

5. _____ is a business organisation that has a separate legal identity from its owners.

Unlimited liability
Partnerships
Agent
Sole proprietorships or sole traders
Company/Corporation

 Check

Figure 4.4 H5P activities.

Watch the following video which explains the classification of assets, the concept of accumulated depreciation, liabilities and equity in more detail.

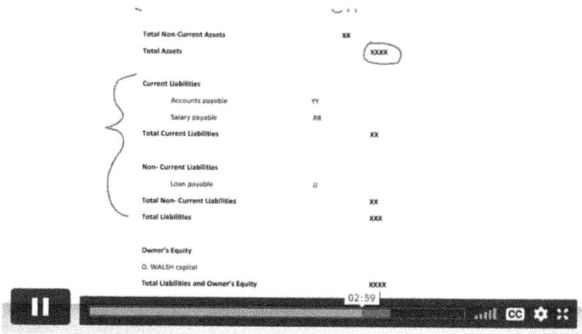

Figure 4.5 Olga's Pencast video.

business school to help students feel a connection to place as they were unable to actually be there.

A student-centred approach to learning was fostered by engaging the students right from the first week, by asking for submissions throughout the module on short learning activities and monitoring the completion of the modules and associated activities through analytics. We ran student focus groups to get feedback on our approach and one group told us 'Seeing the little videos in each module is extremely helpful, it avoids being demotivated when you must sit through 90 minutes of content. Whereas, if you see smaller modules and just work through it, and you check off, … it's more motivating to get through it all' (Student focus group).

Acknowledgements: Our collaborative process was supported by wonderful colleagues including Janine Coupe and Dr Dewa Wardak.

Feedback and its many faces

Maria Ishkova, Anya Johnson, Helena Nguyen and Mesepa Paul

Engaging students in the classroom, especially in a virtual classroom, can be challenging as not all students engage in the same way. Some tend to dominate the discussion (Spencer, 2022), which can make others think they don't have anything else they can contribute, triggering social loafing (Rajaguru, Narendran and Rajesh, 2020). This is a familiar challenge for every educator who aspires to engage their students in the classroom and help them build self-efficacy through the co-creation of a transformative learning experience. This vignette is our experience of building and team-teaching a core unit of study for the Bachelor of Commerce degree in our Business School with 800+ students each semester. It shows how over 4.5 years we evolved our approach to feedback to create a culture of openness to new experiences, requisite vulnerability, trust and psychological safety where students are encouraged and supported to put their best foot forward, interact with each other, their teachers and learn (see Figure 4.6). The FACES of feedback stands for Frequent Actionable Communication (to) Engage Students.

Students' beliefs in the success of their interactions with content, peers and educators are linked to their self-efficacy that builds on performance accomplishments, vicarious experience, verbal persuasion (feedback) and

Figure 4.6 Our team's FACES approach receives its own feedback via the Business School's top teaching award.

physiological states (Bandura, 1977). Fundamental to this, feedback should be constructive, immediate and ongoing (Kuvaas, Buch and Dysvik, 2017). However, it is not always possible to consistently give 'in the moment' or 'tough love' feedback, nor is it sustainable to hold individual student consultations in large courses. This is where a thoughtfully designed software is crucial to deliver personalized, timely and supportive feedback at scale. Our approach is inspired and enabled by the Student Relationship Engagement System (SRES), a cloud-based software developed by the team in the DVC (Education) Portfolio at the University of Sydney and freely available for academics in other institutions (SRES, 2022).

SRES is a limitless online instructor-driven database. We initially used it as an administrative tool to manage our large cohort of students, collating notes on attendance, extensions and other issues in one easily accessible location. Keeping this information in one place enabled patterns to be noticed and proactively provide pastoral care (welfare checks) at scale. Seeing the potential, in our second iteration, we challenged ourselves to create a 'quick notes' feedback interface and set up systematic delivery of frequent personalized feedback that was meaningful and actionable for a student because it was linked to a specific behaviour and shifted the emphasis from feedback to feedforward (Reimann, Sadler and Sambell, 2019).

With each iteration of the course, we evolved our approach. Table 4.1 presents a snapshot of the FACES of feedback we developed and introduced into our unit with Table 4.2 focusing on behavioural feedback.

By providing ongoing feedback and feedforward, we engage in a semester-long action learning cycle that helps students develop a lifelong learner mindset (Yeganeh and Kolb, 2012). This approach helps channel the behaviour of students who (left unguided) would dominate the discussion, allows

Table 4.1 Our FACES of feedback

WHY	FACES	FROM WHO	HOW it is informed	Example
Pastoral care	Personalized, retrospective	Unit coordinators (UC)	Data-driven (attendance records, page views)	*'we noticed … please reach out if you need support'*
Building self-efficacy, encouraging engagement and developing Graduate Qualities (GQ)	Personalized behavioural feedback/ feedforward	Tutors enter the data + UC sets up the delivery	In-class observations	*'thank you for doing …, next time, also try … '*
Deepening the disciplinary expertise, improving critical thinking and communication skills	Assignment-centred	Marker + UC moderates and sets up the delivery	Marking assignments	*'What I loved the most about your paper, was how … In terms of improvements to this paper, you might want to look at …'* + pre-developed comments on each marking criterion
Developing GQ and deepening the disciplinary expertise	Self-feedback	Student	Small continuous assessment submitted before class	Student self-reflection
Developing GQ and self-awareness	Task-centred	Peers	In-class activities designed to ensure high frequency-low fidelity peer feedback	*'one thing I have appreciated about your contribution to class/my learning today'*
Setting the bar	Generalized	Educator	Observations, marking	*'see how the most insightful comments bring in … '*

Table 4.2 A closer look at ongoing behavioural feedback

Participation patterns	Feedback/feedforward focus
Dominating the conversation: Asserting themselves in every discussion to be the first to offer their answer hoping to achieve a higher mark *or* Filling in each pause with their voice as a courtesy to class and/or educator because of their intolerance of silence	Redirecting the student's confidence to take on leadership roles such as encouraging and supporting other's contributions as a pathway to amplify their personal and team success
Minimal visible engagement: Lack of contribution to the overall class discussion from introverted or shy students *or* Lack of engagement from students who do not have confidence in their communication skills	(1) Personalized guidance from educators on how to succeed, challenge themselves and overcome fears endorsed by (2) caring attention from their more confident classmates who have been nudged to focus more on supporting and mentoring peers prompts (3) self-reflection

introverted students to have an impact and builds the self-efficacy of shy students. It brings multiple perspectives to discussions, makes classes engaging and insightful and builds long-lasting connections and friendships between students. Students' motivation for contributing moves from extrinsic towards becoming intrinsic and stimulating personal growth for everyone involved.

Feedback, indeed, has many faces. We are very proud that through the use of SRES we can be confident that all these faces are kind and consistent even at scale.

Acknowledgements: In our SRES journey we are constantly inspired by the innovative ideas and updates from the SRES team led by A/Prof Danny Liu. For more ideas on how to use SRES, we would highly recommend exploring the www.sres.io website.

The three essentials: Human, connected and engaged

Louise Luff, Eagle Zhang, Ben jamin Lay and Emma Della Marta

For our undergraduate second-year financial reporting unit with a mixed local domestic and international offshore student cohort of approximately 350 students per semester, our key question was, 'How can we encourage engagement and build student confidence?' This vignette is about our answer: a reimagined humanistic teaching approach, which, in parallel with TEL tools, effectively connected student to teacher, to each other, and with industry experts to encourage students to engage with their own lifelong learning journey.

Our reimagined teaching approach was framed within a human student to teacher relationship based on trust, openness and caring communication. As trust is built on understanding people, we openly shared insights about our teaching team with students. Welcome, what's coming up and lecture start videos were filmed on Louise's Blue Mountains property where she shared something about her day (see Figure 4.7) and Ben's tutorial groups and the teaching team celebrating his PhD completion and success.

The SRES learning analytics platform was adopted to send a personalized 'welcome to the unit' email that introduced their tutor and included a teaching team photo (see Figure 4.8). This photo is also on the unit's homepage as the thumbnail for the welcome video. Tutorial questions and online quizzes were built in Canvas and its New Analytics function was used at selected times throughout the semester to send 'Are you ok?' Canvas emails to disengaged students, acknowledgements to engaged students and 'you missed Online Quiz 1, please put Online Quiz 2 date in your diary now' reminders.

Each tutor built a supportive rapport with their students and constantly reinforced that the tutorial was a safe, give everything a go environment where it was okay to make mistakes, ask questions and share those 'finally I worked out how to do it' moments (see Figure 4.9). The student to teacher relationship was also used to assess student cognitive load. At appropriate times during semester, a simple and invaluable using your fingers in the gallery window, 'share how

Figure 4.7 Louise shares her day in a what's coming up video.

Figure 4.8 Our teaching team photo.

Introduction and ice breaker

Meet Emma Della Marta

Emma:
- Loves the beach
- Loves travelling overseas (hopefully again sometime soon)
- Is a football fan (go Chelsea!!)
- Has two beautiful dogs (Baci and Macchiato)

Ice breaker

Use the thumb up caption if you have a pet, share a photo or type its name in the chat box

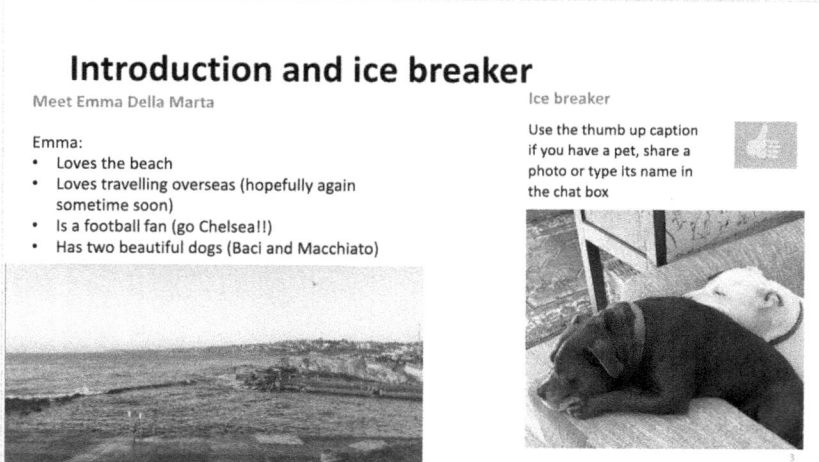

Figure 4.9 A scene from Emma's tutorial.

many assessment tasks you have due this week' tutorial ice breaker was used to identify when the workload in our unit should be reduced.

> *In the online environment being real helps to reduce student anxiety, the unpredictable nature of live remote learning often creeps in, like old dogs snoring. Emma*

To develop students' financial reporting and critical thinking skills and foster student-to-student interactivity, the online whiteboard technology Padlet was developed as a collaborative and reflective learning tool where students learnt from each other (Matthews and Dollinger, 2022). In tutorial groups, students worked on discussion questions entirely in Padlet. Initially the discussion question's key issue was explained by a practitioner in an industry expert interview video, followed by students completing a group written response in a Padlet (see Figure 4.10). The teaching team selected good-work student responses from the tutorial Padlets and provided feedback. These were shared via a subsequent interactive Master Padlet on Canvas and critiqued in the following week's tutorial where students were encouraged to reflect on their original response and, using the Padlet 'like' function, acknowledge the good work student responses. This approach gave students the realization that they could reflect on and change their approach to answering a discussion question over the course of the semester.

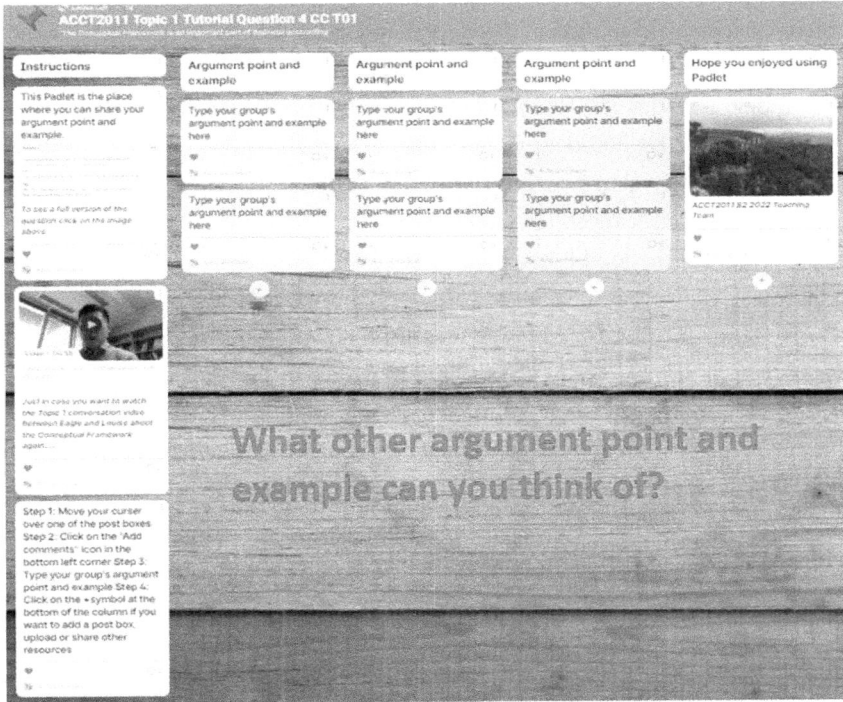

Figure 4.10 Week 2 Tutorial Padlet.

Knowing students are often subject to second-year slump risk (Gregory, 2019), another interactive element we developed was a Practitioner Review and Personalized Feedback task. Through a three-year collaboration agreement, support and feedback from a professional accounting firm, the unit's assessment was transformed into a supportive, collaborative and self-regulated learning task that emulated a team-based workplace experience. Working in groups, students considered a complex financial reporting business world issue and shared their draft responses with practitioners, who, using another adaptation of SRES and the assignment's marking rubric, provided personalized formative feedback and suggestions for improvement. In the final submission, students reflect on how this feedback enhanced their understanding of financial reporting.

Financial reporting requires accountants to make well-considered and complex professional judgements. For students to develop this proficiency, they need to personally make their own decisions as professional financial accountants (Moore, 2013). The Talkit Ltd Project and case study, as an integrated tutorial activity, provided this authentic experience. With the assistance of our Business Co-design team, a professional accounting firm and industry experts, we designed, developed and implemented a case study which required students to analyse the complexities of a complicated accounting issue. To immerse students in a professional accountant role and a virtual office, we filmed an interactive 360-degree tour video of a real accounting firm, embedded it with information pop-ups and developed authentic industry-based working resources, communications and transactions.

These were embedded into a Canvas module that also used interactive H5P, Excel, Google Forms and Padlet technologies. In tutorials, teaching staff worked with students and these resources in a five-step process. The conference call videos from industry experts are the guiding voice in this five-step hierarchy of technical requirements, key accounting concepts, impact on financial statements, influences on professional judgement and making a financial reporting professional judgement so students can develop a critical thinking mindset. Lastly, students submit their own professional judgement to the Talkit Ltd Board of Directors via a Google Form.

It was refreshing to revisit and rethink our conceptions and design the highly effective human, connected and engaged teaching approach. Its interactivity and benefits have been contagious, as like our students, we now look forward to a positive future and working on our next project, Student to Student Talk, where a past student's experience and industry expertise are the guiding narratives.

Acknowledgements: Special thanks to Vickel Narayan for his visionary work on the Talkit Ltd case study, Kimberly Baskin for our always cheerful SRES support and James Friend and his team for their insightful industry expertise.

Conclusion

Through the considered application of TEL, we have designed interactive, student-centred learning approaches which encourage engagement and connection through different forms: with content, with each other and with the teaching team. In telling our stories and sharing our practice we observed the importance of supporting students' digital literacies alongside self-regulated and humanistic approaches to learning that will last them throughout their lives and allow them to take their place in a digitally connected world.

Sources

Adesope, R. and Ahiakwo, M. (2016). 'Perception of educators towards using modular object oriented dynamic learning environment (Module) for teaching', *International Journal of Academic Research and Reflection*, 4 (3): 46–52.

Al-Htaybat, K., von Alberti-Alhtaybat, L. and Alhatabat, Z. (2018). 'Educating digital natives for the future: Accounting educators' evaluation of the accounting curriculum', *Accounting Education*, 27 (4): 333–57.

Anderson, T. (2009). 'The dance of technology and pedagogy in self-paced distance education', 17th ICDE World Congress, Maastricht.

Bandura, A. (1977). 'Self-efficacy: Toward a unifying theory of behavioral change', *Psychological Review*, 84: 191–215.

Biggs, J. and Tang, C. (2011). *Teaching for Quality Learning at University: What the Student Does.* 4th ed. Berkshire: McGraw-Hill Education (UK).

Bower, M. (2017). *Design of Technology Enhanced Learning.* Bingley: Emerald Publishing.

Bryant, P. (2022). 'Transforming business education through connected learning – Part 3', *Co-Design Research Group*.

Churchill, D., King, M., Webster, B. and Fox, B. (2013). 'Integrating learning design, interactivity, and technology', *Australasian Society for Computers in Learning in Tertiary Education*: 139–43.

Gleason, J. P. and Daws, L.B. (2012). 'Interactivity and its effect on student learning outcomes', *Teaching, Learning and the Net Generation: Concepts and Tools for Reaching Digital Learners*, IGI Global. https://www.igi-global.com/gateway/chapter/www.igi-global.com/gateway/chapter/60700 (accessed 9 September 2022).

Gleason, J.P. and Lane, D.R. (2010). 'Interactivity redefined: A first look at outcome interactivity theory', 1–26. Chicago, IL.

Gregory, M.S.-J. (2019). 'Hide-and-seek: Second-year undergraduates lost in the muddy middle', *Handbook & Proceedings of Students Transitions Achievement Retention & Success (STARS)*, 6.

Hamza, C.A., Ewing, L., Heath, N.L. and Goldstein, A.L. (2021). 'When social isolation is nothing new: A longitudinal study on psychological distress during COVID-19 among university students with and without preexisting mental health concerns', *Canadian Psychology / Psychologie canadienne*, 62 (1): 20.

Hesterman, S. (2016). 'The digital handshake: A group contract for authentic Elearning in higher education', *Journal of University Teaching & Learning Practice*, 13: 1–26.

Huber, E. and Shalavin, C.A. (2018). 'Surveying the digital literacy landscape for academic and professional staff in higher education', in *Proceedings ASCILITE 2018*, 142–50). Geelong.

Jackson, D., Michelson, G. and Munir, R. (2020). 'The impact of technology on the desired skills of early career accountants', CPA Australia: 1–35.

Kuvaas, B., Buch, R. and Dysvik, A. (2017). 'Constructive supervisor feedback is not sufficient: Immediacy and frequency is essential', *Human Resource Management*, 56 (3): 519–31.

Matthews, K.E. and Dollinger, M. (2022). 'Student voice in higher education: The importance of distinguishing student representation and student partnership', *Higher Education*, 85: 555–70.

McEwen, C. (2019). 'Student social isolation: Remedying causes and impact in large business schools', Business Co-Design, 52, The University of Sydney Business School. https://ses.library.usyd.edu.au/handle/2123/25446.

Moore, T. (2013). 'Critical thinking: Seven definitions in search of a concept', *Studies in Higher Education*, 38 (4): 506–22.

Nicol, D.J. and D. Macfarlane-Dick (2006). 'Formative assessment and self-regulated learning: A model and seven principles of good feedback practice', *Studies in Higher Education*, 31 (2): 199–218.

Rajaguru, R., Narendran, R. and Rajesh, G. (2020). 'Social loafing in group-based learning: Student-created and instructor-created group perspectives', *Education + Training*, 62 (4): 483–501.

Reilly, J.R., Vandenhouten, C., Gallagher-Lepak, S. and Ralston-Berg, P. (2012). 'Faculty development for E-learning: A multi-campus community of practice (COP) approach', *Journal of Asynchronous Learning Networks*, 16 (2): 99–110.

Reimann, N., Sadler, I. and Sambell, K. (2019). 'What's in a word? Practices associated with "feedforward" in higher education', *Assessment & Evaluation in Higher Education*, 44 (8): 1279–90.

Spencer, R. (2022). '"Hell is other people": Rethinking the Socratic method for quiet law students', *The Law Teacher*, 56 (1): 90–104.

'Student Relationship Engagement System' (n.d.). https://sres.io/licence/ (accessed 9 September 2022).

Sun, H.-L., Sun, T., Sha, F.-Y., Gu, X.-Y., Hou, X.-R., Zhu, F.-Y. and Fang, P.-T. (2022). 'The influence of teacher–student interaction on the effects of online learning: Based on a serial mediating model,' *Frontiers in Psychology*, 13: 1–10.

Warren, T. (2021). 'Microsoft Teams usage jumps to 145 million daily active users', *The Verge*. https://www.theverge.com/2021/4/27/22406472/microsoft-teams-145-million-daily-active-users-stats (accessed 9 September 2022).

Wenger, E. (2000). 'Communities of practice and social learning systems', *Organization*, 7 (2): 225–46.

Yeganeh, B. and Kolb, D. (2012). 'Mindfulness and experiential learning', in J. Vogelsang, M. Townsend, M. Minahan, D. Jamieson, J. Vogel, A. Viets, C. Royal and L. Valek (eds.), *Handbook for Strategic HR: Use of Self as an Instrument of Change*, 152–70, New York: AMACOM.

5

Co-Teaching Literature through the Eyes of the Blind Teacher

Chris Mounsey and Stan Booth

Introduction

This chapter is written for all humanities and creative arts teachers and passes on the experience of Chris, a blind lecturer coming to terms with and overcoming a major impairment. The chapter does not seek sympathy, but passes on the teaching experiences and career outcomes of a successful teaching duo.

The change in practice Chris necessarily underwent after diagnosis, in reading for lectures, teaching and assessing students suggests a number of strategies that fully sighted people might not conceive of.

The idea that an impaired faculty enhances work capability in the humanities should not be surprising for a subject area that is the home of disability studies. However, Chris's conception that no-one is fully able-bodied and no-one is fully disabled has led him to a new conception of VariAbility, which this essay demonstrates: we can all learn from the practice of everyone else. This is demonstrated in the idea that his teaching methodology, which he learned from working with Stan, emphasizes the idea that there should never be a one-size-fits-all outcome for students in the teaching room: an outcome which is not possible in, for example, the STEM classroom.

The double focus in Chris and Stan's teaching room enables and promotes reflexive approaches to teaching, since neither Chris nor Stan claims to be telling the truth about a particular subject under discussion, from which students can gain belief in their own thinking and conclusions. This is further demonstrated by the teaching-led research in which Stan and Chris are engaged, running conferences and editing a series of academic volumes.

Background

I (throughout the words 'I' and 'my' refer to Chris; 'we' refers to Stan and Chris) had been teaching English literature for twenty years when I was diagnosed with a form of macular degeneration which made it difficult for me to read. Like magic, though in the form of twenty-first century technology, books became available to me in electronic formats. I had to learn to read again with text-to-voice; listening is a very different skill from looking at words. Like more magic, changes to university regulations required all student essays to be submitted electronically, so I could read them the same way, whence text-to-voice even makes spelling mistakes audible. Adding comments was slow at first, but when any change happens, there is a time of adjustment, and for me, marking is now much quicker than it was before I lost my sight. Electronic readers can read out loud much faster than eyes can take in information.

But there were some aspects of my work that could not be tackled with technology. Spreadsheets are illegible to me, as are documents with text in boxes (the text-to-voice reader tells me unhelpfully how many lines there are in the box). The choice of Learning Platform made by my university is also geared towards the sighted, and even the IT lead told me that it could not be altered so that I could use it.

As this essay will demonstrate, there is luck in going blind. My diagnosis came in 2010, when the Equality Act became law in the UK, and Harriet Harmon set up a fund called Access to Work which provided me with an assistant, Stan Booth, to help me continue to work as an equal member of staff in a small department at a small university. The Act also stipulated that the university had to make 'reasonable adjustments' to my work pattern, formulated in discussions between myself and the human resources department. This was the genius of the Equality Act; it did not place unreasonable expectations upon employers to prepare in advance for workers with impairments they might employ but it remembered that every impaired person has their own requirements, which cannot be catered for in any sense of one-size-fits-all. I may have no sense of where I am and cannot read spreadsheets or text in boxes or use the university's Learning Platform, but Stan can do all those things. It is from this point that 'I', traditionally a first person pronoun, becomes complicated, as my 'I' is extended. Stan does not believe in creating dependency; he is there purely to support and not replace or replicate. It is a strange synergy, and Stan is not to be confused as an adjunct. Luckily I found the right person for me!

One other thing that disappeared with the onset of my eye condition was facial recognition. This meant that classroom teaching became fraught with my misnaming students. They understood, but I had a strong feeling that underlying students' acceptance of my problem was their feeling that I did not know them as individuals. I thought that this more complex problem might be solved by Stan coming into my classrooms when I taught, but when he came in, he did not simply tell me which student I was talking to, something much more exciting began to happen.

The rest of this essay will proceed with an account of the different aspects of my teaching practice, including the changes that occurred when Stan began to work with me. The reason behind this exhaustive approach is to demonstrate that a blind person can be as effective a teacher as a sighted person, and that perhaps academic employers will become more welcoming to people like me in their establishments. My experience with many universities (as is that of my impaired friends) is that universities are not friendly places to be, but I have written on that elsewhere (Brown, 2021).

Thus, the following paper arises from the chance of my blindness bringing the right person into my classes, which spontaneously produced a synergy between us to the benefit of the students in the classroom. It is important to note that the development of what was to become an unthreatening comedy double act was neither planned and scripted nor has been recorded. When asked to write this paper, Stan and I sat down with a tape recorder, trying to hold the sort of conversation we had in the classroom about what we did in the classroom, but the result was unfocused and full of incomprehensible in-jokes. Developing an environment with two voices and a class of students depends on the context and is not amenable to objective description. Thus, we decided that Chris would write the paper himself, describing the classroom environment that was developed, and so the word 'I' is used throughout and as a reference point to the changes that Stan brought about to Chris's practice. In the end we felt this was more comprehensible to other practitioners than listening to the tone of address that we use. The word 'we' is used four times in the rest of the paper to include Stan at moments when it is unavoidable.

Teaching

My teaching has always been informed by a range of disciplinary perspectives and traditions, grounded in various forms of existential thought and experiential practice, allowing for teaching experience in a variety of different literary genres (eighteenth-century literature, children's literature, women's writing, disability studies, fantasy fiction and sexuality studies). David A. Kolb believes 'learning is the process whereby knowledge is created through the transformation of experience' (Kolb, 1984: 38). Kolb's practice, which I have adapted to my own practice, is made up of four stages:

1. Concrete experience, where the learner actively experiences such as reading a novel, poem or play, or visiting a theatre or a location to experience the living conditions of the writers of the text, e.g. eighteenth-century London.
2. Reflective observation, when the learner consciously reflects back on that experience by attending teaching sessions during which other possible interpretations of the text are presented, and they are questioned by the teacher about their own views.
3. Abstract conceptualization, where the learner attempts to conceptualize what is observed, occurs during seminars when the learner discusses their ideas and interacts with other students who may have different ideas.
4. Active experimentation, where the learner is trying to plan how to test a model or theory by planning an assessment, which may be guided by tutorials.

Kolb's theory aligns with much of my thought and practice, regarding each part of the teaching session and assessment as educational and part of a process of developing oneself as a student and as a person through doing, as opposed to the conception of learning as the development of abstract knowledge through the retention of facts. English literature and culture is my primary research area and the modules I teach always integrate my research process and its outcomes. As such, I have designed and continually re-design a number of modules based on my own research in the areas listed above.

I base sessions, modules and assignments on primary and secondary literature from my own research, lecturing the students on similar questions to my own research questions. Students are thereby taught to become active researchers in the pursuit of their own assessment goals. Often this approach leads to not only research-informed teaching but also teaching-informed research. Thus, for example, my Women's Writing in the Long Eighteenth-century module has led to students gaining many first-class marks (some in the 80+% range) and wanting to stay on to do postgraduate degrees (two students who began in this class now have PhDs) as well as to my publishing two collections of essays, on Delarivier Manley and Eliza Haywood, and planning a third on Penelope Aubin.

I teach classes every semester at Levels 5 and 6, adjusting my engagement with students to ensure a developmental progression from learning core knowledges and how to discuss respectfully with one another through developing individual strategies for student-centred learning that avoid a one-size-fits-all outcome, while remaining within the QA framework for the subject area. In this endeavour, I follow Ira Shor's suggestion that 'education for empowerment is not something done by teachers to students for their own good but is something students co-develop for themselves, led by a critical and democratic teacher' (Shor, 1992: 20). Stan has helped me greatly to become a democratic teacher.

At level 5 I teach large classes, which explore either a literary genre or a period. Following Kolb's first stage 'concrete experience', each class is structured around lecture notes and a wide range of other materials (images, movie clips and artefacts), which maintain the focus on core knowledges; however, as with all of my classes I avoid the use of PowerPoint as this method of dissemination is not flexible and suggests that there is a single goal that each student must learn for each session. The Learning Outcomes for modules are general, as are the Benchmark requirements for each subject area. Honouring both of these suggests there is a particular learning outcome for each individual student. This practice also increases a student's potential employability as they learn how to be independent learners, developing their own critical thinking processes, to become self-reliant and self-motivated.

Example 1

A class on the rise of the novel was reading *Robinson Crusoe*, whose name is an anglicization of 'Kreutznaer', so I suggested that students read the novel as an example of population movement and successful traders. My name is derived from the French, and I used it as an example. At this, Stan intervened in the class and gave the derivation of the names of all the class members, which highlighted our diversity and demonstrated the point which Daniel Defoe made in his poem 'The True-born Englishman' that England is a 'mongrel race', where no race can claim Englishness as their own.

Concomitant with Kolb's second stage, 'reflective observation', it is imperative that students are active in their own learning process and understand themselves as 'a knowledgeable and critical partner in learning' (Bovill and Bulley, 2011: 178). Thus, as a session progresses, I ask students direct questions about the texts under discussion, and encourage respondents to argue with one another if they have differing opinions. I also intervene with new information that may give direction to the developing discussion which precludes the use of PowerPoint as I have no idea what will come up in the discussion, so my teaching has to be flexible and 'democratic' too.

Example 2

If intervention only comes from me, the lecturer, the direction of travel of information remains from teacher to student. But with Stan in the class sitting at the back of the room, the binary becomes much more active and dynamic. Unasked, in one session I was teaching, Stan raised his hand and said blandly, 'I do not agree with you.' This unsettled me, and I felt myself resisting him. But how could I put him down respectfully? 'Can you explain to the class why?' I asked, and he did, so I asked the class which explanation they thought worked best for them, working from student to student. The process took some time, but the benefit was that each student had not only to decide for themselves which explanation worked for them but also to explain why.

Kolb's third stage 'abstract conceptualization' comes next in the form of small group work, during which students discuss an extract from the class text under discussion and report back to the whole group.

Example 3

Having heard the 'mini-debate', as students called it, between Stan and myself, students in smaller groups could then practice the process of building their own argument, based on their own evidence and reasoning, rather than coming to a single group conclusion, which so often is the result of this type of work.

My slightly smaller level 6 groups are made up of students who have experienced our classroom technique and are ready to develop this learning strategy. Thus, each session begins with a general discussion about students' own opinions about a core knowledge, after which discussion, I can tailor the ensuing lecture to the opinions already expressed by the students. In this way I deploy Ramsden's suggestion that '[s]harp engagement, imaginative inquiry and the finding of a suitable level and style are all more likely to occur if teaching methods ... necessitate student energy, problem solving and cooperative learning.' (Ramsden, 2003: 97). My strategy is both subject-specific (the developments in ideas move far too quickly for the academy to record them) and alert to the sensitivities of individual students, who must feel able to discuss all aspects of a subject without fear or discrimination. I have used a similar autoethnographic approach in two recent books, *Developments in the Histories of Sexualities* (Mounsey, 2014) and *Being the Body of Christ* (Mounsey, 2011).

Example 4

In class evaluations for Level 6 teaching, Stan and Chris have become inseparable in the minds of students. But we are very different people and have different ideas and methods of working with students. This is a real advantage, as if a student does not get on with the way I work, they are likely to be motivated by Stan. This has paid off really well for students who, for example, have learning agreements and working with whom Stan has had prior experience.

In sum, all teaching sessions with Stan and Chris are designed to reify the common purpose of academic life and to demonstrate that 'the most important support … derive[s] from a special sense of community … from reciprocal acts of recognition and confirmation' (Kember and Li, 2001: 240). The community of two who begin labelled as teachers and end up as partners in working to find the best in each student's ability.

Assessment

In order to gauge whether students have fulfilled the Learning Outcomes of a module, they are required by the department's rubric to engage with two texts that consider a topic from differing points of view. It was Stan's idea to bring in a third text, of the student's own choice, both to point out the argument and widen the research base of the assessment.

Learning, teaching and class discussions will begin to unpack relevant ideas about the class texts, but students quickly realize that the third text requires that they add their own research if they are to score higher grades in the assessment. Thus, the formative aspect of their learning is structured to that goal and is the first part of the feedback process.

An argument on which a student might base an assessment may be developed in direct classroom interaction. We believe that this is part of the feedback and assessment process since a discussion that leads to this end arises from students' trust that they can experiment with their own ideas in open conversation.

Thus the shift from teaching room conversation to assessment is the fulfilling of Kolb's fourth stage 'active experimentation', and assessment questions are therefore either written in a general form, so they steer the answer rather than demand a particular response, or agreed upon in discussion between the student, Stan and myself, so students' own ideas, backed up with evidence, can be understood to be the way forward, rather than the assessment requiring some predetermined presentation of facts.

Example 5

What has become a general practice between Stan and I is that in discussions with students, I will point the student towards a set of research materials that will lead them to a readily fulfilled essay, and Stan will then 'throw in grenades', that is to say, suggest alternatives which will push a student to think more deeply about their topic should they wish to challenge themselves.

Thus, students are given feedback on written assessments in two forms: before and after the fact. Students are encouraged to bring their early research to a tutorial. My book, *How to Write Successful Essays Dissertations and Exams* (Mounsey, 2013), suggests methods of researching and constructing an introduction, and it is the discussion of a draft introduction during a tutorial that gives the first idea of constructive alignment between the student's ideas and the Learning Outcomes and subject benchmarks of the subject area. This process may be repeated as many times as the student wishes, as drafting progresses.

Example 6

Stan and I have used online tutorials for twelve years, and so we foresaw many of the difficulties which were much discussed during the Covid-19 lockdowns. Briefly, the advantages of having three people in an online tutorial are:

1. They are less threatening than an encounter just between a student and a lecturer.
2. The dynamic of the conversation can shift away from the student, who can listen to us talk about their project.

3. Three people in a room always produce more thoughts than two.
4. Tutorials can be held at mutually convenient times for the student and the lecturers.

Feedback after the fact must be made carefully, so as to respect the differences of individual learners and to promote continued participation by the student, even if an essay has failed to impress, while also being rigorous in terms of the university's marking criteria, which assure QA guidelines are met.

The format for such comments I use is: a positive statement about the best aspect of the essay, general comments about the weaker points if there are any, how the argument might have been made stronger and suggestions as to how the essay style can be improved which might be applied to future essays. Specific comments are made throughout the essay in positive statements. I avoid negative criticism as it serves no other purpose than dishearten students. I use.docx files to make comments, which have been adapted by Stan to make the best use of the vision I have.

In sum the process of feedback, from classroom to returned essay, can be described as 'slow pedagogy ... and slow scholarship and such ideas fit well with the idea of creating larger more integrated assessment tasks that take many weeks to complete, rather than days' (Hartman and Darab, 2012; Payne and Wattchow, 2009).

Access

My time on campus is limited by the hours Stan works. This is no disability, however, as I use the skills my impairment has taught me to enhance the learning environments I create for students by expanding them from the classroom with the assistance of various forms of technology: email, Teams and YouTube.

Communication is one of the most intractable problems in education, and an impaired faculty enhances one's intuition about it and the need for accuracy of language, since I have learned that something which looks reasonable on the page might sound confrontational in text-to-voice, and vice versa. Thus, I have been instrumental in bringing about a university-wide self-disclosure system for both staff and students in which impaired people may explain how best encounters can be managed from the first. The self-disclosure takes the form of an explanation of the expectations of the approach in order to lower the chances of misunderstanding.

Example 7

My email signature is:

> Professor Chris Mounsey
>
> chris.mounsey@winchester.ac.uk
>
> I am partially sighted; please take this into account in your expectations of me.
>
> In particular, please do not send spreadsheets or forms which contain boxes as they are illegible to text-to-voice readers.
>
> Preferred pronouns: he, him, his.

Students with and without impairments must feel they are part of a learning community, and, learning from disability theory, the teaching room, the first point of contact with students, might well fulfil the requirements of Ronald Mace's concept of Universal Design, and be equitable, flexible, familiar, simple to understand, with room for error and large enough. Using this theory, I try to manage the teaching room, as well as informal access to me, to produce the same sort of mutual respect which the self-disclosure statement aims to generate.

Stan and I always get to the room as early as possible, and have music or a video playing with lowered lighting as a way of making the teaching space unthreatening for the students as they enter, the relative dark giving them a place to hide if they feel insecure during class. Stan and I engage in informal conversation with the early birds, which leads to a wider and more focused conversation with the whole group, with the music or video off, but the lights still low, to set up the questions that the teaching session will explore. The lecture and seminar format is not, to my mind, the best way of teaching as it suggests that there are a number of facts and ideas that students need to know, which they can discuss only within the parameters delineated by the lecture. The initial conversation about the issue of the session is aimed to make students aware that their opinion and experience are welcome in class and valuable to their teacher, and it keeps the class lively as the trust which working in this way imparts to students brings forth opinions which cannot be resolved into a synthesis: students thus learn to disagree with one another and still get on. As Lupton argues, 'teaching in this way is an art which "allow[s] for the action unfolding, for spontaneity, for responding to students' needs"' (Lupton, 2013: 160).

However wide-ranging and lively a discussion, students' interest cannot be held without a sense of how the information might be used in an assessment. In the lecturer-centred part of the teaching session, which follows on from the discussion, I illustrate the thoughts and concerns the students have brought with them, explore how they fit with existing scholarship and how they might be deployed in an assessment.

I disseminate my more formal lectures and other materials on YouTube, as it is a resource through which students can revisit what I've said on complex topics in other ways than those I have used in the classroom. For example, a lecture I gave on androgyny at: https://www.ycutube.com/watch?v=cG7GRnc5gxc which might be used by students to follow up the session on 'trans' in my Sexuality and Morality module.

Research

I agree with Wood and Su that it is only possible to teach effectively if one is publishing in the subject area one teaches. 'Research and scholarship are not separate from excellent teaching but are wholly conjoined to it, as reflected for example in the words … "good research should lead to good teaching."' (Wood and Su, 2017: 166). This is because, I believe, that while teachers in higher education (HE) must fulfil the QAA subject benchmarks, the very nature of HE requires that it cannot be guided by some sort of national curriculum of pre-determined goals and strategies, but rather develops out of the experience of the lecturer who is well informed by both quality assurance and is up to date with their subject area. This I do by following two pathways: continual professional development and developing the subject benchmarks through excellent scholarship.

To fulfil the requirement of continual professional development, I engage in constant peer-review of my teaching activities. Since my sight condition means that I have a Stan with me in all classes, I take advantage of the situation and discuss each teaching session with another professional with whom I explore what went well and what did not. I also find out how sessions went by talking to the students themselves, and acting on their suggestions.

Further formal engagement with QA comes from Department and Programme meetings, which Stan and I attend online, and from which I learn about the latest developments. I have also been active in the degree validation process (I wrote the Revalidation document for the MA in English Literature, 2022). This required constant interaction with Stan to make sure that the documents, all of which used boxes, were accurately filled in.

Conference attendance might be regarded as a hinge point between the two pathways to subject and pedagogy, as all conferences I attend are made up of at least one-third pedagogy sessions. Conferences also provide the first-informed audience for projects that began in the classroom. But first, a conference paper needs to be researched, and in this process, Stan is vital, not only in finding materials and making it legible in text-to-voice but also as an informed discussant as the paper progresses.

For my eighteenth-century studies modules I attend national and international conferences hosted by the British Society for Eighteenth-century Studies, the American Society for Eighteenth-century Studies and the International Society for Eighteenth-century Studies, presenting the next forms of teaching sessions before they become journal articles or book chapters. At the same time, I also learn about other developments in aspects of the period that I am not writing on, by attending panels and lectures.

In the field of sexuality and body studies, which feed my Level 6 module Sexuality and Morality, I am a world-leading scholar. I organize two series of conferences, VariAbilities and Queer Bodies, each of which is in its sixth iteration. Connected with these are my monograph series, *Peculiar Bodies*, published by the University of Virginia Press, and my essay collection series published by Routledge*: Routledge Advances in the History of Bioethics*. Both series are paradigm shifts in the field and will change the benchmarks for humanities subjects by challenging existing practice. The monograph series already has six books in its list, the first of which is mine: *Sight Correction: Vision and Blindness in the Eighteenth Century.* I have based a number of chapters from this book on teaching sessions, and I always ask students to write my next book for me. The essay series has six books in the list, a number of volumes of which I have edited with Stan. Working together has generated an unexpected outcome in that we can produce an index together in less than four hours.

How our teaching methodology fits with the ten evidence-informed educational principles from the UK's Teaching and Learning Research Programme:

1.   Effective teaching and learning demands consistent policy frameworks, with support for learning for diverse students as their main focus.
      Students who experience diverse teachers learn that there are no barriers to their own diversity and that there is no single way to succeed.
2.   Effective teaching and learning depend on the research and learning of all those educators who teach and research to support the learning of others.
      Chris and Stan edit a book series called *Routledge Advances in the History of Bioethics*. This brings on the assistant while also reminding the students that their work might be good enough to be published.

3. Effective teaching and learning recognizes the significance of informal learning in developing specific expertise.

   Stan's interventions are always informal, and the collapsing of lectures into seminars adds to the informal nature of the learning experience. Chris and Stan were awarded Outstanding Lecturer of this year by their students.

4. Effective teaching and learning foster both individual and social processes and outcomes.

   Learning to speak in front of other students and to enter into discussions which may result in the parties not agreeing is a really important endpoint. We do not all have to agree.

5. Effective teaching and learning promote the active engagement of the student as learners.

   Because there is no single focus in the teaching room, every student understands that their input might be as important as that of the lecturer.

6. Effective teaching and learning need assessment to be congruent with learning.

   Students in all of our classes choose a text to work on in conjunction with a module text. This adds to the independence of the student's learning experience in the process of assessment.

7. Effective teaching and learning require learning to be systematically developed.

   Our methodology begins in the second year, where the students are fostered more carefully. By the third year, students know what they are getting, and our class sizes get bigger.

8. Effective teaching and learning recognize the importance of prior or concurrent experience and learning.

   The first forty minutes or more of a teaching session begins with direct questions to the students, so they bring in their own experiences of the topic under discussion, whence the lecture section is tailored to their needs and prior experience.

9. Effective teaching and learning engage with expertise and valued forms of knowledge in disciplines and subjects.

   The lecture section is always included, to make sure that students are aware of the academic context of the topic under discussion.

10. Effective teaching and learning equip learners for life in its broadest sense.

    Our methodology reminds students of the importance of their contributions, and as such informs them of their importance to the group project, to the community in which they find themselves, and to life.

Conclusion

In the world of management training, a whole world of writing has been done on the sort of practice that Stan and I came upon inadvertently. Jan Jones's book, *The CEO's Secret Weapon* (Jones, 2015), describes the importance of the role that Stan has taken up in my teaching but also in the corporate management structure. Rather than being a lackey or a 'yes-man', Jones suggests that the assistant can be more important and effective if they act as a sounding board who is taken seriously. To be effective, the assistant has to be treated as an equal, respected and cherished as a person, and believed when they suggest a useful interpretation.

Twelve years into our partnership, Stan and I have moved through arguments and battles to an understanding based on mutual respect. It's a good place to be.

Jan Jones, *The CEO's Secret Weapon: How Great Leaders and Their Assistants Maximize Productivity and Effectiveness*, Springer, 2015.

Sources

Bovill, C. and Bulley, C.J. (2011). 'A model of active student participation in curriculum design: Exploring desirability and possibility', in C. Rust (ed.), *Improving Student Learning (ISL) 18: Global Theories and Local Practices: Institutional, Disciplinary and Cultural Variations*, 176–88. Oxford: Oxford Brookes University, Oxford Centre for Staff and Learning Development.

Brown, N. (2021). *Lived Experiences of Ableism in Academia: Strategies for Inclusion in Higher Education*. Bristol: Policy Press.

Hartman, Y. and Darab, S. (2012). 'A call for slow scholarship: A case study on the intensification of academic life and its implications for pedagogy', *Review of Education, Pedagogy, and Cultural Studies*, 34: 49–60.

Jones, J. (2015). *The CEO's Secret Weapon: How Great Leaders and Their Assistants Maximize Productivity and Effectiveness*. Cham: Springer.

Kember, D.K. Lee and Li, N. (2001). 'Cultivating a sense of belonging in part-time students', *International Journal of Lifelong Education*, 20 (4): 326–41.

Kolb, David A. (1984). *Experiential Learning: Experience as the Source of Learning and Development*. Englewood Cliffs, NJ: Prentice-Hall, Inc.

Lupton, M. (2013). 'Reclaiming the art of teaching', *Teaching in Higher Education*, 18 (2): 156–66.

Mounsey, C. (2011). *Being the Body of Christ*. Sheffield: Equinox.

Mounsey, C. (2013). *How to Write Successful Essays Dissertations and Exams*. Oxford: Oxford University Press.

Mounsey, C. (2014). *Developments in the Histories of Sexualities*. Lewisburg: Bucknell University Press.

Payne, P.G. and Wattchow, B. (2009). 'Phenomenological deconstruction, slow pedagogy, and the corporeal turn in wild environmental/outdoor education', *Canadian Journal of Environmental Education*, 14: 15–32.

Ramsden, P. (2003). *Learning to Teach in Higher Education*. 2nd ed. London: Routledge Falmer.

Shor, I. (1992). *Empowering Education: Critical Teaching for Social Change*. London: University of Chicago Press, 20.

Wood, M. and Su, F. (2017). 'What makes an excellent lecturer? Academics' perspectives on the discourse of "teaching excellence" in higher education', *Teaching in Higher Education*, 22 (4): 451–66.

6

Using Reflection to Cultivate Creativity in Faculty Members

Jonna Myers and Amanda F. Evert

Introduction

The purpose of this chapter is to encourage faculty members to reflect on their roles and responsibilities as creatives and as educators. This chapter is written specifically for teachers walking the tightrope between the art of their craft and the structure of their discipline. It is designed to transform our understanding of reflection from theoretical comprehension into practical application. Several questions are offered in this chapter to stimulate authentic reflection in the reader. These questions serve as 'springboards' helping us to think deeper about how we teach, learn, engage and create. Several barriers and blind spots are also discussed. These barriers can stifle our reflection and smother our creativity, so it is important that we learn to name and combat these untruths. Ultimately, this chapter calls faculty members to step into the difficult yet beautiful act of introspection. This reflective approach to teaching is all about cultivating creativity. Practising the art of reflection ensures that we never stop learning or growing.

It is impossible to fully explore the roles of creativity in higher education without taking an in-depth look at faculty members and the many ways that they promote, discuss and model creativity. It shines through in their course design, lecture delivery, assignment structures, research foci, community engagement and professional service. Still, for many in higher education, the notion of creativity remains elusive.

In recent decades, gurus and pop psychologists have offered recipes, acronyms and analogies crafted to help educators capture the mythical unicorn that is creativity. However, creativity is not a rare event upon which one might be lucky enough to stumble, nor is it a black-and-white equation where the 'correct' inputs robotically produce an earth-shattering innovation. Rather, creativity is a process. It's messy, personal and unique. Your relationship with creativity is yours alone. Thus, it is important to recognize how your own experiences, preferences and strengths shape your understanding and application of creativity. *That* requires some authentic introspection.

The purpose of this chapter is to highlight some of the scholarship that addresses the relationship between reflection and creativity, as well as the importance of reflection for the professional and personal development of faculty members. Then, several specific reflection questions are shared. These questions are designed to help you assess your personal relationship with creativity and how you can incorporate and stimulate creativity in your unique context.

The relationship between reflection and creativity

There is a substantial body of literature which addresses the correlation between self-reflection and creativity (Cohen and Ferrari, 2010; Shrimpton et al., 2017; Verhaeghen et al., 2014). This relationship is highlighted in scholarship from an array of fields including medicine (Chan, 2013; Lyon et al., 2013), psychology (Copeland, 2016) and business (Sunley et al., 2019). Within the field of adult education, the idea of reflection has shaped influential theoretical frameworks like Mezirow's Transformative Learning (1978, 1991), Bookfield's Critically Reflective Teacher (1995) and Schön's Reflective Practitioner (1983). Each recognizes the important connection between creativity and reflection in the context of educational settings.

In the context of faculty development, research shows that many faculty members desire opportunities to reflect on their roles and responsibilities (Marshall, 2005; Shadiow, 2013). However, whether for lack of time or a knowledge of how-to, most faculty members do not regularly engage in reflection unless formal programming or developmental efforts require it of them (Kolbe and Rudolph, 2018). Our hope is that this chapter will stir your desire to do the difficult, profound work of reflection for the purpose of experiencing new understanding in your own personal and professional development

How to catch a unicorn: Reflection in 'real life'

The reflection questions in this chapter are designed to be practical. There are no trick questions or wrong answers, just opportunities to think *deeper*. As with most things in life, the more effort you put in, the more you will learn. As you reflect on these questions, I humbly recommend the following tips to maximize impact:

- Use a variety of mediums to answer these questions – words, phrases, pictures, icons, music and COLOR. Write in landscape rather than portrait. Type it, write in ink and doodle. Try to have some – gasp! – fun.
- Craft your answers across multiple sittings. Start an answer, then put it away. Revisit it again. Draft, revise, hone, etc. Sometimes our best epiphanies need to ruminate.
- Invite discussion from family, friends, colleagues, etc. We are social constructivists, after all.

These strategies are intentionally informal because genuine reflection most frequently flows out of spaces that are relaxed, organic and spontaneous (Gu-Ze'ev, Masschelein and Blake, 2001; Hilsdon, 2005; Hobbs, 2007). This idea is echoed in Standard 3 as identified by the UK's TLRP, which states that to be an effective educator and create effective learners, we must often employ informal tactics. Many students (and faculty members!) have been conditioned to believe that the process of learning occurs only within the walls of a classroom while teachers lecture, and students take notes. Calling students and faculty members into a reflective relationship with learning promotes an engagement with the material that is reinforced by the TLRP's Standard 5: Effective teaching and learning promotes the active engagement of the student as learner. Reflection engages the whole person by asking learners to connect new ideas with their own experiences, understanding and goals. Informal environments foster safety, which frees up learners to focus their energies on engaging in meaningful ways with the material, with their peers and with themselves. As you read and react to the following questions, I invite you to do so in ways that actively engage you in informal and authentic ways.

Reflection question #1: What moment, or moments, have made you feel most connected or engaged as a teacher?

This question comes directly from the work of Brookfield (1995), who asserts that critical reflection helps teachers to define their own ideological biases in teaching. He contends that reflection must be somewhat autobiographical in nature; it reveals something innately personal that connects one's emotions with professional behaviours. The purpose behind this question is for you to begin to think about your sense of self as an educator – what do you value? Which experiences make you think, 'This is why I became a teacher'?

Dear reader, I implore you to ponder this question beyond the surface-level answers that may initially come to mind. If you are anything like me, it is almost too easy to give this question a perfunctory answer that does not require any real reflection at all. Can you articulate the pieces of your professional roles that you most enjoy? What parts of your job challenge you? Can you name the most rewarding moments of your career? Are there 'light-bulb moments' on the faces of your students? Awards you have won? Publications? Scientific discoveries? Each of these examples leads us to new understanding of what motivates us to engage with our work.

Reflection question #2: Imagine your brain as a magical, colourful filing cabinet. It's covered in magnets, postcards and photos that collectively represent YOU. Can you picture it? What memories, words, phrases and pictures are filed in the drawer labelled 'creative?'

This is where we begin to reflect on our unique frames of reference and how those experiences shape our understanding of creativity. Think of this question as the construction of a comprehensive definition. Words are not sufficient to describe the idea of creativity. Instead, it requires all the complexity and nuance that we can muster with our senses, our emotions, our memories and our expectations for the future. It makes sense for us to creatively visualize all the terms, ideas and emotions that reflect what we think of when we think of creativity. Creative thoughts lead to creative learning.

As you seek to answer this question, I might also encourage you to reframe it a bit: What cannot (or should not) be filed in the drawer labelled 'creative'? Are there pieces of your personal or professional self that are 'off-limits'? How do you know? Will this always be true?

Reflection question #3: What does today's world need your students to create?

I must caution you here. With a question like this, the temptation is to default into an answer that looks more like a checklist of learning objectives rather than the product of critical reflection. But we must think *deeper*, my friends. What are the questions plaguing practitioners in your field? What are the political, economic, technological and managerial challenges that your students will encounter in their professional contexts? These questions reflect our need to work together as educators to create a cycle of effective teaching and learning. As the second educational standard shows, educators do not stop learning simply because they are on the other side of the classroom. Teaching does not rely solely on presenting information to an audience; an educator's lesson must be backed up with personal research and knowledge if it is to have any impact in the classroom. When we have a better understanding of the types of creativity needed from our students, especially after conversing with other educators, we can start to strategically craft environments where students can experiment and practise in relevant ways, which will allow for new and varied learning experiences.

Reflection question #4: In what ways can you facilitate spaces where your students feel safe, confident and equipped to create?

Safety and risk are both compelling and necessary parts of creativity (Tu et al., 2019). However, the line between the two can be murky for all of us. Therefore, the impetus behind this question is to provoke reflection around your teaching practices. How can we encourage our students to recognize risks and to discern where to engage with them while also maintaining appropriate boundaries? What tools (literal and metaphorical) outfit your students to create solutions, innovations and new understandings? The TLRP's Standard 7 asserts: Effective teaching and learning require learning to be systematically developed. This framework helps educators to produce contexts that systematically call on students to take risks in ways that are also safe. Educators do not fall into a meaningful mishmash of safety and risk *by accident*; rather, they must systematically and strategically manufacture it over time.

What's next? Name your barriers

You are holding this book, and you have made it this far. Clearly, you are ready to reach new heights in your own personal development and in your students' course experiences with creativity. Part of this journey is recognizing and overcoming barriers that may keep you from tapping the deepest recesses of your vibrant, unfettered creativity. Naming these challenges helps us to recognize them for what they are and to begin to tackle them. Below is a partial list of some potential barriers, as well as tips and tricks for overcoming those barriers. Fear not: these struggles are felt by so many around the world. That's why we need each other – and books like this one. Standard 10 states that effective teaching and learning equip learners for life in its broadest sense. I submit that life in the modern world demands creativity. Overcoming these barriers makes us better teachers, learners and people.

Barrier #1: Creativity feels indulgent.

We are busy. The demands of life require digital calendars, reminder apps and text messaging services just to keep up with our daily to-dos. Thus, making the time and space to enjoy creativity feels indulgent. What's the point, right? But we must remember that feeding our creativity is like giving ourselves a daily serving of mental superfood. When we feed our creativity, we model for our students the importance of growing and maintaining our creative muscles.

Sit down with your calendar and carve out fifteen minutes for creative time. I know, I know – you don't have fifteen minutes to spare. Nor do I. Just humour me, okay? Sit down at your desk/table/coffee shop/favourite sofa and set a timer for fifteen minutes just to *create*. Doodle, rap, write a poem, colour, sing, rhyme, dance or make up an outlandish story. You will be shocked when the timer ends AND sad that the time passed so quickly. The gift of fifteen creative minutes is not a waste of time, nor is it indulgent. It is good for you.

Barrier #2: Creativity feels scary.

Dreaming about becoming more creative and doing the work of increasing your creativity skills are two very different things. Honestly, it is easier to daydream about success than it is to try, fail and then to muster the courage to try again. Many of our self-imposed barriers stem from our fear of failing at this whole creativity thing. What if I make something stupid? What if my idea doesn't work? What if people laugh at me? It's important to remember this very cliché truth: it's okay to fail. In fact, it is inevitable. In some way, shape or form, failure is coming for all of us.

Despite how frightening/embarrassing/uncomfortable failure can be, there is an odd solace in knowing that we will be in good company. If you read the biographies of the greatest creative minds, you will find they all struggled with this fear at some point in their journey. Learning to be okay with failure is an important step in attempting anything new. Not everything you create will be widely accepted or admired, but every rejected piece will lead to a refinement of your process and, as a result, better work. The fear of failure will guide your creativity. Just make sure it does not paralyse you.

Barrier #3: Creativity feels lonely.

Another common apprehension that often accompanies the call to create is loneliness. For those in the act of creating, it's scary to call friends and colleagues into an underdeveloped idea. For others, it can be difficult to articulate your artistic vision. Some even feel a fervent intrinsic need to protect their ideas from those who might steal their work, damage it or fail to capture its brilliance and beauty. Thus, we isolate ourselves by taking a defensive posture and keeping others at an arms' length. If you start hissing 'My preciousss!' at passers-by, it is time for a sabbatical.

Breaking news: Teaching is not a solo sport. Nor is learning. Or creating. So, set aside a part of your creative time to actively search for your people.

Dust off your LinkedIn account, join an association, post on a discussion board and check out an online event; you *will* find your people. Virtual spaces have created nearly infinite opportunities to find like-minded creators with similar visions for the world. Those in the communities you find will be much more receptive to your ideas, even if they may not initially understand or agree with them.

Conclusion

It is quite possible that the role of creativity within higher education will forever remain illusory – seemingly close, while simultaneously so far off. But this conversation around the role of reflection in developing our creativity is important because faculty members play an imperative role in promoting cultures of creativity within the field of higher education. I am convinced that reflection is a critical tool in helping faculty to think deeper about learning, teaching and assessment in higher education.

You're off to great places! Today is your day! Your mountain is waiting, so ... get on your way!

– *Dr Seuss*

Sources

Brookfield, S. D. (1995). *Becoming a Critically Reflective Teacher*. San Francisco, CA: Jossey-Bass.

Chan, Z.C.Y. (2013). 'A systematic review of creative thinking/creativity in nursing education', *Nurse Education Today*, 33 (11): 1382–87. https://doi.org/10.1016/j.nedt.2012.09.005.

Cohen, J.R. and Ferrari, J.R. (2010). 'Take some time to think this over: The relation between rumination, indecision, and creativity', *Creativity Research Journal*, 22 (1): 68–73. https://doi.org/10.1080/10400410903579601.

Copeland, C.T. (2016). 'Take some time to feel this over: Relations between mood responses, indecision, and creativity', *Creativity Research Journal*, 28 (1): 11–15. https://doi.org/10.1080/10400419.2016.1125247.

Gu-Ze'ev, I., Masschelein, J. and Blake, N. (2001). 'Reflectivity, reflection, and counter-education', *Studies in Philosophy and Education*, 20 (2): 93–106.

Hilsdon, J. (2005). 'Rethinking reflection', *The Journal of Practice Teaching and Learning*, 6 (1): 57–70.

Hobbs, V. (2007). 'Faking it or hating it: Can reflective practice be forced?', *Reflective Practice*, 8 (3): 405–17.

Kolbe, M. and Rudolph, J.W. (2018). 'What's the headline on your mind right now? How reflection guides simulation-based faculty development in a master class', *BMJ Simulation & Technology Enhanced Learning*, 4 (3): 126–32.

Lyon, P., Letschka, P., Ainsworth, T. and Haq, I. (2013). 'An exploratory study of the potential learning benefits for medical students in collaborative drawing: Creativity, reflection and "critical looking"', *BMC Medical Education*, 13 (1): 1–10.

MacLaren, I. (2012). 'The contradictions of policy and practice: Creativity in higher education', *London Review of Education*, 10 (2): 159–72.

Marshall, J.L. (2005). 'Learning about teaching in communities: Lessons for faculty development', *Teaching Theology & Religion*, 8 (1): 29–34.

Mezirow, J. (1978). 'Perspective transformation', *Adult Education*, 28 (2): 100–10. https://doi.org/10.1177/074171367802800202.

Mezirow, J. (1991). *Transformative Dimensions of Adult Learning*. San Francisco, CA: Jossey-Bass Publishers.

Schön, D.A. (1983). *The Reflective Practitioner: How Professionals Think in Action*. London: Routledge.

Shadiow, L.K. (2013). *What Our Stories Teach Us: A Guide to Critical Reflection for College Faculty*. San Francisco, CA: John Wiley & Sons.

Shrimpton, D., McGann, D. and Riby, L.M. (2017). 'Daydream believer: Rumination, self-reflection and the temporal focus of mind wandering content', *Europe's Journal of Psychology*, 13 (4): 794–802.

Sunley, R., Harding, L. and Jones, J. (2019). 'Realising creativity in management education: Putting student energy into action', *The International Journal of Management Education*, 17 (2): 172–81.

Svojanovsky, P. (2017). 'Supporting student teachers' reflection as a paradigm shift process', *Teaching and Teacher Education*, 66: 338–48.

Tu, Y., Lu, X., Nam Choi, J. and Guo, W. (2019). 'Ethical leadership and team-level creativity: Mediation of psychological safety climate and moderation of supervisor support for creativity', *Journal of Business Ethics*, 159 (2): 551–65.

Verhaeghen, P., Joormann, J. and Aikman, S.N. (2014). 'Creativity, mood, and the examined life: Self-reflective rumination boosts creativity, brooding breeds dysphoria', *Psychology of Aesthetics, Creativity, and the Arts*, 8 (2): 211–30.

Part Two

Outside the Classroom: Module Design, Employability, Well-being and Post-Uni Care

Revisioning and Humanizing Assessment in Teacher Education

Katherine Bates, John Buchanan, Fiona Dobrijevich,
Sue Lane and Tracey-Ann Palmer

Introduction

Without sacrificing congruity, assessment should be no less imbued with creativity than the learning it measures. The creativity that teachers customarily apply to their teaching and learning experiences does not routinely transfer to assessment practices. Numerous reasons exist for this misalignment. These include ease and speed of marking, high-stakes testing and competitive league tables. For this chapter, five Initial Teacher Education (ITE) teachers from creative arts (visual arts, music, movement and dance), English, history/ geography and science engaged in professional learning conversations about one another's approaches and underpinning philosophies and how our pre-service teacher assessment approaches might apply, and be challenged, cross- and trans-disciplinarily across the arts and humanities. Our conversations, shared documents and recommendations constitute our data, with Habits of Mind (HoM) (Costa and Kallick, 2008) guiding our analysis. First, we established preliminary assessment criteria with a mix of 'standardized' and 'individualized/ idiosyncratic' features. Idiosyncratically, generative assessment is experimental, exploratory, experiential and embodied. Standards-wise assessment demands evidence-based academic rigour. We argue that both spheres interplay to extend the learner.

At the intersection of our framework, learning, while demanding engagement, transcends mere entertainment, assisting to internalize and communicate the material and concepts applicable to the field. Overlying this, reflective approaches to our teaching and active reflection for adult learners whom we teach complement the learning and assessment process. Our conversations explored learner confidence, competence and engagement, and how they complement or compromise one another. We considered how academic assessment might build positive behaviours and dispositions in ITE. By deploying a reflective approach when sharing our teaching practices, we identified the need to design assessments that are both resilient and agile in the face of external changes. A faculty approach to assessment in ITE might contribute to diminishing the exclusion felt by some in approaching the arts and humanities.

Assessment foundations

Assessment in ITE should develop (a demonstrated understanding of) pre-service teachers' academic progress and consider personal dispositions, ways of thinking and problem-solving that serve the development of their capabilities as future teachers (Bryan and Clegg, 2019; Buchanan, 2013). This view transitions assessment from gauging newly acquired content knowledge to one which also values the development of ways of being and thinking in what we consider as a 'graduate-ready' teacher. We know that their growth as problem-finders and -solvers corresponds to their mastery of strong pedagogical content knowledge (van Driel and Berry, 2010). We also know that useful patterns of thinking developed during university study can develop intelligent behaviours, skills and dispositions that can be applied in other adult education contexts and when teaching students in schools (Costa and Kallick, 2008).

Assessment across ITE constitutes a demonstration of curriculum content knowledge and skills, as well as affective states of functioning that enhance pre-service teachers' graduate preparedness, professional resilience and self-efficacy (Pfitzner-Eden, 2016; Shuck et al., 2008). Accordingly, we adopted a twofold approach to assessment design to include professional and personal capabilities. HoM (Costa and Kallick, 2008) offered a means to identify the humanistic assessment dimension.

We identified several HoM within our existing assessment approaches. Conceptually, they served our purposes in several ways. They illuminated the useful behaviours we had identified to support long-term academic and personal growth, and their usefulness for reflecting on our own assessment practices (Figure 7.1). The application of HoM in tertiary assessment is also consistent with The Australian Curriculum's three-dimensional curriculum model,

Figure 7.1 The sixteen Habits of Mind (Images by Dobrijevech, 2022).

comprising discipline content, General Capabilities and Cross-Curriculum-Priorities (Australian Curriculum and Reporting Authority [ACARA], 2022). Our assessment approach also aligns with 'futures-thinking' by supporting learners' intellectual resources for developing resilience, problem-solving and adapting to global issues impacting humanity beyond academic outcomes. In acknowledging that the application, understanding and implementation of capabilities and competences need to be advanced across education (Frank,

2019), ITE is a critical player in developing pre-service teachers' capacities, behaviours and dispositions which they can apply in their future teaching (de Bruin and Harris, 2017).

Background

To inform our understanding of assessment, we draw on its etymology, that of 'sitting beside' someone in advocacy, not adversity. Shelton et al. (2020) advocate humanizing assessment practices. We recognize the double meaning of this – the 'humanization' of such practices might better humanize. Such approaches:

1. are 'as iterative, diverse and meaningful as our students' with less focus on one correct answer.
2. connect to the social reality of relevance to our students' lives and contexts beyond the university walls, for example, by allowing flexible deadlines.
3. engage in multimodal learning, participant agency and choice (Shelton et al., 2020: 126).

One common thread across these elements appears to be imbuing assessment tasks with democracy. Affording extension of choice to adult learners can add, rather than remove, rigour, requiring familiarity with more than one topic, mode and approach, to make informed choices. Moreover, pre-service teachers' choices are almost certain to educate us as teachers; some choices will not have occurred to the facilitator. Nevertheless, there remain challenges. Encouraging creative and critical thinking requires time to tolerate unease and unfamiliarity with creativity, and time for repeated practice to innovate and produce (Flew, 2012). While all our approaches provide practicing through a constructivist frame, time-pressured pre-service teachers may resist, preferring hand-me-down classroom ideas (Harris, 2014). This situation is compounded by pre-service teachers' limited confidence in *taking responsible risks*, favouring modelled templates with 'right answers'. Another challenge is developing the teacher–student relationship; assessment is arguably the most colonizing edge of an educational process that we strive to make liberating and de-colonizing.

Nevertheless, each profession embodies certain expectations. When these remain unmet, consequences can be substantial. While errors made by teachers are likely to be less consequential than those by pilots or doctors, they can nonetheless be dire. Students, parents and the public have a right to expect certain competencies and bodies of knowledge from those who teach. Having deadlines in the workplace is not unreasonable per se. These tensions inform our study.

Assessment in ITE needs to be relevant to current curriculum models, research and education trends for meeting the needs of twenty-first-century learners in an Australian context (Kemmis et al., 2013; Lamb et al., 2017). Maintaining this pursuit of excellence and preparedness for entering the workforce therefore requires assessments in ITE to also be contemporary and multifaceted with a clear sense of relevance for the modern learner. They must also provide opportunities to demonstrate applications of pedagogues that support future-focused learning that is resilient and transformative (Nolan and Molla, 2021; Teacher Education Ministerial Advisory Group [TEMAG], 2014).

Methodology and approach

We have sought here to challenge and enhance our own and each other's practice through 'professional learning conversations' (Schuck et al., 2008). From this viewpoint, we met for eight one-hour online or face-to-face meetings over three months to exchange thoughts and ideas. We recorded our online sessions and selectively transcribed them. We analysed the data thematically, with the development of shared meaning being an iterative process during and after each meeting.

Data comprised relevant excerpts from our online conversations, student feedback and artefacts, including assessment designs, assessment mapping analytics and pre-service teacher assessment samples. These sources in/formed our collaborative self-study (Louie et al., 2016). We focused particularly on our dialogue as a method for interrogating our assessment practices (East, Heston and Fitzgerald, 2009). We engaged in a probing professional learning discussion focusing on the case studies. For our purpose, the conversations focused on exchanging ideas that did not need to reach consensus but acted to reconfirm or challenge, recalibrate and improve our situated practice concerning rigorous assessment that remains contemporary, engaging and valid (Louie et al., 2003; Shulman, 1986). In doing so, we sought to remain *open to continuous learning,* as 'assessing ourselves and changing our own practices so that we're all growing and evolving' (Bates, 3 February 2022).

Our conversations were analysed thematically, and our experiences were evaluated through the HoM lens, among other theories and issues, such as humanism, constructivism, commitments at University, and education jurisdiction levels. Our analysis began with a mapping exercise of associated HoMs, which follows the case studies below.

Findings

In acknowledging the challenges of somewhat siloed disciplines, examples of our assessments in each discipline were shared among us to identify the differences and similarities. This section presents the five case studies we discussed as exemplars of our practice.

Case study 1: Music, Movement and Dance

Coordinated and taught by Sue Lane

Although ungraded, a pre-session survey of pre-service teachers at the beginning of the subject Music, Movement and Dance allows the lecturer to understand the individual's skill and confidence needs. In subsequent tutorials, creative experiences are 'unpacked', allowing further self-assessment, opportunities for *thinking interdependently* and reflecting on activities regarding classroom application. The final non-graded voluntary survey allowed pre-service teachers at all experience levels to reflect on their personal growth and academic learning. In their responses (June 2021), pre-service teachers commented:

> By participating in activities that I would use in my classroom, I was able to see first-hand how effective the strategies are.
>   I really enjoyed the practical experience that the subject provided, as it has increased my confidence in teaching music and dance in the classroom.

Formal assessment requires pre-service teachers to demonstrate their application of the Music and Dance curriculum following repeated experiences and practice with peers. This process creates the music and dance space as a safe environment

HoM	1	5	11
	13	15	16

Figure 7.2 HoMs Identified in subject coordinated and taught by Sue Lane. (See Figure 7.1.)

where participants can *take reasonable risks* and *persist* through activities. This approach particularly supports those 'dreading doing this subject', demonstrated by capacity-building, pushing through perceived limits, and developing academic skills and personal growth, as reflected by a student (non-graded survey, June 2021):

> I was so nervous about doing music and dance in front of my peers. I have done a full 180 on it … The skills you expected were achievable even for someone who doesn't feel like they have a sense of rhythm!

Pre-service teachers were encouraged to *create, imagine and innovate* as they considered new ideas to explore in the classroom. Discovering the process of exploration 'taught [them] so many new things to incorporate into [their] teaching' (non-graded survey, June 2021). Repeated practices also encouraged participants to develop a plan, experiment with the plan and reflect after completion. As a major component of metacognition, *thinking about their thinking* through reflection and discussion, and *remaining open to continuous learning* supported participants in acknowledging their skills, and refining and revisiting tasks, which also resulted in personal development.

Case study 2: Visual Arts

Developed and taught by Fiona Dobrijevech

Visual Arts curricula in primary schools include problematic descriptions that retain notions from the 1960s purporting creativity as some kind of 'substance' rather than a pedagogical and relational process (Caldwell and Vaughan, 2011; Thomas, 2019). To transcend these notions about who is creative and what is creativity, the assessment in Visual Arts designed by Fiona Dobrijevich includes detailed and clear criteria, which promote autonomy and support rather than stifle authentic art learning. The clarity and detail in task objectives and assessment criteria resulted in building pre-service teachers' self-efficacy. As described by Fiona (Pers. Comm, 20 January 2022), they 'talk about the idea of scaffolding, and building up skills and practising. There is a lot of learning involved', practising *communicating with clarity and precision*. An elaboration of one assessment that adopts this approach now follows.

Pre-service teachers participated in five different in-class drawing exercises, *gathering data through the senses*. They submitted a folio of drawings, then a more complex and resolved piece demonstrating skill development and *persistence* in completing multiple drawing lab experiences forming the drawing compilation assessment. The assessment criteria comprise three categories: conceptual analysis, experimentation with materials and of no less importance, the application of study to resolve challenges and complete their pieces. Notable in their

Figure 7.3 HoMs Identified in subject developed and taught by Dobrijevech. (See Figure 7.1.)

productions was the application of *creativity, imagining, innovating* and *thinking flexibly* (Figure 7.4).

The learning tasks provided participants with the same experimental and exploratory drawing experiences, the same design complexity and the same stimuli. The resulting products were assessed against the three criteria. Grades were assigned to conceptual analysis and experimentation. The third category assessed pre-service teachers' sublime aesthetics and how they reimagined the sublime

Figure 7.4 Preparatory drawing exercises and final complex pieces.

by responding to and representing visual and social aspects in images through *wonder and awe*. Thus, particular HoM were organically embedded in the learning and purposefully acknowledged in assessment criteria. The open-ended nature of the tasks resulted in the production of different but equally valued reasons, i.e., realistic representation, idiosyncratic approach, expressive use of media, application of visual elements, and the ability to recognize and respond to sublime aesthetics by *gathering data through all the senses*.

Case study 3: English Education

Developed and taught by Katherine Bates

The subject 'English Education 2' runs in the second year of a four-year Bachelor of Primary Education degree and is one of three cumulative core subjects for the English discipline over their study. This subject requires the completion of two assessments that demonstrate skills in applying strategies introduced in the teaching and learning components of the course. An elaboration of one of those assessments follows. The assessment task had two parts requiring an application of social semiotic theory, English subject content knowledge, multimodal resources and strategies.

Figure 7.5 HoMs Identified in subject developed and taught by Katherine Bates. (See Figure 7.1.)

1. Design four learning sequences that explore a quality picture book over one week.
2. Compose an originally produced three-minute multimedia text (Vox Pop) explaining the importance of explicitly teaching visual literacy across the curriculum.

The production of the three-minute Vox Pops requires pre-service teachers to apply *prior knowledge* about theory, pedagogy and digital technology, *thinking interdependently* to demonstrate content knowledge. Their digital productions also needed to *communicate their ideas clearly and with precision.* Despite being the same task, the open-ended approach used various sub-genres, target audiences and visual styles allowing organic *innovations* within the confines of the required task, i.e., a breakfast show interview, a children's news programme and a short silent film inspired by Charlie Chaplin's popular culture (Figure 7.6).

Pre-service teachers' production choices contributed to the intellectual quality of the assessment and provided opportunities for them to express individuality. It required *flexible thinking* to produce a submission beyond replication. It also enabled them to work in different dimensional spaces, locations and with different people (Kligyte et al., 2022). The pre-service teachers said that the activity pushed them beyond their comfort zones and required them to *take risks.* A small percentage found *responsible risk-taking, creating, imagining and innovating* 'stressful' requiring deeper personal growth of constructive behaviours that apply *persistence* to problem-solve and complete the task.

Case study 4: History/Geography education

Developed and taught by John Buchanan

This subject prepares pre-service teachers to teach History and Geography K-6. The assessment task's main aim is to fuel and extend pre-service teachers' *creativity.* This operates through the conception and production of a text, consistent with chosen syllabus topics/outcomes and by observing how their peers did likewise, through viewing and discussions.

VOX POP Products	Title and link
	Contemporary Visual Literacy Popular culture silent film
	Monday Breakfast Breakfast show interview
	Visual Literacy Vox Pop Children's news program

Figure 7.6 Multimodal productions (included with permission) in the course designed and taught by Katherine Bates.

Task: This assessment task comprises three components:

a. Production of an original teaching resource (in virtually any mode, i.e. written, pictorial, 3D, performance, etc.).
b. An explanation of the work and its conception/design/production.
c. At least one example of the resource's application in a K-6 classroom is to meet one or more History/Geography syllabus outcomes.

To scaffold this task, I shared some picture books I've written, such as *The Ugly Potato*, which warns against wasting food. Excerpts below.

Figure 7.7 HoMs Identified in subject developed and taught by John Buchanan. (See Figure 7.1.)

Daily, across the planet, we waste millions of tonnes of food.[1]
Either it's thrown out by farmers or supermarkets for being the
wrong shape, or size or colour, or it's thrown into dumpsters, or
into our own garbage bins. All this is good food. Below you can
see bananas being thrown away on a conveyor belt for being the
wrong size, shape or colour.[2]

---

[1] Food and Agriculture Organization of the United Nations. http://www.fao.org/save-food/resources/keyfindings/en/

[2] The most humiliating thing is the sign at the bottom of the conveyor belt:

Figure 7.8 Introduction to example assessment response devised by John Buchanan.

The Ugly Potater (And how I became an escaper)

I'm an ugly potater[3].[4]
I got dimples and spots, and a crater!
Got a cauliflower ear,
And lumpy bits here,
'n' me bottom could be a bit straighter.

I do think it's unfair to hate a
Spud like me, with bad skin like a 'gaitor.

Figure 7.9 Opening lines of example assessment response devised by John Buchanan.

Pre-service teachers were given some class time to discuss their proposals in small groups and raise questions or comments with the whole class if desired. Following the marking and the return of assignments, the pre-service teachers create an 'art gallery' of their works, placing them on their desks and circulating around the room to experience their peers' works. A whole-class discussion discerns new ideas they gleaned from these. Next, the pre-service teachers form groups of about three to discuss their resources. During Covid-19, the small groups operated in breakout rooms, with (regrettably) less whole-class sharing. The task, being deliberately ill-defined, encourages *problem-posing* (choosing and designing a text), *empathy* (creating characters in a narrative), *independent thinking* and *communicating clearly and precisely*. Pre-service teachers' examples included a narrative from one of Sydney Harbour's endangered penguins and words of wisdom from an elder Wollemi pine tree to a seedling.

Case study 5: Teaching across the curriculum

Developed and taught by Tracey-Ann Palmer

After noting the risk of siloed nature of assessments, an educational team designed a sustained, transdisciplinary, project-based learning sequence that culminated in an authentic assessment task. It was designed to assess pre-service teachers' discipline knowledge and their ability to apply and communicate that knowledge *creatively* and publicly. The assessment task required self-selected

HoM	1	5	9

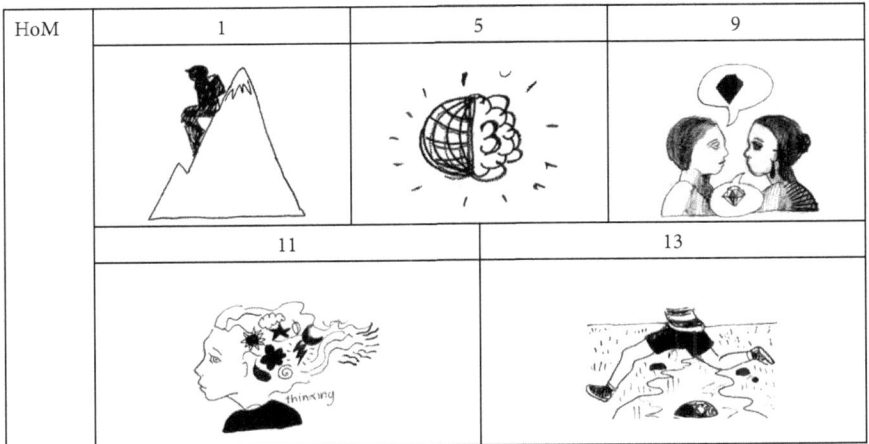

11	13

Figure 7.10 HoMs Identified in subject developed and taught by Tracey-Ann Palmer. (See Figure 7.1.)

small groups of pre-service teachers to collaboratively design and create a museum-style 'exhibit' and an accompanying 'explainer station' that described the intention of the exhibit. The task was trialled in two subjects: Curriculum Integration and English Methods. The exhibits were designed throughout the semester and enabled visitors to engage and explore the 'concept of change actively'. Pre-service teachers were supported through scaffolded workshopping, provisioned with time and expert direction, including guest speakers.

The exhibits were on public display over two days in the foyer of the faculty building. They employed various strategies to engage passers-by, including colourful displays, puzzles and interactive learning technologies. Giving pre-service teachers this type of ownership in what and how they engaged with the task was critical in fostering *creativity and innovation*. Unanticipated positives arose from commentary explaining that the task required them to *think about their thinking* in a formal reflection and taught skills applicable to the classroom in how to engage with an audience to *communicate with clarity and precision*. The production of an embodied experience was critical to the initiative's success.

Initially, several pre-service teachers expressed discomfort concerning the *risk* of presenting their work in a public setting and this created a 'disruptive' moment in their ITE experience. With support and *persistence*, this discomfort dissipated, being replaced by motivation and inspiration. The pre-service teachers noted that they were inspired by the ideas and guest speakers every week. They became comfortable with their display changing and evolving. The teaching team reflected on the experience and expressed similar delight in the outcomes for pre-service teachers (and themselves) in developing positive HoMs to take into their future classrooms.

Discussion

This section describes the alignment of our approaches with HoMs and extricates key learnings from our discussions that may inform similar creative assessment endeavours in ITE. We mapped our assessment tasks against the sixteen HoMs (Costa and Kallick, 2008). We compared when, where and how assessments had aligned with the HoMs (Table 7.1). Patterns emerged which highlighted our

Table 7.1 Mapping across assessment

	Habits of Mind (Costa and Kallick, 2008)	Case Studies: The Assessments				
		1	2	3	4	5
1	Persisting	■	■	■		■
2	Managing impulsivity					
3	Learning with understanding and empathy				■	
4	Thinking flexibly		■			
5	Metacognition (thinking about thinking)	■				■
6	Striving for accuracy					
7	Questioning and posing problems				■	
8	Applying past knowledge to new situations			■		
9	Thinking and communicating with clarity and precision			■	■	
10	Gathering data through all the senses	■				
11	Creating, imagining and innovating	■		■	■	
12	Responding in wonderment and awe					
13	Taking responsible risks	■		■		■
14	Finding humour					
15	Thinking interdependently	■		■	■	
16	Remaining open to continuous learning	■				

multi-dimensional approach to assessment that also offered interdisciplinary and transdisciplinary reach with certain HoMs prevailing across disciplines and the most predominant being:

- Persisting
- Thinking and communicating with clarity and precision
- Creating, imagining and innovating
- Taking responsible risks, and
- Thinking interdependently.

The most salient HoM across all assessments, *'Creating, Imagining and Innovating'*, captures perceptions about self, others and contexts to encourage thinking beyond facts and replication of assessment models, to one where pre-service teachers consider alternatives, generating original work. Our discussions also highlighted that pre-service teachers require more unpacking and explaining for assessment tasks and the importance of encouraging habits that *enabled responsible risk-taking, creating* and *innovating*. The embodied experiences in Creative Arts, for example, support students to, in their words, 'learn through seeing and doing ... (building) confidence in teaching music and movement in the classroom' (Music, movement and dance, non-assessable survey [June 2021]). Sue (20 January 2022) summed this up by stating, 'in a sense, that *is* creativity – learning how to apply your learning in other settings, with other content, in other spaces'. More generally, navigating the unknown is a creative process, sometimes undervalued for its opportunities to provoke, brainstorm, err and reflect on learning for wisdom-gaining and self-education (George et al., 2018; Harris, 2014).

To further encourage responsible risk-taking during embodied experiences, we observed differences in how this capability was attributed to assessment. Some subjects made clear the inherent and implicit expectation of embodiment in their learning experiences and assessment. Others had entire creative tasks as the gradable assessment, with others acknowledging creativity, embodiment and risk-taking in the grade weighting. Despite these differences, the overarching intent was to encourage organic freedom to express, experiment and innovate, rather than focus on performance accuracy.

In addition, parallels were discovered across our subjects with common intellectual behaviours interwoven into our assessments for well-rounded collective capacity-building (Altan et al., 2017; Sava et al., 2020). For example, self-efficacy was targeted across several subjects. Tracey-Ann (21 April 2022) noted that the tasks in science 'allowed preservice teachers to be creative within the task, but they have to be comfortable with the structure of the task, afforded through the scaffold around the task'. Similarly, Katherine highlighted that a significant number of preservice teachers felt 'quite uncomfortable ... [within the English subjects], they panic because they don't want to be on show'. However, repeated practice, sharing and *taking responsible risks* proved to build confidence and reduce anxiety. Sue and Fiona noted significantly low confidence in the arts. With arts education implemented inconsistently in Australian schools due to varying levels of teacher uncertainty, particularly in the primary years (Garvis and Lemon, 2013; Lane, 2019; Russell-Bowie, 2012), ITE must therefore consider building adult learners' dispositions to develop useful behaviours for dealing with the unknown and encouraging an *openness to continuous learning*. Katherine (20 January 2022) commented that we sought an organic balance between 'confidence and competence – developing self as an adult, and as an educator, that then allows them to be creative in learning spaces'.

For many pre-service teachers lacking prior experience in different curriculum areas, much of their learning requires them to move into uncertainty well beyond their zone of proximal development (Vygotsky, 1978). While, by definition, assessments deal with 'new territory' and new learning takes us to the edge and beyond our comfort zone – in our experience, pre-service teachers with limited experience or confidence perceive the gap between the known and unknown as too large a leap. Accordingly, building pre-service teachers' capacity to *persist* and deal with the unknown is critical; we know little of what is ahead for ourselves – even less so for our pre-service teachers.

As individuals, we had identified subliminally that pre-service teachers' personal development was critical to consider and, as a collective, we had intuitively targeted pre-service teachers' self-efficacy. Our findings support existing research that argues the higher a teacher's self-efficacy, the greater the likelihood they will experiment with instructional methods and innovative practices (Bandura, 1997). Left unchecked, low pre-service teacher confidence and self-perceptions about their skills can impact the potential for offering meaningful experiences and innovations to their future students (Caldwell and Vaughan, 2011; Lane, 2019).

An emergent framework

The analysis also highlighted the fusion, yet distinctness of standardized and individualized learning and assessment features, acknowledging that the result of academic labour, while creative, involves attaining academic norms and serving multiple social purposes and goals. In reimagining transdisciplinary education, we recognized the liminal space in pre-service teachers' learning – that often unsettling, fluid space where learners 'surrender' past identities and learning experiences to accommodate uncertainty and confusion before sense-making and expressing new learning creatively (Kligyte et al., 2022). It was here that the HoM came to the fore, and accordingly, we identified commonalities across the academic, social and personal goals of assessment, irrespective of discipline resulting in an emergent multi-dimensional assessment framework (Figure 7.11). Commonalities of approach and theories that endow assessment with freedom-within-structure formed two overarching spheres. Each sphere contains multiple facets that contribute to pre-service teachers' graduate readiness against performance standards and useful dispositions for their future teaching. It visualizes our assessment intentions which seek to honour integrity in two senses: striving for coherent internal structure and fidelity to the world beyond in which our students will operate. Harris (2014) observes, 'whereas standardised learning and testing require good rote memorisation, competition versus collaboration, a notion of right answers versus new solutions, and achievement versus innovation, creativity encourages multiplicity, diversity, undirected experimentation and often a lack of resolution'. Our instincts incline towards creativity here; Harris continues, 'creativity rhizomatically reproduces itself, and in so doing, reimagines the system in which it occurs' (p. 26).

Thus, our assessment mapping identified facets that address ways of thinking and being for applying personal dispositions to deal with the unknown, to be responsive and persistent and to create and innovate without adding another layer of compliance, pushing creativity into a meaningless kaleidoscopic box-ticking exercise. We espouse the value of utilizing creative assessment to bridge the spheres of standardized and individualized learning objectives. Our approach enables us to create real-life learning experiences for our pre-service teachers that help them to develop authentic skills, knowledge and positive dispositions to take into their future classrooms.

Conclusions

Our discussions and mapping exercise highlighted particular HoMs that were applied repeatedly, as well as gaps. This may not be the cause for concern for several reasons. We do not represent the totality of the teaching in our initial

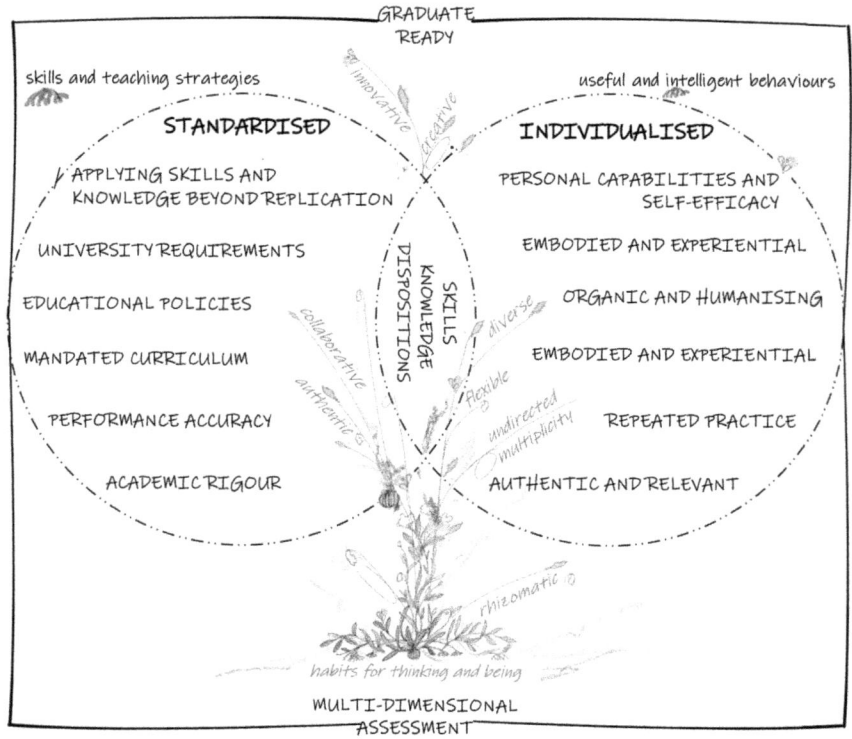

Figure 7.11 Emergent framework.

Teacher Education programme. Moreover, the HoMs were selected as but one way of examining our assessment tasks. Indeed, beauty and terror inhere to heuristics; we strive to transcend box-ticking. Nevertheless, the activity has led us to further interrogation of these tasks, individually, with one another, and with others teaching in the programme, towards a more all-encompassing approach. We identify here some continua that might further guide our and others' assessment approaches:

(i) Higher-order thinking versus basics

Assessment should reflect the complexity that is teaching. It should be enabling and generative, to prompt higher-order thinking, rather than conforming to basal banality. It should challenge and extend learners.

(ii) Creative and open to differentiation, yet rigorous and discriminating

Assessment needs to embody rigour and distinguish among various students' attainment of outcomes. Moreover, we do not enjoy free rein regarding the content of our subjects and assessments. We are answerable to institutional, national and state governing bodies. Ultimately, assessment serves the interests of subject outcomes, rather than the reverse. Yet, there is no reason why an assessment task should not be an engaging, creative experience. Indeed, engaging in the task is likely to result in more incisive thinking and feeling, and in the case of primary education, more willingness to teach associated topics. Differentiation, too, has its limits, in that all students should aspire to mastery of all modes of communication and designing high challenge alongside high support.

(iii) Inter- or transdisciplinary, yet distinct.

Compiling this chapter introduced us to one another's creative worlds of seeing, thinking, teaching, learning and assessment. It has opened us to new possibilities for assessing assessment. But while each subject area is characterized by certain disciplinary, intellectual approaches that can inform other subject area approaches, we do not seek to blend them. We seek, perhaps, a middle road between purism and puree.

This brings us back to the ideal of creativity. While there are necessary constraints on the how and what of teaching, we harbour concerns that current moves towards increased standardism may serve to constrain creative, innovative, humanizing approaches that seek to meet the needs of non-standard learners. We recognize a tension between offering all students equal access to 'the canon', and for the canon and its proponents to be open to students' diverse ways of seeing, knowing and learning.

Sources

Aditomo, A., Goodyear, P., Bliuc, A.-M. and Ellis, R.A. (2013). 'Inquiry-based learning in higher education: Principal forms, educational objectives, and disciplinary variations', *Studies in Higher Education*, 38 (9): 1239–58.

Altan, S., Lane, J.F. and Dottin, E. (2017). 'Using habits of mind, intelligent behaviours, and educational theories to create a conceptual framework for developing effective teaching dispositions', *Journal of Teacher Education*, 70 (2): 1–15.

Australian Curriculum Assessment and Reporting Authority (ACARA) (2022). *General Capabilities* (Vol. 9). Sydney: ACARA. https://www.acara.edu.au/curriculum/foundation-year-10/general-capabilities.

Bandura, A. (1997). *Self-efficacy: The Exercise of Control*. New York: WH Freeman and Company.

Bryan, C. and Clegg, K. (2019). *Innovative Assessment in Higher Education: A Handbook for Practitioners*. 2nd ed. London: Routledge.

Buchanan, J. (2013). *History, Geography and Civics: Teaching and Learning in the Primary Years*. Victoria: Cambridge University Press.

Caldwell, B. and Vaughan, T. (2011). *Transforming Education through the Arts*. New York: Routledge.

Costa, A.L. and Kallick, B. (2004). *Discovering and Exploring Habits of Mind*. Victoria: Hawker Brownlow Education.

Costa, A.L. and Kallick, N. (eds.) (2008). *Learning and Leading with Habits of Mind: Sixteen Essential Characteristics for Success*. USA: Association for Supervision and Curriculum Development.

de Bruin, L.R. and Harris, A. (2017). 'Fostering creative ecologies in Australasian secondary schools', *Australian Journal of Teacher Education*, 9: 23–43.

East, K., Fitzgerald, L.M. and Heston, M.L. (2009). 'Talking, teaching and learning: Using dialogue in self-study', in *Research Methods for the Self-Study of Practice*, 55–72. Dordrecht: Springer.

Flew, T. (2012). *Creative Industries: Culture and Policy*. London: Sage.

Frank, J. (2019). *Teaching in the Now: John Dewey on the Educational Present*. West Lafayette: Purdue University Press.

Garvis, S. and Lemon, N. (2013). 'Are the arts important in schooling? Clear messages from the voices of pre-service generalist teachers in Australia', *Australian Journal of Music Education*, 2: 98–104.

George, S.V., Richardson, P.W. and Watt, H.M.G. (2018). 'Early career teachers' self-efficacy: A longitudinal study from Australia', *Australian Journal of Education*, 62 (2): 217–23. https://doi.org/10.1177/0004944118779601.

Harris, A. (2014). *The Creative Turn: Towards a New Aesthetic Imaginary*. Rotterdam: Sense Publishers.

Kemmis, S., Wilkinson, J., Edwards-Groves, C., Hardy, I., Grootenboer, P. and Bristol, L. (2013). *Changing Practices, Changing Education*. Singapore: Springer Singapore Pty. Ltd.

Kligyte, G., Buck, A., Le Hunte, B., Ulis, S. and Wilson, B. (2022). 'Re-imagining transdisciplinary work through liminality: Creative third space in liminal times', *The Australian Educational Researcher*, 49: 617–34.

Lamb, S., Maire, Q. and Doerke, E. (2017). *Key Skills for the 21st Century: An Evidence-based Review*. Education: Future Frontiers, Analytical Report. New South Wales: State of New South Wales, Department of Education.

Lane, S. (2019). *We Need to Put the Arts on the Map! Exploring the Perspectives of Primary Educators about the Teaching of the Arts in Australian Primary Schools* (uon:35605) [Doctoral thesis, University of Newcastle]. https://nova.newcastle.edu.au/vital/access/manager/Repository/uon:35605.

Louie, B. Y., Drevdahl, D. J., Purdy, J. M. and Stackman, R. W. (2003). 'Advancing the scholarship of teaching through collaborative self-study', *The Journal of Higher Education*, 74 (2): 150–171.

Louie, B.Y., Drevdahl, D.J., Purdy, J.M. and Stackman, R.W. (2016). 'Advancing the scholarship of teaching through collaborative self-study', *The Journal of Higher Education*, 74 (2): 150–71. https://doi org/10.1080/00221546.2003.11777194.

NESA (NSW Education Standards Authority) (2021). *Curriculum Requirements*. Sydney: NSW Government.

Nolan, A. and Molla, T. (2021). 'Building professional capabilities through transformative learning', *Asia-Pacific Journal of Teacher Education*, 49 (4): 450–65.

Pfitzner-Eden, F. (2016). 'Why do I feel more confident? Bandura's sources predict teachers' latent changes in teacher self-efficacy', *Frontiers in Psychology*, 7: 1496–86.

Russell-Bowie, D. (2012). 'Developing preservice primary teachers' confidence and competence in arts education using principles of authentic learning', *Australian Journal of Teacher Education*, 37 (1): 60–74.

Sava, S., Borca, C. and Clitan, G. (2020). *Collective Capacity Building: Shaping Education and Communication in Knowledge Society*. Boston: Brill Sense.

Schuck, S., Aubusson, P. and Buchanan, J. (2008). 'Enhancing teacher education practice through professional learning conversations', *European Journal of Teacher Education*, 31 (2): 215–27.

Shelton, C., Aguilera, E., Gleason, B. and Metha, R. (2020). 'Resisting dehumanising assessments: Enacting critical humanising pedagogies in online teacher education', in B. Gleason (ed.), *Teaching, Technology, and Teacher Education during the Covid Pandemic: Stories from the Field*. Association for the Advancement of Computing in Education, 125–8. https://oaks.kent.edu/covid19ksu/teaching-technology-and-teacher-education-during-covid-19-pandemic-stories-field.

Shulman, L.S. (1986). 'Those who understand: Knowledge growth in teaching', *Educational Researcher*, 15 (2): 4–14.

TEMAG (Teacher Education Ministerial Advisory Group) (2014). *Action Now: Classroom-ready Teachers*. Sydney: Teacher Education Ministerial Group, Department of Education.

Thomas, K. (2019). 'Celebrating the ingenuity and mystery of the cultural achievement of creativity: Animating the workings of the art classroom', in *The Paradox of Creativity in Art Education*. Cham: Palgrave Pivot. https://doi.org/10.1007/978-3-030-21366-4_6.

Van Driel, J. H. and Berry, A. (2010). 'Pedagogical Content Knowledge', in P. Peterson, E. Baker and B. McGaw (eds.), *Encyclopedia of Education*, 656–61. Amsterdam: Elsevier.

Vygotsky, L.S. (1978). *Mind in Society: The Development of Higher Psychological Processes*. London: Harvard University Press.

8

Learning from Experience: Creating the Right Online Environment for Creative Teacher Education

Tony Reeves, Nicholas Houghton and Ray Martin

Introduction

This chapter will be of interest to staff involved in providing professional development in UK Higher Education Institutions (HEIs). This includes, but is not limited to, leaders of PGCerts in Teacher Education, leaders of AdvanceHE-accredited provision and staff involved in delivering these programmes. The chapter provides a case study of a PGCert in Creative Education at a creative arts university, but the course's grounding in social science literature renders the case study relevant to those involved with professional development in multidisciplinary institutions.

The chapter focuses on a course that was intended to prepare tutors to work in a creative institution. As such, the curriculum and activities described in this chapter were designed to relate to the creative disciplines in which the trainee tutors were working. The issues raised in the chapter highlight the tensions of delivering a programme of creative learning, teaching and assessment in a university context.

As the PGCert in Creative Education was grounded in concepts emanating from the literature on creative arts higher education, the course was clearly located in the arts. The activities and experiences described in the chapter all reflect issues that are specific to arts education in universities.

The chapter provides a reflective account of the design and delivery of a PGCert. In doing so, it models the type of reflection expected of teaching staff in higher education. The examples provide a launchpad for reflective discussions on ways of designing and delivering reflective teaching in a university context. The case study itself explores the role and sustainability of PGCerts in creative arts higher education.

The 1997 Dearing Report suggested all HEIs should have an in-house PGCert or be able to access one (Recommendation 13, paragraph 72). This recommendation was very quickly addressed by both 'old' and 'new' universities, and by 2010, David Gosling saw the growth of training in HEIs as 'extraordinary' (Gosling, 2010: 1).

A flurry of small-scale research projects appeared offering conflicting evidence for the value of these teaching courses, and it was difficult to draw any firm conclusions about their efficacy. Findings from two reviews suggested a move from a teacher-centred to a more student-centred practice (Gibbs and Coffey, 2004; Gosling, 2010), and there was early evidence that teachers felt more confident after engaging in PGCert courses (Butcher and Stoncel, 2012). Ball (2015) wonders if the real educational needs of teaching staff are being addressed.

Following the introduction of the Teaching Excellence Framework in 2017, there have been increasing calls for evidence of value for money in higher education (HE) teaching. Kushnir and Spowart (2021) note that research is still limited and are calling for a large cross-university study to determine the value of such courses as the PGCert. However, what teaching excellence might be and what the PGCert might bring to this remain contested (Butcher and Stoncel, 2012).

As with many universities, this policy context formed the backdrop to the PGCert in Creative Education at University for the Creative Arts (UCA). Initially developed in 2011 by our predecessor, Dr Gill Nah, the course played a central role in providing staff with a teaching qualification. But following the abolition of the Teaching and Learning team in 2012, the course became the sole outpost for those staff wishing to discuss and explore aspects of their teaching practice. In a culture that very much reflected that of the 'pressure vessels' described by Morrish (2019), the former members of the team were distributed across the university with no formal mechanisms for continuing their work. This led to the development of an almost 'underground network' of staff, who continued to promote good practice in learning and teaching in a clandestine manner. This experience was central to the positioning of critical pedagogy in the course curriculum as a way to prepare students for the power and politics of higher education, but more on that later on.

Designing the learning experience

The introduction of the Teaching Excellence Framework (TEF) in 2016 had renewed the emphasis on the need for a coordinated approach to learning and teaching. When the three of us took over the reins of the course in June 2018, we therefore had the opportunity to revalidate the curriculum and review the course philosophy and delivery. The starting point wasn't the fact we needed an online course, but rather to look at what we thought needed to be learned and what the philosophy of course would be.

As far as possible we started from scratch. Although we acknowledge that it's impossible to eradicate all we knew from previous, similar courses, we didn't want our course to be a revision of any previous course. Instead, our aim was to develop a course informed by current research and best practice. If we ended up re-inventing the wheel, so be it. If nothing else, doing it this way ensured we had ownership – and that we would know what we were doing and why.

After much discussion, we decided to use seven principles to underpin the course design:

- Connecting: informed by the work of Fung (2017) on the idea of the connected curriculum, we believed the curriculum should connect students with each other and with the world beyond the course;
- Critical: the need for criticality and critical reflection is widely recognized as central to teacher professional development (Bright, 1996; Brookfield, 1995; Dewey, 1933; Schön, 1996);
- Creative: the focus of the course on teaching in creative disciplines meant the curriculum needed to be grounded in creativity and creative practice;
- Co-constructed: this was informed by our intention to place team-based learning (Michaelson et al., 2004; Sookhoo and Thurston, 2018) at the centre of the learning experience;
- Inclusive: it was essential that we didn't just talk about the importance of inclusivity, but we also had to model it through the course design;
- Intercultural: in order to prepare students for an increasingly internationalized classroom, the curriculum needed to model the importance of intercultural awareness through language, resources and learning experiences;
- Research informed: in order to promote critical reflection, everything we did on the course needed to be grounded in relevant research.

This work was to prove crucial, because these principles enabled us to verify whether each specific aspect of the learning experience aligned with our guiding principles.

In addition, we used specific learning theories to inform the development of the curriculum. These were:

- Social constructivism (Vygotsky, 1978): we believed that the concepts of the 'more knowledgeable other' and 'Zone of Proximal Development' are highly relevant to teacher education;
- Facilitation (Rogers, 1951): Rogers's argument for showing students 'unconditional positive regard' is a strong theoretical basis upon which to build a culture of inclusivity;
- Empowerment (Freire, 2005): we felt it necessary to make students aware of the role of power in education, both in the classroom and in the university more widely.
- Connected Curriculum (Fung, 2017): Fung's work on the idea of 'students as researchers' informed the design of the individual and team projects, as it highlights the value of providing students with authentic assessment tasks.

Curriculum design

Having established the theories and principles underpinning the course, we then began designing the curriculum. The course was initially designed to be a hybrid experience, informed by the research of Hill and colleagues (2009) who observed the value of groups meeting in person before collaborating online. This required a learning environment that could support the multiple elements of the curriculum design. For the online learning environment to be effective, it would first be necessary to establish trust between the participants (Gibson and Manuel, 2003; Hart and McLeod, 2003; Wilson, Straus and McEvily, 2006). Given that the participants would only meet twice in person, there was a need to maximize the value of the two days where participants met on campus, one at the start of each of the two modules.

To establish and build trust, we used a series of five weekly warm-up activities that were designed to enable participants to get to know each other before meeting in person. These activities were as follows:

1. Join the LinkedIn group, download the pre-readings and videos and watch the three short interviews with previous graduates. The readings and videos introduced participants to the concept of creative education, and the interviews provided them with an insight into the learning experience through the eyes of recent graduates.

2. Share your 'Desert Island Discs'. This is a shortened version of the long-running BBC Radio 4 programme in which guests share the records they would take with them if they were to be stranded on a desert island. We asked participants to share the records, the book and the luxury item they would take with them. This activity provided an insight into people's personal tastes, enabling them to both bond emotionally and discover new books and music.

3. Respond to the question: 'What does creative education mean to you?' This used the dynamic of accountability to get participants to engage with the pre-readings and videos, and provided a gradual introduction to the kind of critical discussion we wanted participants to experience on the course.

4. Create a model of the next four months of your professional life. Informed by the work of Chrissi Nerantzi and Alison James on using LEGO for reflective practice, the course team used LEGO to literally model the key moments in the first few months of the course. The aim of doing so was to visualize the learning experience for participants in a fun way and encourage them to do the same. They did not disappoint, and many created paintings and sculptures using household objects which showed deep reflection about the personal and professional obstacles they would need to navigate in the coming months while they studied.

5. Join a technical testing session. This final warm-up activity was designed to minimize the time spent resolving technical issues during the Day 1 meeting and also to familiarize participants with Zoom. Participants were asked to join a Zoom session, share their screen, use the chat and practise raising and lowering their hand. This meant that when they joined their first online session they would already have some experience of how to use these key features.

The curriculum design itself was informed by the principle of 'little and often', which is one of the ADSHE 'seven principles for supporting neurodivergent students in Higher Education' (Association of Dyslexia Specialists in Higher Education). The largely online nature of the learning experience meant it would be very easy for participants to just turn up for the live sessions and do little work in between. To avoid this problem, every week had a clear rhythm. The week began with a short video from the course leader sent out on Monday morning which introduced the weekly readings and highlighted the key points. Participants were asked to watch this video and explore one or more of the weekly readings during Monday and Tuesday, and share one key insight on the LinkedIn group. These readings were intended to generate pre-lecture interest in the topics, and also to reduce cognitive load. This is particularly for neurodiverse and international students – for educationalist Dylan Wilian, 'Sweller's Cognitive Load Theory is the single most important thing for teachers to know' (cited in Lovell, 2021). This generated engagement with the reading material and insights that could then be discussed in the synchronous Wednesday session.

The key points for the weekly sessions also included a 'teaching tip', the aim of which was to provide practical strategies for inclusive teaching and assessment that participants could put straight into practice. Using the 'little and often' principle, these ideas were then curated to ensure ideas and concepts covered previously were reviewed and to introduce new ideas. Sometimes they were quotes from one of our students so that they could claim some ownership of the material. The inclusivity tips included notes on protecting our PGCert students from themselves and from the health-sapping demands HEIs now make on their staff. Apart from anything else, how can they inspire and support their students – even adequately – if they are dealing with their own mental crises?

The group then met on Wednesday mornings for two hours on Zoom, and the focus of the session was to encourage further debate and discussion of the reading material. These sessions were grounded in Rogers's theory of facilitation, in which the course team aimed to facilitate discussion and questioning rather than simply impart information.

A second synchronous session took place on Thursday evenings. During this one-hour session, participants worked in teams to complete a series of team-based learning projects (these will be discussed in more detail later in the chapter). Finally, participants were set a short weekly task to complete and upload to their learning log over the weekend.

The 'little and often' approach was also informed by the concept of Universal Design for Learning (Fornauf and Erikson, 2020), which advocates the use of 'multiple means of engagement' with course materials. By providing participants with multiple ways to access learning during the week, the aim was to model an approach that participants could use with their own students.

Learning environment

As participants only gained access to the Blackboard Virtual Learning Environment (VLE) at the point of enrolment, we felt there was a need to engage them in discussions and activities before the start of the course to deliver the socially constructed aspect of the learning experience. To achieve this, we opted to use the LinkedIn platform to support the social aspect of the learning experience. This was because almost all participants already had LinkedIn accounts and because LinkedIn offered the ability to create free, private 'group' spaces. The LinkedIn group was to prove central to the learning experience, as it created a less formal, more democratic 'social' space where debates could be had and opinions could be shared easily.

The group provided a necessary counterpart to the more formal VLE, which felt more the domain of the university. The VLE played a useful role in transmitting information to participants including weekly readings, links for online sessions and key documents. Participants were also each given a blog on the VLE, which we renamed as a 'learning log', and this is where they uploaded their weekly tasks. All learning logs were visible to all participants, and they were able to comment on each other's learning logs.

The weekly, two-hour live sessions were delivered via Zoom, which in 2018 was still a relatively unknown platform. The course team needed a robust platform to support the synchronous session and team-based activities, and Zoom's effectiveness in supporting social, collaborative learning had been demonstrated by its use on the popular AltMBA course run by marketing guru Seth Godin. The reliability of Zoom and its ease of use for participants unfamiliar with the platform were integral to the success of the course.

Finally, the connected curriculum aspect of the course was supported by the use of a Wordpress blog. This provided a public-facing space in the form of a journal called the *Journal of Useful Investigations in Creative Education*. This provided a way to share work created by participants after it had been peer reviewed and revised. The journal was to play a key role in making the individual and team projects feel more authentic and to create the feeling of 'students as researchers' (Fung, 2017).

Assessment

The course team also applied the little and often approach recommended by ADSHE to assessment and feedback, and there were several reasons for this.

In previous iterations of the course, participants had produced essays for their assessment. But as participants were almost always taking the course alongside their day job of teaching, the problem was that these essays were often written hastily in the final week of a module. In addition, a significant number of participants experienced dyslexia, which further hindered their ability to produce an essay in a short space of time.

A further problem with the use of end-of-module essays was that students couldn't use the summative feedback provided to improve their work. Inspired by the research of Hattie (2009) into visible learning, the course team changed assessment to a series of weekly tasks, with students uploading each task to an individual blog on the VLE. Hattie notes that effective teaching requires that 'the teacher comes to class to evaluate the impact of their teaching' (ibid. 2015: 87). The blogs made it possible to see what students had learned (or not learned) on a weekly basis and for teaching to be adapted in response. Hattie's research also indicates that 'the biggest effects on student learning occur when teachers become learners of their own teaching and when students become their own teachers'. The weekly blog-based assessment tasks meant that students were able to see and provide formative feedback, on each other's work. Every few weeks, one of their weekly tasks would be to provide feedback, and at the end of the module they would choose and submit five of their best pieces of feedback as part of their assessment. This approach reduced their dependency on the course team for feedback and guidance, enabled them to practise writing effective feedback based on what they had learned, and enabled us to provide feedback on their feedback. In view of the largely online nature of the course delivery, the ability to 'see' how students were progressing on a weekly basis was invaluable for the course team. It also meant that when a student didn't post any work for a couple of weeks, we were able to follow up and ask them if they needed any help, or whether there were any issues preventing them from engaging with the course.

The accreditation of the course by AdvanceHE in 2018 also led the course team to explore the use of a 'professional dialogue' to assess learning (Pilkington, 2018). At the end of each module, participants met with members of the course team for a thirty-minute conversation about their work. The conversation was structured around the assessment criteria, with each question asking participants to elaborate on what they had learned in relation to each criterion. The dialogues both provided a valuable insight into how participants had internalized their new knowledge and ensured they were able to engage meaningfully with the assessment criteria. To prepare for their professional dialogue, each participant had a thirty-minute 'diagnostic conversation' with the course team a few weeks before the end of each module. In preparation for this, they self-assessed their weekly tasks using the assessment criteria to map the evidence they had produced. During the diagnostic conversation, the course team was able to guide each participant towards appropriate ways of addressing any gaps they had identified. All diagnostic and professional conversations happened using Zoom, and this made it possible for participants to share their screens while talking through their work.

Team projects

In addition to their individual weekly tasks, participants also worked in teams of six to produce a series of five team tasks. Having attended an event on team-based learning (TBL) at the University of Sussex in 2018, the course team saw the potential for team tasks to make participants accountable to each other. Given that the learning experience would take place almost entirely online (and fully online during the 2020–1 academic year), TBL offered a way to keep participants engaged through the use of social, collaborative learning. The idea for online team work had also come from the highly successful online course AltMBA, a four-week course in which participants from across the world worked intensively in online teams to complete a series of assignments.

Inspired by TBL and AltMBA, the course team developed a series of team tasks that participants could complete through online collaboration. Guided by the work of Hattie (2009) and Fung (2017), the tasks were designed to make learning visible and, where possible, to share the learning in 'public'. This harnessed the dynamic of 'students as researchers' advocated by Fung, along with the intention to make the tasks feel meaningful and authentic. The first team task was a team presentation of a learning theorist, which made learning about learning theories more active. The second task was a team podcast about Specific Learning Differences (SpLDs), during which each team member interviewed someone with experience of supporting students with SpLDs. They then used Zoom to record a thirty-minute conversation between the team members about the outcomes of their investigation. Team task 3 required teams to research assistive technologies and create a series of short instructional videos to explain their value. These were shared on the public-facing Wordpress blog as a learning resource.

For their fourth team task, participants developed a toolkit for decolonizing assessment in the arts. This proved to be an effective way to engage participants in the complex topic of decolonizing the curriculum, and turn their new knowledge of assessment into a practical resource that they could share with their colleagues. The team tasks culminated in an online conference entitled VOICE (Visualizing Online Inclusive Creative Education). This was a live event which was openly available for anyone to attend and was promoted through participants' own professional networks. Each team undertook research into a topic of their choosing and developed a conference poster of their findings. During the conference, the course team facilitated a discussion with each team about their research and its impact on the participants' approach to teaching and supporting learning.

On reflection, the team tasks can be viewed as the element of the course that made it work effectively online. The social, collaborative nature of the tasks involved what Wenger (1999) describes as the 'joint activities and discussions' required for a community of practice to emerge. Although the team tasks did not strictly follow the TBL format (Fink, 2004; Michaelsen and Sweet, 2008), by linking performance in team tasks to an assessment criterion, the tasks succeeded in producing the accountability which Stein and colleagues (2015) highlight as a core component of TBL.

Teaching team

In designing the course, the team was acutely aware of the research that PGCerts often fail to provide practical solutions to the day-to-day practical issues faced by academic and professional support staff working in HE (Smith, 2011; Trowler and Cooper, 2002). In response, the course team strove to model every concept and theory that was taught on the course to enable participants to experience its effects. For example, team tasks enabled participants to see how social constructivism (Vygotsky, 1978), discovery learning (Bruner, 1961, 1966) and communities of practice (Wenger, 1999) worked in reality. The 'little and often' approach and the use of blogs enabled participants to experience concepts of visible learning, peer learning and formative feedback (Hattie, 2009).

Feedback from participants through informal evaluation and the Postgraduate Experience Survey showed that one of the most transformative approaches modelled by the course team was that of facilitation (Rogers, 1951). Through his work on client-centred therapy, Rogers developed concepts including unconditional positive regard (UPR), self-actualization and congruence. These concepts require the therapist to maintain a high level of awareness of the specific needs of their client in order to facilitate an effective process of transformation. By aligning Rogers's work with the legal requirements of inclusivity, the team was able to model practical strategies for providing student-centred learning. As the course progressed, the weekly tasks created by participants revealed the extent to which Rogers's theory of facilitation was having an impact on their approach to teaching. By the end of the course, participants' work indicated that the majority demonstrated a clear shift away from teaching as delivering content and towards teaching as facilitating learning.

The ability for the course team to team-teach also provided participants with different viewpoints and perspectives during the course. In both the LinkedIn group and the live Zoom sessions, the team was able to discuss and debate concepts and approaches and also demonstrate differences of opinion. This modelled the kind of critical dialogue we wanted participants to engage in and enabled participants to develop their confidence in sharing and debating their own views about teaching and supporting learning.

The team also strove to model good practice in assessment and feedback, such as through providing swift responses to participants' weekly tasks (Ross, Jordan and Butcher, 2006) and through the use of professional dialogues (Pilkington, 2018). By harnessing the potential of the cohort and asking them to provide feedback on each other's learning logs, the team was able to mitigate the extensive workload created by providing weekly feedback on each participant's work. In doing so, participants were able to experience the value of peer learning and peer assessment.

Power

As stated at the beginning of this chapter, the course operated within a particularly challenging institutional culture that was at best indifferent, and at times hostile, to providing support for teaching and learning. In view of this, the course team felt the need to prepare participants as fully as possible for the realities of the professional environment they hoped to enter. Paolo Freire's theory of critical pedagogy (1968) provides a way to analyse the role of power in teaching and learning, and the course team felt this was a useful mechanism to examine how power works in both the classroom and the wider university.

However, the revolutionary rhetoric of Freire's writing risked overshadowing more practical aspects of teaching and learning such as inclusivity and assessment. The course team therefore decided to introduce critical pedagogy in the final weeks of the course as a way to create momentum in the learning design and provide a climax to the learning experience. This proved to be effective, as participants were able to use critical pedagogy to reflect on their learning during the course and on their role within the wider university. By the end of the course, many participants were showing evidence of their growing awareness of the dynamics of power in teaching and learning, and we felt we had at least provided them with some critical tools with which to navigate the increasingly turbulent landscape of higher education.

Analysis

So far, we have described our approach to designing and delivering the 'right' environment for online creative education. Certainly, the feedback from participants through conversations and survey results, as well as the high quality of work produced, indicated that the course was working effectively. But on reflection, we have had to confront a growing feeling that the environment we were modelling, and which we hoped our participants would adopt, was increasingly unsustainable in the current climate of higher education.

As long ago as 2007, Brown and colleagues highlighted the growing pressure of course administration on academic staff working in universities. More recent research has suggested that UK HE has become an 'anxiety machine' which is producing an 'epidemic' of poor mental health among HE staff (Morrish, 2019). The massification and marketization of HE since the early 2000s have resulted in the increasing commodification of learning and the desire to extract greater value out of decreasing resources (Taberner, 2018). However, Taberner observes that one of the unintended consequences of this shift has been a significant growth in the occupational stress of those working in universities (Alvesson and Spicer, 2016; Lynch and Ivancheva, 2015; Parker, 2014; Visser, 2016). Such stress was experienced by the course team, as during our tenure the number of participants doubled while teaching hours were cut. This presented us with a dilemma: should we give participants the quality of pedagogy they deserve, and for which the course was designed, or respond to the reduction in teaching hours and work sustainably? Each week, we reminded participants to 'be kind to themselves' and to try not to do the impossible. Yet we increasingly found ourselves unable to deliver the course we had designed. In order to meet the high standards of teaching and feedback we had set for ourselves, we risked inadvertently modelling a way of working that was unsustainable.

To be credible, a PGCert in Higher Education should strive to model sustainable, inclusive practice in teaching and assessment. While we set out to model good practice in online creative education, there was a growing danger that we were modelling the burnout and anxiety we were trying to help our learners avoid. In his article 'Living the Neo-liberal University' (2015), Stephen Ball observes how he felt 'other to himself precisely at the place where he expected to be himself' (Butler, 2004). We found ourselves in a similar position: while striving to enthuse our participants about the academic world they hoped to enter, we were increasingly unable to sustain the good practice in teaching and assessment we strove to model.

It is here that Freire's theory of critical pedagogy played a key role in influencing the course leader's decision to resign. To use Freire's language, the choice was either to become the 'oppressor' by accepting and perpetuating the unrealistic working conditions that are expected of academic staff, or to side with the 'oppressed' and reject these pressures.

Conclusion

In this chapter, we have attempted to demonstrate the characteristics of an effective hybrid, then fully online course in creative education. We began by explaining the rationale behind the course design and the principles and learning theories which formed the pillars of the learning experience. We then went on to demonstrate how enacting these principles and theories led us to a point where maintaining our professional integrity placed us in conflict with the best practices we sought to model. Research into the experience of academic staff in UK universities continues to paint a sobering picture of a sector in turmoil, with managers placing unrealistic demands on individuals and course teams. It is against this neoliberal backdrop of marketization and commodification that PGCerts in Education are likely to find themselves in an increasingly difficult position: either to model a culture of 'do as I say, not as I do' or to confront the reality of overwork and stress that the literature indicates are the new norms of the sector.

Sources

Alvesson, M. and Spicer, A. (2016). '(Un) conditional surrender? Why do professionals willingly comply with managerialism', *Journal of Organisational Change Management*, 29 (1): 29–45.

Ball, S. (2015). 'Living the neo-liberal university', *European Journal of Educational Research, Development and Policy*, 50 (3): 258–61.

Bright, B. (1996). 'Reflecting on reflective practice', *Studies in the Education of Adults*, 28 (2): 162–84.

Brookfield, S. (1995). *Becoming a Critically Reflective Teacher*. San Francisco: Jossey-Bass.

Brown, R. et al. (2007). 'Working without a script – Rethinking how academics can work 23 collaboratively in changing contexts', in L. Drew (ed.), *Proceedings of the GLAD 07 Conference: The Student Experience in Art and Design Higher Education: Drivers for Change*. Group for Learning in Art and Design, 25–40.

Bruner, J.S. (1961). 'The act of discovery', *Harvard Educational Review*, 31: 21–32.

Bruner, J.S. (1966). *Toward a Theory of Instruction*. Cambridge, MA: Belknap Press.

Butcher, J. and Stoncel, D. (2012). 'The impact of a Postgraduate Certificate in Teaching in Higher Education on university lecturers appointed for their professional expertise at a teaching-led university: "It's made me braver"', *International Journal for Academic Development*, 17 (2): 149–62.

Butler, J. (2004). *Undoing Gender*. New York and London: Routledge.

Dewey, J. (1933). *How We Think: A Restatement of the Relation of Reflective Thinking to the Educative Process*. Boston: Heath.

Fink, L. Dee (2004). 'Beyond small groups: Harnessing the extraordinary power of learning teams', in L.K. Michaelsen, A.B. Knight and L.D. Fink (eds.), *Team-based Learning: A Transformative Use of Small Groups in College Teaching*, 3–26. Sterling, VA: Stylus.

Fornauf, B. and Erikson, J. (2020). 'Towards an inclusive pedagogy through Universal Design for Learning in Higher Education: A review of the literature', *Journal of Postsecondary Education and Disability*, 33 (2): 183–99.

Freire, P. (2000). *Pedagogy of the Oppressed* (30th anniversary edition). New York: Bloomsbury.

Freire, P. (2005). *Pedagogy of the Oppressed*. London and New York: Continuum.

Fung, D. (2017). *A Connected Curriculum for Higher Education*. London: UCL Press.

Gibbs, G., and Coffey, M. (2004). 'The impact of training of university teachers on their teaching skills, their approach to teaching and the approach to learning of their students', *Active Learning in Higher Education*, 5 (1): 87–100. https://doi.org/10.1177/1469787404040463

Gibson, C.B. and Manuel, J.A. (2003). 'Building trust: Effective multicultural communication processes in virtual teams', in C.B. Gibson and S.G. Cohen (eds.), *Virtual Teams That Work*, 59–86. San Francisco, CA: Jossey-Bass.

Gosling, D. (2010). 'Professional development for new staff – How mandatory is your Post Grad Cert?', *Educational Developments (SEDA)*, 11 (2): 1–4.

Hart, R.K. and McLeod, P.L. (2003). 'Rethinking team building in geographically dispersed teams: One message at a time', *Organizational Dynamics*, 31 (4): 352–61.

Hattie, J.A.C. (2009). *Visible Learning: A Synthesis of 800+ Meta-analyses on Achievement*. London: Routledge.

Hibbert, P. and Semler, M. (2016). 'Faculty development in teaching and learning: the UK framework and current debates', *Innovations in Education and Teaching International*, 53 (6): 581–91.

Kushnir, I. and Spowart, L. (2021). *University Teacher Development Courses in the UK Neoliberal Higher Education Context*. www.abdn.ac.uk/eitn (accessed 7 April 2022).

Lovell, O. (2021). *Cognitive Theory in Action*. https://vimeo.com/471302773 (accessed 9 March 2022).

Lynch, K. and Ivancheva, M.P. (2015). 'Academic freedom and the commercialisation of universities: A critical ethical analysis', *Ethics in Science and Environment politics*, 15 (1): 1–15.

Morrish, L. (2019). *Pressure Vessels: The Epidemic of Poor Mental Health among Higher Education Staff*. HEPI Occasional Paper 20.

Michaelsen, L., Knight, A. and Fink, L. (2004). 'Team-based learning: A transformative use of small groups in college teaching', Centers for Teaching Excellence – Book Library. 199. https://digitalcommons.georgiasouthern.edu/ct2-library/199.

Michaelsen, L. and Sweet, M. (2008). 'The essential elements of team-based learning', in L.K. Michaelsen, M. Sweet and D.X. Parmelee (eds.), *Team-based Learning: Small-group Learning's Next Big Step*, 7–27. San Francisco: Jossey-Bass.

Nerantzi, C. and James, A. (2019). *LEGO for University Learning: Inspiring Academic Practice in Higher Education* (open access book). Zenodo, Open access publication.

Parker, M. (2014). 'University Ltd.', *Organisation*, 21 (2): 281–92.

Pilkington, R. (2018). 'Investigating the use of "professional assessed dialogues" when assessing academic practice: revealing learning, managing process and enabling judgments', *International Journal for Academic Development*, 24 (1): 47–60.

Rogers, C. (1951). *Client-Centered Therapy: Its Current Practice, Implications and Theory*. London: Constable.

Ross, S., Jordan, S. and Butcher, P. (2006). 'Online instantaneous and targeted feedback for remote learners', in C. Bryan and K. Clegg (eds.), *Innovative Assessment in Higher Education*, 123–31. London: Routledge.

Schön, D. (1996). *Educating the Reflective Practitioner*. San Francisco: Jossey Bass.

Smith, J. (2011). 'Beyond evaluative studies: Perceptions of teaching qualifications from probationary lecturers in the UK', *International Journal for Academic Development*, 16 (1): 71–81.

Sookhoo, D. and Thurston, C. (2018). 'Effectiveness and experiences of team-based learning in nurse education programs: A mixed methods systematic review protocol', *JBI Database of Systematic Reviews and Implementation Reports*, 16 (10): 1912–21.

Stein, R. E., Colyer, C. J. and Manning, J. (2016). 'Student accountability in team-based learning classes', *Teaching Sociology*, 44 (1): 28–38. https://doi.org/10.1177/009205 5X15603429

Taberner, A.M. (2018). 'The marketisation of the English higher education sector and its impact on academic staff and the nature of their work', *International Journal of Organizational Analysis*, 26 (1): 129–52.

THES Annual Work-based Survey (2016). THES 4 February 2016: 42.

Trowler, P. and Cooper, A. (2002). 'Teaching and learning regimes: Implicit theories and recurrent practices in the enhancement of teaching and learning through educational development programmes', *Higher Education Research & Development*, 21 (3): 221–40.

Visser, M. (2016). 'Management control, accountability, and learning in public sector organisations: A critical analysis', in L. Gnan, A. Hinna and F. Monteduro (eds.), *Governance and Performance in Public and Non-profit Organizations*, Volume 5, 575–93. Bingley: Emerald.

Vygostsky, L. (1978). *Mind in Society: The Development of Higher Psychological Processes*. London: Harvard University Press.

Wilson, J.M., Straus, S.G., and McEvily, B. (2006). 'All in due time: The development of trust in computer-mediated and face-to-face teams', *Organizational Behavior and Human Decision Processes*, 99 (1): 16–33.

9

Embedding Mental Well-being in Modules

Geoff Mills

Introduction

This chapter takes the position that student well-being and academic success are closely aligned; as such it is aimed primarily for, and will be of most practical value to, the student-facing academic. More widely, this chapter is for anyone in a position to influence the shape and direction of a HE student's educational experience. Consequently, graduate teaching assistants, aspiring lecturers, university administrators, policymakers, student mental health professionals and, of course, the students themselves are all invested in the issues I explore in this chapter.

My argument for a reorientation in pedagogical strategy, where well-being is placed at the heart of the HE agenda, calls for fresh ways of approaching the business of teaching, learning and assessment. I propose a number of ways in which teaching methodologies can be creatively aligned with the latest data we have on well-being. Whilst the sciences lend themselves to an examination of well-being from a clinical perspective, the arts and humanities offer greater room for more abstract or speculative modes of enquiry: I provide illustrative examples of courses in which teachers working in these fields have achieved a creative interplay between subject-specific expertise and a focus on well-being.

Finally, the chapter challenges the academic to question their go-to teaching methods, and the conventional educational objectives which may underpin them. Further, I invite module designers to reflect whether a radical shift in focus towards well-being might better serve the core missions of the university as we move towards the future.

What is well-being?

As Houghton and Anderson observe in a widely referenced HEA report, 'Mental wellbeing, as a concept, can seem so all encompassing that it stands invisible in plain sight' (Houghton and Anderson, 2017: 10). Despite being possibly the 'closest psychological construct to happiness, the most fundamental of human goals' (Marshall and Morris, 2011: 61) that we have, the term is often associated with stereotypical, distressing forms of mental illness, and many inside the university still think of it as a peripheral educational concern best dealt with by healthcare specialists who reside outside the formal spaces of the curriculum. With this chapter I hope to dislodge such outmoded thinking and replace it with the conviction that issues of well-being reside not at the fringes but at the heart of the academy, that a focus on well-being is central to the social, academic and economic purpose and success of the university, and that while a 'whole university approach' to well-being is being increasingly advocated by a large number of influential global organizations, the most transformative potential rests in the hands of those who have the highest contact with the students themselves, i.e. the academics who design and deliver the curriculum.

A number of organizations do a good job of pinning down this nebulous concept. The World Health Organization (WHO), for example, defines mental health as a 'state of wellbeing in which every individual realises his or her own potential, can cope with the normal stresses of life, can work productively and fruitfully, and is able to make a contribution to her or his community' ('Mental Health: Strengthening Our Response', 2022).

Byrne and Surdey draw on several definitions to give a broader scope to our conception of well-being:

> At a personal level, it relates to one's physical, social and mental state and how satisfied we are with our lives, that what we do in life is worthwhile and our day-to-day emotional experiences. At the societal level, wellbeing encompasses objective and subjective features, including the natural environment, personal wellbeing, our relationships, health, our contribution to society, where we live, personal finance, the economy, education and skills and governance. Wellbeing changes over time, as society and the relative importance of different aspects of life evolve.
>
> (Byrne and Surdey, 2021: 14)

In other words, well-being concerns all of us and reaches into every aspect of our lives.

What has well-being got to do with HE?

The picture now is a crowded and competitive one. In the year 2020/21, there were 2.75 million ('Higher Education Student Statistics', 2022) students registered at institutions of HE in the UK and the sector is grappling to define its roles and responsibilities in relation to the ever-increasing, growingly diverse, number of students entering its doors. What it hadn't anticipated was the challenge it would face in dealing with huge numbers of students self-reporting mental health issues. The pandemic has exacerbated the problem. In a recent poll conducted by Humen (Pandey, 2022), nearly half the students interviewed believed that mental health difficulties adversely affected their university experience. There is also evidence to suggest that university students have a higher risk of developing mental health problems ('About Student Mental Health', 2022), ascribed in part to the fact that the highest prevalence of mental disorders occurs in the 16–24-year-old age group (Baik et al., 2017: 4).

The moral imperative alone should motivate the HE institutions to act in response to this crisis, but there are further compelling motivations. Mounting evidence indicates that student success is intrinsically linked to good mental health. In learning environments alert to issues of mental well-being, a positive feedback loop begins to operate: students with good mental health become better learners, and engaged and motivated learners report higher levels of mental well-being.

This mental health crises may have many complex underlying causes, but what some see as HE's relentlessly competitive, rankings-obsessed, functionalist drive towards measurable outcomes exists at the expense of the difficult to measure but no less important emotional aspects of the learning process.

Like other reports the University Mental Health Charter (2019), developed in consultation with thousands of staff and students across the UK, lays down a framework to support universities in their adoption of a whole university approach to mental health and well-being (Hughes and Spanner, 2019: 10). This mission, valuable in its own right, also looks towards the transformative impact this would have on academic performance. The charter states:

> At their core, universities are communities united in pursuit of meaningful learning and wisdom. They can and should be places that naturally support good mental health and good wellbeing for all. Equally, there is a clear transactional relationship between the core missions of universities and the wellbeing of staff and students. Creativity, problem solving and good quality academic learning, are all higher order cognitive functions that benefit from good mental health.
>
> (Hughes and Spanner, 2019: 7)

Why should course designers bring well-being into the classroom?

Although a whole university approach is advocated, in reality it is in the assessed academic programme that the most transformative potential lies. I make this argument because:

1. The only guaranteed, and most valued, point of meaningful contact between a student and the university occurs inside the classroom. A What Works report concludes that 'students are most likely to feel like they belong to their programme, and this decreases at departmental, school and institutional levels' (Thomas, 2012: 6).
2. A Student Minds report indicates that 'responding to student mental health problems is now an inevitable part of the academic role' (Hughes et al., 2018: 5), a situation which has a 'significant, negative impact on the wellbeing' (Hughes, 2018: 9) of the academic. A university culture which supports a culture of embedded well-being would help relieve the stress on the academic in the long term.
3. One graduate, reflecting on her struggle at university, explained to me: 'There needs to be an acknowledgement of the fact that some people aren't able to take the steps to reach out for help themselves, the uni has to make the first move' (Northern England University Graduate, 2022). The well-being-embedded module seeks to create an explicitly supportive space which pre-empts dips in well-being and clearly signposts the course of action a student can take if further support is needed.

How does the course designer embed well-being into the module?

In a 2018 report a large cross section of academics 'broadly supported the idea that wellbeing should be embedded in the curriculum' (Hughes, 2018: 53), though there was a concern that it would become overly generic. Indeed an increasing number of HE institutions have chosen to offer generic modules in well-being, delivered by healthcare specialists, which run alongside a student's chosen subject specialism. This approach, however, lies outside this scope of this chapter. While many science courses, and in particular the health sciences, lend themselves to the examination of well-being from a professional and clinical perspective, well-being has trickled more slowly and tangentially into the disciplines outside the scientific sphere. Here I explore how those who work inside the arts and humanities can infuse well-being targeted pedagogy into already existing content and/or find creative ways to fuse their own subject specialism with well-being to make it an explicit thematic focus of the module. Consequently I split this section into two: process (the *how*) and content (the *what*).

Well-being as process

Collaboration and a sense of belonging

A student's sense of belonging is critical to both retention and success (Thomas, 2012: 1). A Student Minds report is firm in its conviction that it is 'the human side of higher education that comes first – finding friends, feeling confident and above all, feeling a part of your course of study and the institution – that is the necessary starting point for academic success' (Thomas, 2012: 1). For those who remain on the course, social and academic interaction remains key. Loneliness, the 'strongest overall predictor of mental distress in the mental population ... reduces cognitive function, mood and immunity and loneliness has a direct negative effect on academic performance' (Hughes and Spanner, 2019: 7).

The What Works Network is strident in its call for change. It challenges institutions to 'look afresh at their priorities and to consider: how the curriculum might be reorganised to provide for sustained engagement between teachers and students; how teaching can be organised to create student learning communities; and how to convey the message to students that they belong' (Thomas, 2012: 1). Belonging is fostered most effectively by a student-centred approach to learning. For example:

- **Peer-to-peer support:** Proactive facilitation of peer-to-peer academic networks. This can be built into the module or supported outside it. PASS (Peer Assisted Study Sessions), for example, is a scheme which encourages cross-year support between students on the same course. The more experienced students receive training to lead study sessions which help deepen subject understanding, develop study skills, provide moral support and ease the transition into university life. This scheme has been adopted by many universities worldwide.

- **Collaboration:** The setting up of staff/student collaborative exchanges. For example, in 2010 the University of Lincoln launched a project to facilitate the 'student as producer', to 'emphasise the role of the student as a collaborator in the production of knowledge' ('Student as Producer', 2010). In the Student as Producer manifesto, it states: 'Undergraduate students will work alongside staff in the design and delivery of their learning and teaching programmes, and in the production of work of academic content and value' ('Student as Producer', 2010).
- **Contact with staff:** An academic's readiness to communicate a non-judgemental attitude of acceptance, as well as a genuine readiness to invite students into their world (by learning names, asking questions, listening, giving considered responses) does much to bridge the gulf and draw students in.
- **Opportunities for learning outside the classroom:** Field trips, excursions and team projects diversify the learning experience and bring students together in unexpected and enjoyable ways outside the predictable dynamic of the classroom.

Deep learning

Students who engage in deep learning seem to possess higher levels of well-being (Postareff et al., 2016: 441–57). Intrinsic motivator – a thirst for the subject, a relish for the learning process – becomes its own reward system, prompting a positive feedback loop. In such cases students are driven to read beyond the mandatory content and to make connections with other disciplines and the world beyond (Haggis, 2003: 9–104). Motivated students work harder, achieve more, and so build up a reservoir of positive emotion which enables them to function better in other areas of their life. According to Fredrickson's broaden-and-build theory, 'positive emotions promote discovery of novel and creative actions, ideas and social bonds, which in turn build that individual's personal resources; ranging from physical and intellectual resources, to social and psychological resources' (Fredrickson, 2004: 1367).

Surface learning, however, is more likely to be motivated by extrinsic factors, e.g. high grades, pursuit of prestige, increased employment prospects, the approval of a course leader. The surface learner is less likely to experience that totally immersive 'flow state' in which time seems to disappear, a phenomenon Mihaly Csikszentmihalyi, one of the co-founders of positive psychology, often observed in creatives at work: 'The best moments in our lives are not the passive, receptive, relaxing times … The best moments usually occur if a person's body or mind is stretched to its limits in a voluntary effort to accomplish something difficult and worthwhile' (Csikszentmihalyi, 1990: 3).

Contemplative pedagogy is an educational approach designed to foster more meaningful and enduring connections to the course content. It aims to bring a heightened form of attention, reflection and awareness to the study process so that students 'find more of themselves in their courses' (Barbezat and Bush, 2014: 9). Contemplative pedagogy slows the urgent pace of goal-oriented learning down and licenses the student to engage with the material at a personal, emotional or creative level. Examples of contemplative activity include providing space for thoughtful silence, meditative listening, retreats, subject-specific forms of storytelling and improvisation, volunteer work as well as academic/personal journaling and self-reflection. Contemplative learning practices have taken a stronger foothold in the United States, however the UK is following suit. In 2019, for example, Winchester University launched the Winchester Institute for Contemplative Education and Practice (University of Winchester, 2022), while at Exeter University Irene Salvo is leading a project called Mindful Classics which seeks to explore the ways teachers can embed contemplative pedagogy into the study of Antiquity (Institute for Advanced Teaching and Learning (IATL), 2022).

Autonomy

A sense of agency and autonomy, or a form of 'rule by the self', is important to a student's sense of well-being. Research by Deci and Ryan demonstrates that students feel empowered as learners when they are given the range to explore, take the initiative or play an active role in the formation of their learning goals (Deci and Ryan, 2000: 227–68).

In practical terms course design, led by teachers who are demonstrably passionate about their subject, might then be structured to encourage autonomous forms of learning, where the student is given freedom to explore topics of personal interest. By contrast there is a need to reduce controlling teaching styles e.g. motivating students by triggering anxiety of future outcomes ('these employers demand that you have a 1st class degree'), manifesting obvious approval of students who fall in line with their way of thinking, or marginalizing those who don't.

Experienced teachers may even feel comfortable opening up a discussion about the module while it is in progress. From such discussions it may be possible to gauge how students are feeling, which aspects of the module they are enjoying or struggling with, and why. In this way students may feel they have influence over the direction of the course as it develops. Plenary feedback of this nature enables students to *be* heard and *feel* heard.

Assessment and feedback

Academic work is the aspect of university life students reported as having the most impact on their well-being (Grant, 2002). In relation to assessment, the specific aspects students struggled with were clustered deadlines, exams and coursework (Grant, 2002). Assessment needs to be positively aligned with the factors which influence well-being. Does the assessment encourage and reward deep learning, for example? Particularly in early modules, does the timing and design of the assessment align with a scaffolded curriculum? If it is too easy, students become disinterested and demotivated. Likewise if it is pitched at too high a level early on in their academic career. Informally assessed projects, activities and assignments, built into a scaffolded curriculum and supported by transition pedagogy, can help with goal setting and confidence building. This also gives the course leader the opportunity to show where and how the student has progressed and what goals they should be setting themselves in advance of the formal assessment. Strategic goal setting can bolster a student's sense of purpose and achievement, as well as support a more optimistic view of the future (MacLeod, Coates and Hetherton, 2007: 185–96). Students become frustrated and lose motivation if they struggle to understand how and why the assessment is relevant, both within the context of the module and the course structure as a whole (Kirschner and Hendrick, 2020). In other words, if assessment is to be meaningful it needs to be integrated into a course that is narratively cohesive.

Well-being as content

In this section I focus on the *what* rather than the *how*. I highlight courses where the content achieves a creative interplay between the course leader's expertise and a thematic focus on well-being. Leading the way is The Engelhard Project for Connecting Life and Learning at Georgetown University. It is a large-scale initiative that has been infusing health and wellness topics into courses across the undergraduate curriculum since 2005. What began as an experiment has now evolved into one of the most distinctive features of their undergraduate provision. Below I have included three abridged examples of courses it offers as they appear on the Engelhard website.

Theatre as social change

Performing Arts, Human Science

Well-being topics: drugs and alcohol, depression and suicidality, stress and coping, sexuality, support systems, friends and community

In Theatre as Social Change, Georgetown students work with an afterschool group of High School students to develop, write and perform a high school play. One of the underlying goals of this collaboration is to explore ways to use the performance as a platform to discuss and explore solutions to social issues that concern the high school student community. Georgetown students, while still being students themselves, are also taking on roles as mentors, co-collaborators, peers, instructors and guests. This course creates the structure and space for students to reflect on and process their experiences in the community (The Engelhard Project for Connecting Life and Learning, 2022).

Introduction to ethics – Karen Stohr, Philosophy

Well-being topics: friendships, sexual relationships and sexual violence, alcohol and substance abuse, bystander intervention.

Stohr wants her students to see 'how ethics can help them live their lives better and make their community and their world better.' She also sees Engelhard as a tool for better learning.

In a unit on community ethics, Stohr assigns readings by Immanuel Kant that raise moral problems with drunkenness and sexual objectification. Stohr then asks her students to reflect on what it takes to be fully self-respecting and fully respecting of others in the context of social life at Georgetown (The Engelhard Project for Connecting Life and Learning, 2022).

Social entrepreneurship – Sarah Stiles, sociology

Well-being topics: wellness as a lifestyle

In her Engelhard course on Social Entrepreneurship, Sarah Stiles asks her students to commit to as personal wellness routine for the semester.

In order to help her students learn to apply theories of social change and to see social entrepreneurship as a lifestyle, Sarah Stiles asks her students to commit to a personal wellness routine – both physical and mental – during the semester. Students partner one another as 'accountability buddies' and keep journals of their progress towards their wellness goals.

> Additionally, students collaborate with local organizations to undertake social entrepreneurial projects to engage with real problems in the D.C community, and apply course strategies with an eye to creating systemic change (The Engelhard Project for Connecting Life and Learning, 2022).

In 2021 Munster Technological College piloted a six-week initiative in which the five ways to well-being (connect, be active, take notice, keep learning and give to others) (Aked et al., 2022) were incorporated into existing classes across a range of disciplines. Academics were given training and resources and were tasked with infusing the five actions into their course content. Out of the 143 students who completed the post-course poll, over 80 per cent said they had implemented the well-being strategies and over 90 per cent indicated that they would do so in the future (Byrne, 2021: 26).

The Drama department at Exeter University offers a module in theatre and health which examines, among other complementarities, the relationship between theatre, well-being and mental health (Theatre and Health (DRA2045), 2022). Finally, in what I regard to be a showcase for well-being course design, the University of Warwick hosts an innovative interdisciplinary module called Understanding Wellbeing Theory and Practise (IATL, 2022). Led by Elena Riva, Director of Education at the Institute for Advanced Teaching and Learning, the module is taught collaboratively by academics representing biomedicine, sociology, economics and the arts & humanities as well as a resident well-being adviser. Flexibility is built into the assessment, which takes the form of a traditional academic essay or a 2–4 minute video plus a 400-word commentary. The remaining 50 per cent of the assessment is devised by the individual student and explored in the form of 'an article, a short film, a talk, a play, a workshop, a painting, a podcast and so on' (IATL, 2022). The module is open to all undergraduates and deploys a wealthy spread of the teaching methodologies discussed in this chapter, including scaffolded pedagogy, fieldwork, cross-curricular narrative cohesion, self-reflection, contemplative pedagogy, autonomous learning, experiential learning and student/staff collaboration.

Conclusion: Creativity and the well-being revolution

We have seen how different forms of creativity lie at the heart of the well-being revolution. Pedagogic practice implemented to boost well-being within the module requires the course leader to apply contextually appropriate teaching methods. To keep students interested and engaged, both course design and delivery need to be diverse, inventive, flexible, playful and dynamic as well as constructively aligned with the data we have on well-being. A yet greater creative challenge lies in the task of designing a course in which student well-being constitutes an explicit part of the content. How to fuse a teacher's research interests with issues of well-being? Or how, in the words of Edward Maloney at Georgetown University, to create 'meaningful connections between intellectual pursuits and the lived experiences of our students' ('The Engelhard Project', 2015: 2). This creative enterprise, which lies at the intersection of well-being, teaching and learning, inevitably leads to the generation of more opportunities for the students themselves to respond and engage creatively. Creative play lifts well-being, increases engagement and promotes the sort of deep learning that is an absolute precondition to the generation of new ideas, new knowledge and new solutions. In 1969 Chomsky observed:

> In its relation to society, a free university should be expected to be, in a sense, 'subversive.' We take for granted that creative work in any field will challenge prevailing orthodoxy. A physicist who refines yesterday's experiment, an engineer who merely seeks to improve existing devices, or an artist who limits himself to styles and techniques that have been thoroughly explored is rightly regarded as deficient in creative imagination. Exciting work in science, technology, scholarship, or the arts will probe the frontiers of understanding and try to create alternatives to the conventional assumptions.
>
> (Chomsky, 2022)

By way of an ouroboric loop the university, having trained its followers to 'probe the frontiers' of knowledge in mental health and well-being, is beginning to challenge its own 'conventional assumptions', its own 'prevailing orthodoxies' and reform itself from within. Fuelled by a spirit of creative subversion, a growing number who work within its ranks believe that the academy is uniquely placed to lead a cultural shift in which well-being is valued not only for itself and its transformational impact on student learning, but for the powerful ripple effect it will have on the world beyond the campus gates.

Sources

'About Student Mental Health'. *Mind.* https://www.mind.org.uk/information-support/tips-for-everyday-living/student-life/about-student-mental-health/ (accessed 30 August 2022).

Aked, J., Marks, N., Cordon, C. et al. Rep. (2022). 'Five ways to wellbeing', *New Economics Foundation*. https://neweconomics.org/uploads/files/five-ways-to-wellbeing-1.pdf (accessed 29 August 2022).

Baik, C., Larcombe, W., Brooker, A., Wyn, J., Allen, L., Brett, M., Field, R. and James, R. (2017). *Enhancing Student Mental Wellbeing: A Handbook for Academic Educators.* Enhancing Student Wellbeing. https://melbourne-cshe.unimelb.edu.au/__data/assets/pdf_file/0006/2408604/MCSHE-Student-Wellbeing-Handbook-FINAL.pdf.

Barbezat, D. and Bush, M. (2014). *Contemplative Practices in Higher Education: Powerful Methods to Transform Teaching and Learning.* San Francisco, CA: Jossey-Bass.

Byrne, D. and Surdey, J.R. (2021). *Embedding Well-being across the Curriculum in Higher Education.* Union of Students in Ireland & National Forum for the Enhancement of Teaching and Learning in Higher Education, July. https://usi.ie/wp-content/uploads/2021/10/Supporting-Well-being-in-Practice-October-2021.pdf.

Chomsky, N. (2022). 'The function of the university in a time of crisis', *Noam Chomsky.* https://chomsky.info/1969/ (accessed 20 August 2022).

Csikszentmihalyi, M. (1990). *Flow: The Psychology of Optimal Experience.* 1st ed. New York: Harper and Row.

Deci, E.L. and Ryan, R.M. (2000). 'The "what" and "why" of goal pursuits: Human needs and the self-determination of behavior', *Psychological Inquiry*, 11 (4): 227–68.

'The Engelhard Project for Connecting Life and Learning'. The Engelhard Project | Profiles. https://engelhard.georgetown.edu/profiles/ (accessed 20 June 2022).

Fredrickson, B.L. (2004). 'The broaden–and–build theory of positive emotions', *Philosophical Transactions of the Royal Society of London. Series B: Biological Sciences*, 359 (1449): 1367–77.

Grant, A. (2002). 'Identifying students' concerns: Taking a whole institutional approach', in N. Stanley and J. Manthorpe (eds.), *Students' Mental Health Needs*, 83–106. London: Jessica Kinglsey Publishers.

Haggis, T. (2003). 'Constructing images of ourselves? A critical investigation into "approaches to learning" research in higher education', *British Educational Research Journal*, 29 (1): 89–104.

'Higher Education Student Statistics: UK, 2020/21 – Student Numbers and Characteristics', *HESA*, 25 January 2022. https://www.hesa.ac.uk/news/25-01-2022/sb262-higher-education-student-statistics/numbers.

Houghton, A.-M. and Anderson, J. Publication (2017). *Embedding Mental Wellbeing in the Curriculum: Maximising Success in Higher Education.* Higher Education Academy. https://www.advance-he.ac.uk/knowledge-hub/embedding-mental-wellbeing-curriculum-maximising-success-higher-education.

Hughes, G. (2022). *Supporting Student Well-being through Curriculum Design and Delivery.* Heriot Watt University. https://lta.hw.ac.uk/wp-content/uploads/Guide-NO20_Supporting-Student-Well-being-Through-Curriculum-Design-and-Delivery.pdf (accessed 19 June 2022).

Hughes, G and Spanner, L. Publication (2019). *The University Mental Health Charter*. Student Minds, 2019. https://www.studentminds.org.uk/uploads/3/7/8/4/3784584/191208_umhc_artwork.pdf.

Hughes, G., Panjwani, M., Tulcidas, P. and Byrom, N. Rep. (2018). *Student Mental Health: The Role and Experiences of Academics*. Student Minds, January. https://www.studentminds.org.uk/uploads/3/7/8/4/3784584/180129_student_mental_health__the_role_and_experience_of_academics__student_minds_pdf.pdf.

'Institute for Advanced Teaching and Learning (IATL)'. Understanding Wellbeing Theory and Practice. University of Warwick. https://warwick.ac.uk/fac/cross_fac/iatl/study/ugmodules/understandingwell-beingtheoryandpractice/ (accessed 28 August 2022).

Kirschner, P.A. and Hendrick, C. (2020). *How Learning Happens: Seminal Works in Educational Psychology and What They Mean in Practice*. Abingdon: Routledge.

MacLeod, A.K., Coates, E. and Hetherton, J. (2007). 'Increasing well-being through teaching goal-setting and planning skills: Results of a brief intervention', *Journal of Happiness Studies*, 9 (2): 185–96.

Marshall, L. and Morris, C. (eds.) Publication (2011). *Taking Wellbeing Forward in Higher Education Reflections on Theory and Practice*. Brighton: University of Brighton Press.

'Mental Health: Strengthening Our Response'. World Health Organization. https://www who.int/news-room/fact-sheets/detail/mental-health-strengthening-our-response (accessed 29 August 2022).

(Northern England University Graduate) (2022). Interview with author, 11 July.

Pandey, M. (2022). 'Mental health negatively affecting almost 50% of UK students in survey'. *BBC*, 29 June. https://www.bbc.com/news/newsbeat-61968952.

Postareff, L., Mattsson, M., Lindblom-Ylänne, S. and Hailikari, T. (2016). 'The complex relationship between emotions, approaches to learning, study success and study progress during the transition to university', *Higher Education*, 73 (3): 441–57. https://doi.org/10.1007/s10734-016-0096-7.

Publication (2015). *The Engelhard Project: A Decade of Connecting Life and Learning*. https://engelhard.georgetown.edu/static/Engelhard_Program_Book.pdf.

Salvo, I. (2022). 'Mindful classics: Embedding contemplative pedagogy into the study of antiquity'. University of Exeter. https://classics.exeter.ac.uk/research/projects/mindfulclassics/ (accessed 27 August 2022).

Stanley, N., Manthorpe, J. and Grant, A. (2002). 'Identifying students' concerns: Taking a whole institutional approach', Essay, in *Students' Mental Health Needs*. London: Jessica Kingsley Pub.

Stepchange: Mentally Healthy Universities (2018). Universities UK. https://www.universitiesuk.ac.uk/sites/default/files/field/downloads/2021-07/uuk-stepchange-mhu.pdf#page=12.

Steuer, N. and Marks, N. Publication (2008). *University Challenge: Towards a Well-Being Approach to Quality in Higher Education.* New Economics Foundation. https://neweconomics.org/uploads/files/176e59e9cc07f9e21c_qkm6iby2y.pdf.

Student as Producer (2010). Lincoln University. https://cpb-eu-w2.wpmucdn.com/blogs.lincoln.ac.uk/dist/e/185/files/2010/09/Student-as-Producer.jpg.

'Theatre and Health (DRA2045)' University of Exeter Drama. University of Exeter. https://drama.exeter.ac.uk/modules/dra2045/description/ (accessed 28 August 2022).

Thomas, L. Publication (2012). *Building Student Engagement and Belonging in Higher Education at a Time of Change: A Summary of Findings and Recommendations from the What Works? Student Retention & Success programme.* Paul Hamlyn Foundation, July 2012. https://www.phf.org.uk/publications/works-student-retention-success-final-report/.

University of Winchester (2022). 'Winchester Institute for Contemplative Education and Practice'. https://www.winchester.ac.uk/research/winchester-institute-for-contemplative-education-and-practice/ (accessed 25 August 2022).

10

Combining Creativity and Employability in Higher Education

James Wadsworth

Introduction

Lauder (2015) suggested that the development of creativity as a skill in higher education (HE) students is valued by graduate employers and can support individuals through the unpredictability of work environments. How creativity is perceived by students, academics and employers is, however, less than clear and, subsequently, development of creativity during their course of study is challenging, both to the students themselves and to the academics entrusted with facilitating this growth. This chapter will provide some contextualization from the UK HE sector with regard to creativity and employability and explore the perceptions that students, academics and employers attach to creativity in the employment context, including those particular to arts and humanities subjects. This chapter should, therefore, be of interest to students, academics and graduate employers, who should use the following narrative and recommendations as a platform for reflection and to inform learning, teaching and assessment practices which will promote the development of creativity in HE students.

Where is the sector now?

The development of creativity can be undertaken in a variety of educational and societal contexts, including that of HE, and indeed, creativity has long been considered a fundamental underpinning of HE. This is suggested by Jackson (2013), who says:

> If the moral purpose of higher education is to enable individuals to prepare themselves for the complexities and challenges of their future life, then surely enabling learners to develop their creative potential must be an important part of this purpose.

The position and existence of creativity within the UK HE context are, to some extent, defined by the policies which drive the sector. While UK HE institutions do operate in an autonomous manner, they are not impervious to governmental policy which influences their operation, including in relation to creativity.

The concepts of marketization and competition promoted in the Success as a Knowledge Economy white paper (BIS, 2016) appear to present something of a conceptual barrier to creativity in UK HE due to, as Baer and Garrett (2010) identified, the risk-taking nature and potential inefficiencies of creativity being at odds with the consumerist values of accountability and standards. This presents a challenge to the UK HE sector, where values of creativity and the encouragement of such activity in students are conflicted by governmental policy that tends towards measurement and conformity, to the point where institutional funding could be restricted should certain thresholds not be met. This challenge appears to be confounded by the differing requirements of employers who desire creativity in their graduate workforce (Gray, 2016).

Graduate employers deem transferable core skills, including creativity, as a necessity for the workforces of the future alongside professional, subject-specific skills (Universities UK, 2018). The Institute of Student Employers (ISE) (2018) noted that global employer perceptions of creativity as an employability skill are high yet, at the same time, also reported that employer satisfaction of this graduate skill to be deficient. The ISE report also highlighted a divergence between student and employer perceptions of the value of creativity, suggesting 'a clear lack of understanding between the two groups'.

Recognizing that creativity is a valuable personal skill and held in high regard by graduate employers, the general deficiency of bespoke literature in this area and the absence of specific governmental policy are challenges to the HE sector and, hence, the findings here will, in part, provide guidance as to the meaning given by academics, students and employers to creativity and subsequently recommend learning practices to guide development.

Are we agreed?

Creativity, as a concept, appears to be in receipt of much anecdotal comment and formal research, being explored using a variety of perspectives from the fundamental theoretical foundations (e.g., Wallas, 1926) to applied studies in bespoke contexts (e.g., Sternberg et al., 2014); however, an agreed understanding of creativity as an employability skill is not evident in the research literature. It could, therefore, be postulated that the development of creativity, which has generic value for graduate employability, may be challenging for those charged with establishing, nurturing and promoting it, including those in HE.

In a study of 150 stakeholders from a medium-sized post-92 UK university, academics, final-year HE students and graduate employers engaged in constructivist grounded theory approaches to explore and define the meaning given to creativity in the employment context. Representing science-, social science- and arts-based backgrounds, stakeholders conveyed their perceptions of creativity via survey activity, photo elicitation techniques and semi-structured interviews. Thematic analysis of the resulting data and extrapolation/ pattern coding identified the agreed, tripartite perceptions of creativity in the employment context, which informed the model (Figure 10.1).

The meaning given to creativity demonstrates consensus in two core principles of creativity and four enabling factors which surround the core principles. The two core principles of *processing thoughts* and *producing a valued entity* illustrate that creativity is perceived as a sequence of processing thoughts from initial genesis to application of the synthesized entity. Participants were clear that this entity need not necessarily be a tangible artefact but must be valued by stakeholders if it is considered to be creative, and the notion that the produced entity of creativity should equate to a complete, never-seen before, novelty was not the case, tending towards Plucker and colleagues' (2004) conclusions that creativity is about creating the 'unobvious'.

Figure 10.2 illustrates the sequencing of thought processing. *Conceptualizing* is the initiating element of the creative process and is the genesis of individual ideation and initial thinking about a scenario. The second element of the creative process is *clarifying* if the *conceptualizing* has validity, refining the initial thoughts and defining the aim or purpose of the creativity in the scenario. Subsequent to *clarifying*, a *designing* stage seemingly exists, where individuals' ideas are *'mapped out'* within the established parameters of the situational context. *Synthesizing* follows, whereby an individual, subsequent to the '*mapping out*', will contrive artefacts or thoughts to meet the requirements of the *designing* stage. An individual will then enter an *evaluating* stage, whereby creative outputs are analysed, critiqued and refined. The final element of the creative process, *applying*, then assumes that individuals who are being creative will now apply the refined artefact or thought to the scenario associated with this particular process.

The two core principles of creativity as an employability skill identified do not appear to operate in isolation and are best achieved when supported by surrounding factors, specifically collaborating with others, understanding the subject, facilitative situational factors and the personal characteristics of those attempting to be creative.

Collaborating emerges as a facilitative factor as it gives permission to exchange and develop thoughts with others throughout the process. *Collaboration* is underpinned, however, by the notion of trusting other individuals in a humanistic manner and also having trust in the subject understanding of a collaborator. Furthermore, for collaboration to be pragmatic and effective, a shared appreciation between collaborators of when not to be collaborative is important.

While random acts of creativity are seemingly possible without *subject understanding*, it is more likely that creative entities will have value if produced by individuals who have an understanding of the subject domain the creative

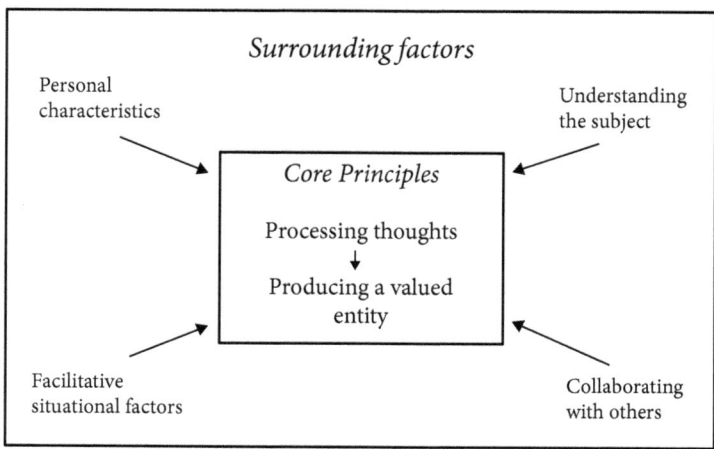

Figure 10.1 A conceptual model of creativity in the employment context.

act is situated within. However, creativity can also be restricted by subject understanding which is highly developed, as a danger exists of following dogmatic tradition, thus limiting the ability to seek new possibilities.

The processing of creative thoughts is likely to be more effective. An individual has a more developed sense of curiosity, passion, perseverance, communication and organization, as these *personal characteristics* facilitate the seeking of alternative ideas, maintain focus on the task despite failure or criticism and allow the conveyance of creative ideas to others (thus more effectively establishing their value to other stakeholders).

Personal creativity tends to be more fluent when personal agency is enabled by co-actors surrounding an individual, who acknowledge the individuality of a person as opposed to conforming to established traditions. While agency is necessary, it is seemingly important to remember that unfettered agency and individuality are neither pragmatic nor efficient, and the boundaries of this freedom need to be defined in any given situation.

While shared meaning, from the perspective of academics, students and employers, is evident, variability of specific perceptions is evident, indicating an element of plurality in how creativity is defined and should be recognized by stakeholders. Tables 10.1 and 10.2 illustrate the common aspects of plurality by stakeholder group and subject domain, which are helpful in understanding creativity and also permitting a degree of pragmatism when making recommendations for future practice development.

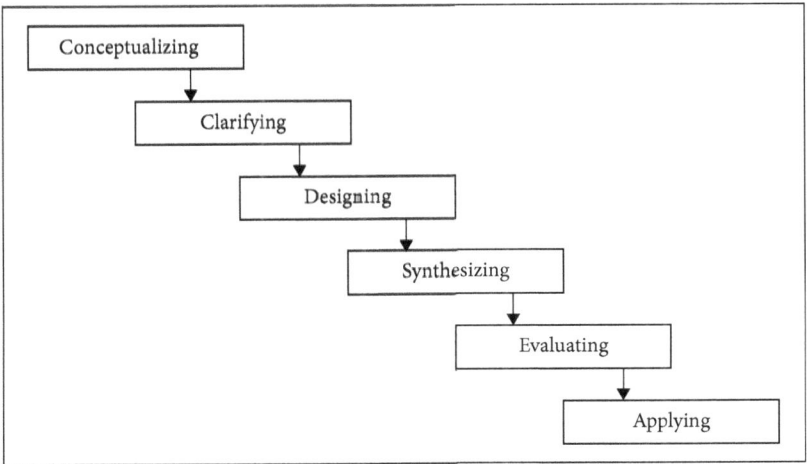

Figure 10.2 Sequencing of creative thought processing.

As illustrated in Table 10.1, academics tend to feel constrained (during the design phase of the creative process) by their own previous experiences and those of others. With regard to situational factors, academics prefer flexibility in the boundaries which frame the creativity related to the task, whereas students and employers prefer clear boundaries to work within. In respect of collaboration, both academics and employers agree that how a person is valued in a working relationship is important; however, students tend to view collaboration more simply as a means to develop ideas further. Employers also identify that mutual trust in a group member's individual subject knowledge is important. While agreeing that personal characteristics are key, academics specifically value the ability to resiliently persuade others of their creative entities, whereas employers tend to value resilience to critique of creative ideas and thoughts.

In terms of the plurality between subject domains, arts-based stakeholders are more likely to use feelings and experiences when clarifying the initial thoughts and defining the aim of the creativity. When contriving artefacts or thoughts to meet the requirements of the creative task, science-based stakeholders prefer to practically test solutions in something of a trial-and-error manner, whereas social scientists seemingly prefer to create theories and ideas in an internal, abstract way.

The manner in which evaluation of an entity is undertaken by different subject groups seemingly varies, with science-based participants preferring a structured personal critique against agreed standards, social sciences participants seeking to make sense of the entity and link with other entities, and arts-based stakeholders requiring subjective critiques from peers. It is widely agreed that an entity which results from a creative process should have value; however, science-based stakeholders seemingly ascribe more materialist, demonstrable value as opposed to the more humanist values noted by the arts-based stakeholders. The perception of subject understanding deemed to be required by individuals when being creative also appears to vary. Science-based stakeholders feel that subject understanding should be generally, if not necessarily specifically, related to the area of study to facilitate valued creativity (e.g., the underpinnings of cell biology being understood and applied in biology, chemistry or physics). Arts-based stakeholders, however, tend to believe that excessive subject understanding constricts the creative potential of a person as they are likely to follow precedent rather than thinking in novel or divergent ways.

The plurality of perceptions by subject domains (Table 10.2) illustrates useful consensus compared to the analysis by participant type. It is noticeable that

Table 10.1 Plurality of creativity by stakeholder grouping

Stakeholder group Model element	Academics	Students	Employers
Designing *(processing thoughts)*	**Constrained by previous experience**	*Variable specific perceptions**	*Variable specific perceptions*
Facilitative situational factors	**Flexible boundaries**	**Clear boundaries**	**Clear boundaries**
Collaborating with others	**Personal value and safety**	**Developing ideas**	**Personal value and safety Trust subject knowledge**
Personal characteristics	**Resilient persuasion**	*Variable specific perceptions*	**Resilient to critique**

* No commonality evident in perceptions related to the model element.

Table 10.2 Plurality of creativity by subject domain

Stakeholders Model element	Science based	Social Science based	Arts based
Clarifying *(processing thoughts)*	*Variable specific perceptions*	*Variable specific perceptions**	**Feelings and experiences**
Synthesizing *(processing thoughts)*	**Testing practically**	**Abstract theorization**	*Variable specific perceptions*
Evaluating *(processing thoughts)*	**Structured personal critique**	**Sense making Linking to other entities**	**Subjective peer critique**
Producing a valued entity	**Practical, capitalist values**	*Variable specific perceptions*	**Humanist values**
Understanding the subject	**More generic**	*Variable specific perceptions*	**Constriction of excessive understanding**

*No commonality evident in perceptions related to the model element.

science-based participants prefer structure and tangible practicality, whereas social scientists seemingly like to make sense and operate in an abstract context, with arts-based individuals apparently reliant on more humanistic values within themselves and their peers.

How do we improve?

The development of creativity in an individual, per se, is challenging and is compounded further by the contextual influences on UK HE when attempting to develop creativity as a graduate skill. Using an adaptation of Beghetto's (2017) model of teaching creativity as a vehicle, recommendations are proposed to pragmatically inform the future practices of students, academics and graduate employers and assist in the development of creativity.

Teaching *about* creativity

In the initial element of the model, Beghetto (2017) noted that 'teaching about creativity' should be concerned with educating students as to the theories which surround creativity, and hence, it would seem logical that students, academics and employers should be made aware of the agreed perceptions of creativity as an employability skill, including those illustrated in Tables 10.1 and 10.2.

Recommendation 1: Understand the local model and plurality

Prior to any teaching about creativity, those responsible for the teaching about creativity (primarily academics and to some extent employers) should consider and understand the model of creativity (cross reference) and the concept of plurality so as to better understand the preconceptions about creativity, which influence the three stakeholder groups.

Recommendation 2: Transfer the understanding

Following the absorption of the model and plurality by academics and employers, subsequent transfer of this understanding of the six elements of the model and the differing values attributed to the resulting entity to undergraduate students should occur. Recognizing the plurality of understanding, academics must acknowledge to students and employers that in the designing phase of the creative process, academics perceive that creativity is constrained by previous experience; thus, the parameters and affordances of this experience should be explained clearly to students when, for example, setting assessed work.

Recommendation 3: Reflect on personal characteristics

Similarly, the key personal characteristics of undergraduates which facilitate creativity (curiosity, passion, perseverance, communication and organization) should be made clear to undergraduate students during general study skills sessions. However, to encourage student understanding and contextualization of these characteristics for themselves, academics and employers should create opportunities for students to reflect on how they demonstrate these personal characteristics, for example, in assessments (academics) or via work experience (employers). Within the perseverance agreed upon by the participants, academics and employers pluralized their view by recognizing resilience as a key part of the characteristic, in terms of persuading others and being resilient to the criticism of others. With this plurality in mind, activity should provide opportunities where students are required to reflect upon where they are to justify their ideas and have been exposed to criticism of these thoughts. While the justification of ideas and the receiving of criticism is not necessarily a new concept in UK HE, this activity should be reflected upon in the context of it being an employability skill and realization be made by the students that it is contributory to the creative process.

Recommendation 4: Illustrate the importance of personal agency and individualism

Enabling personal agency and the acknowledgement of individualism are evident as key situational factors to promote creativity and, mirroring the above recommendation, should also be facilitated by academics and employers in applied contexts. Space and time should be routinely created in the undergraduate learning experience which encourages agency and the reasonable challenging of tradition without fear of any penalty to academic marks. Furthermore, students should also self-evaluate their individualism and personal agency against varying employment scenarios, facilitated by, ideally, graduate employers. With regard to the plurality associated with the facilitative situational factors, students and employers prefer clearer boundaries of operation, whereas academics are more flexible. While this recommendation meets the academic expectation of flexibility, it is incumbent upon academics to clarify this with students and employers and manage the individualism and agency to permit a degree of freedom, at the same time as providing parameters which define the limits of acceptability for students and employers.

Recommendation 5: Emphasize collaboration

Collaboration with others assists in providing humanistic safety and confidence when generating ideas and, furthermore, fosters greater divergence of thinking and ideas. Therefore, academics should transfer this conceptual understanding to students via tutorial or employability sessions, subsequently designing and implementing simulated goal-oriented activities, which require students to collectively employ the processing thoughts model and collaboratively contrive a valued entity. On completion of these activities, students should reflect upon the processes and outcomes of the activities to gain a greater realization of collaboration being an aspect of creativity in an employment context. These activities and reflections should attempt to encapsulate all values of collaboration previously mentioned.

Teaching *for* creativity

The second element of Beghetto's (2017) model referred to the development of students' creativity specific to their subject domains: *'teaching for creativity'* (p. 2). Recognizing the plurality of creativity as an employability skill, the teaching for creativity should focus on the specific development of academics' knowledge and skills in their specific subject domains.

Recommendation 6: (Science) Encourage practical synthesis

When teaching for creativity in science-based subjects, students should be exposed to an experience which develops creativity with the following specific nuances in mind. At the point of reaching the penultimate stage of the processing thoughts model (synthesizing), science-based participants tend towards practical testing of their creative thoughts; therefore, academics and, where appropriate, employers, for example, during work placement activity, should create situations in their teaching where students can physically contrive artefacts to represent and test the processed thoughts and ideas.

Recommendation 7: (Science) Establish clear criteria

Subsequent to recommendation 6, science-based participants seemingly prefer a structured evaluation of the entity which is personally undertaken by the creator. At the evaluating stage of the creative process, academics should facilitate evaluation for science-based students via clear criteria to personally test the worth of their contrived entity. As the academic maturity of science-based students develops, academics should also encourage the empowerment of students to seek their own criteria for the evaluation of their entity, thus facilitating personal agency and the managed challenging of tradition. It is incumbent upon academics and employers to make students aware that the criteria for this evaluation should be generally congruent with more practical and pragmatic values such as efficiency, cost reduction, feasibility and reliability.

Recommendation 8: (Science) Facilitate inter-disciplinarity

The final nuance in the development of creativity as an employability skill for science-based undergraduates is concerned with subject understanding. For science-based domains, subject understanding can be more generalized (e.g., the understanding of human cells can be creatively applied in biology, physics and chemistry), and therefore, academics and employers must, when facilitating creative endeavours, illustrate the fundamental cognate links between scientific subjects. Efforts should be made to enhance students' creativity by engaging them in inter-discipline curricula activities and promoting collaboration with a wider range of students.

Recommendation 9: (Social science) Provide space for abstract thinking

The plurality of perceptions in the social sciences indicates two key aspects in the processing of thoughts which should be taken into account when considering the development of creativity. At the synthesizing stage of the process, social science students tend to perceive synthesis as abstract rather than tangible and, therefore, it is recommended that students need to think, internally theorize and draw together their thoughts into a synthesized entity. Furthermore, students should also be provided with time and space within a curriculum to practise this abstract theorization, be that via an activity in a lecture or seminar, or as a distinct task.

Recommendation 10: (Social science) Make sense and transcend

Further to recommendation 9, the theoretically synthesized entity should be evaluated by making sense of the entity and linking it to other entities. Academics and employers must initially provide guidance for students on how to make sense of the reasoning which underpins the created entity, how the entity can, theoretically, be appraised for its value and how the entity is linked across within and across subject domains. As with the scientific recommendations, the responsibility for the application of these skills should, as academic and employability maturity develop, ascend from the academic staff and employer to the student.

Recommendation 11: (Arts) Give worth to personal feelings

The development of creativity as an employability skill via teaching for creativity in arts-based subjects has three specific recommendations, grounded in the plurality perceived by the arts-based stakeholders. The first focuses on the clarifying stage of the processing thoughts model, as arts-based stakeholders tend to suggest that personal feelings are points of reference when clarifying the conceptualization of initial thoughts. Thus, it is recommended that arts-based students are made aware of this notion and are encouraged to engage with personal feelings at this stage, supported by academics and employers in ensuring that confidence in this personal rather than external referencing is developed.

Recommendation 12: (Arts) Facilitate peer critique

Subsequent to recommendation 11, arts-based stakeholders tend towards the subjective peer critiquing of entities as the preferred form of evaluation. It is recommended that students be exposed to external peer review of their creative entities consistently within a course of study, including evaluation from academics, fellow students, subject experts and employers, thus also developing the resilience to criticism. This recommendation is helpful in this sense as it affords students the opportunity to better understand stakeholder values in creative products, thus allowing enhancements to an entity under current critique but also future products.

Teaching *with* creativity

'*Teaching with creativity*' (Beghetto, 2017) refers to where creativity is developed by academics using the theories of creativity to teach their subject matter in creative ways and by role modelling the principles of creativity to others. Kleiman (2008) suggests that academics should be the 'agents' in the development of students' creativity. The following recommendations will, therefore, assume this role modelling in each case and offer guidance as to how academics, students and employers can teach with creativity, with the intention of turning unfamiliarity or tacit knowledge of creativity as an employability skill to a conscious application of the processing thoughts model and the factors which surround it.

Recommendation 13: Develop personal characteristics

With regard to the personal characteristics which facilitate the processing thoughts model (curiosity, passion, perseverance, communication and organization), it is recommended that academics and employers facilitate the development of these five characteristics by creating opportunities in their teaching and assessment which require students to demonstrate these characteristics within formative and summative assessments (academics) and via work experience or extracurricular activity (employers). Furthermore, the plural notion of resilience gives rise to the suggestion that the formative and summative assessment activities noted above should provide opportunities for students to develop resilience by communicating and justifying their ideas and thoughts and subsequently being exposed to managed criticism of these ideas and thoughts.

Recommendation 14: Promote agency and individualism

The facilitation of desired situational factors supports the processing of thoughts model and, therefore, creativity. When teaching with creativity, it is recommended that the notions of individualism and personal agency should be promoted, where practicable, by careful assessment design and the allocation of marks during summative assessments for the demonstration of individualism by, for example, allowing the exploration of literature and methods that challenge usual traditions in a subject. Similarly, summative assessments should also foster personal agency by permitting personal choice and managed risk taking in the design of coursework structuring and submission, and via the requirement for divergent idea creation within assessments which can subsequently be honed by the student to form a final entity.

Recommendation 15: Foster collaborative endeavours

Collaboration is a key surrounding factor which supports the processing of creative thoughts, as it promotes idea development and humanistic safety for those attempting to be creative. To raise awareness and provide students with the experience of collaborative work, academics should design and embed curricula activities which routinely require groups of undergraduate students to work collaboratively on tasks that require creativity and divergence, while also having a clear purpose and parameters to work within. These collaborative activities should also have periods of individual consolidation to clarify personal ideas before convening again with colleagues to finalize ideas.

Recommendation 16: Be curious of assigned values

The outcome of the processing thoughts model is a valued entity, falling into one of two general categories, practical or humanist, as defined subjectively by a stakeholder. Given this subjectivity, it would seem prudent to ensure that these values are understood by academics, students and employers, and, therefore, it is recommended that academics regularly engage with employers to ascertain the specific values within related employment sectors and convey this to their students in their teaching. Furthermore, as students progress through their undergraduate journey, academics should transfer responsibility for the ascertaining of the employer values from themselves to the students, thus facilitating knowledge of the values while also developing the personal characteristic of curiosity.

Recommendation 17: Accept the risk of failure

Recommendation 17 provides guidance for academics as a distinct recommendation but should also be viewed as a key underpinning for the preceding recommendations. Undertaking creative activities in the pursuit of a novel entity can result in failure and, if associated with negative consequences, can lead to more risk-averse behaviours and reduce creativity. Therefore, it is recommended that academics and employers permit greater acceptance of failure by providing managed space for students to undertake the processing of thoughts in a risk-free manner, particularly during summative assessment thus demonstrating commitment to creativity development as an employability skill. It is acknowledged that, due to prior experience, students may initially not engage with this approach; therefore, it is suggested that a tapered approach be employed where the guidance and support for creativity begin at a highly structured level and are reduced over the course of a student's programme of study.

Final conclusion and thought for the future

It would seem that UK HE may benefit from greater definition and thinking about creativity in the employment context and how this skill can be developed in graduates in an ever-changing twenty-first century. The model presented here highlights the multifaceted nature and processes of creativity, concepts which are not necessarily new when compared to creativity research per se but are perhaps original in the context of graduate employability. The plurality of meaning given creativity by the key stakeholders' perspective also gives further clarity to specific subject variability, and it is hoped that the recommendations based upon this model are pragmatic in informing practice and, ultimately, the development of creativity but also serve as a prompt to continue the inquiry into creativity in a continually evolving context.

Sources

Baer, J. and Garrett, T. (2010). 'Teaching for creativity in an era of content standards and accountability', in R.A. Baghetto and J.C. Kaufman (eds.), *Nurturing Creativity in the Classroom*, 6–23. New York: Cambridge University Press.

Beghetto, R.A. (2017). 'Creativity in teaching', in J.C. Kaufman, J. Baer, and V.P. Glăveanu (eds.), *Cambridge Handbook of Creativity across Different Domains*, 549–64. New York: Cambridge University Press.

Business, Innovation and Skills (BIS) (2016). *Success as a Knowledge Economy: Teaching Excellence, Social Mobility and Student Choice*. BIS/11/994. London: Crown copyright. Available from: https://www.gov.uk/government/uploads/system/uploads/attachment_data/file/523546/bis-16-265-success-as-a-knowledge-economy-web.pdf (accessed 5 October 2016).

Gray, A. (2016). 'The 10 skills you need to thrive in the Fourth Industrial Revolution', *World Economic Forum*. https://www.weforum.org/agenda/2016/01/the-10-skills-you-need-to-thrive-in-the-fourth-industrial-revolution/ (accessed 14 June 2019).

Institute of Student Employers (ISE) (2018). *The Global Skills Gap in the 21st Century*. QS Intelligence Unit UK. https://www.qs.com/portfolio-items/the-global-skills-gap-in-the-21st-century/ (accessed 23 September 2019).

Jackson, N. (2013). *Developing Students' Creativity through a Higher Education*. https://www.creativeacademic.uk/uploads/1/3/5/4/13542890/developing_students_creativity_through_a_higher_education.pdf (accessed 15 November 2020).

Kleiman, P. (2008). 'Towards transformation: Conceptions of creativity in higher education', *Innovations in Education and Teaching International*, 45: 209–21.

Lauder, H. (2015). 'Human capital theory, the power of transnational companies and a political response in relation to education and economic development', *Compare: A Journal of Comparative and International Education*, 45 (3): 490–3.

Plucker, J., Beghetto, R.A. and Dow, G.T. (2004). 'Why isn't creativity more important to educational psychologists? Potentials, pitfalls, and future directions in creativity research', *Educational Psychologist*, 39: 83–96.

Sternberg, R.J., Jarvin, L., Birney, D.P., Naples, A., Stemler, S.E., Newman, T., Otterbach, R., Parish, C., Randi, J. and Grigorenko, E.L. (2014). 'Testing the theory of successful intelligence in teaching grade 4 language arts, mathematics, and science', *Journal of Educational Psychology*, 106 (3): 881–99.

Universities UK (2018). *Solving Future Skills Challenges*. London: Universities UK. https://www.universitiesuk.ac.uk/policy-and-analysis/reports/Pages/solving-future-skills-challenges.aspx (accessed 24 April 2019).

Wallas, G. (1926/2014). *The Art of Thought*. 2nd ed. Tunbridge Wells: Solis Press.

11

Enhancing the Post-University Experience via Graduate 'Writing Weekends'

Glenn Fosbraey

Introduction

In 2012, I launched the first of many 'Writing Weekends' for Creative Writing graduates, where alumni could gather together and continue the workshop aesthetic of university life, while socializing, collaborating and reminiscing about university in between quizzing, chatting, playing mini-golf and board games. According to one student who took part in the 2019 weekend, 'Old friendships were brought up to date. New friendships were founded. And through mutual encouragement, writers found time to pull their proverbial fingers out and get down to some non-proverbial work.' In 2020 and 2021 in the midst of Covid-19, the writing weekend moved online, but the aesthetic remained the same: like-minded people spending time writing, workshopping, quizzing, chatting and reliving uni memories. In 2022, the in-person weekends returned with two occurrences, one in May and one in November. Over the ten years since it started, seventy different Creative Writing Graduates have attended at least one event, with many of those going on to attend multiple weekends (and in three cases, all of them so far).

This chapter is a case study of the 2023 'Writing Weekend' for BA Creative Writing graduates. Written for academics and anyone with an interest in setting up such events, this chapter examines the communal writing experience, the impact of location on writing, the concept of taking learning beyond the classroom, and how Universities can stay in touch with and assist their graduates after they have finished their studies.

Post-university as a transitionary period

*The writing bug is an infectious one. Allowed to
spread in a breeding ground of creative minds
feeding and bouncing and sparking off one another,
it can go viral. Fellow writers sharing thoughts, ideas,
characters, plots; driving each other to their
notebooks in an epidemic of inspiration. Then comes
the quarantine of graduation. Thrust into sudden
isolation, the creative virus may not flourish as it used to.
Finding the time, energy and wit to put pen to paper can
be difficult. Writing in a vacuum, without a gauntlet of
critically-minded peers to run ideas past, can dishearten
the most prolific of us.*

– Daniel Luxton, University of Winchester Creative Writing Graduate,
from his blog post 'a fine meeting of minds – a look at
graduate writing weekends.'

For many graduates, the period immediately after university can be a difficult one as they come to terms with one chapter of their lives closing and another beginning. 'Student Minds, who produced a report using graduate focus groups alongside City Mental Health Alliance, spoke to over 300 recent graduates, and say 49% of those surveyed said their mental wellbeing declined after leaving university, while 44% felt their friends were doing better than them and 40% felt socially isolated' (Baxter-Wright and Davies, 2019). And the Covid-19 pandemic hasn't helped with this, and 'for many […] has magnified the anxiety and distress that can make [… post-University] life feel like an emotional black hole' (Delzell, 2022). But, as professional counsellor Libby O'Brien says, 'The first thing to understand is that you're not alone [… and] feeling anxiety, depression, or some degree of "stuckness" and discomfort after graduating is normal' (Delzell, 2022). The Careers team at The University of Winchester work hard to make the transition from University to employment as smooth as possible, offering 'Careers Advice for Life' where all alumni – whenever they graduated – are entitled to use the Careers and Opportunity Hub's resources. Graduates can book individual guidance appointments or come onto campus to use the resources in the Careers and Opportunities Hub. All alumni can register for free and use CareerConnect to find jobs, volunteering opportunities, attend webinars and book Careers Guidance Discussions with the university's

Employability Advisers. As well as this there is also 'The Winton Society', the official alumni association of the University of Winchester community, an evolution of the Winton Club which was formed in 1874. The society offers a continued connection with Winchester for its alumni and has over 35,000 members from ninety countries across the world. It helps develop that sense of belonging to not only Winchester but a world-wide community through professional development and networking opportunities. This year we launched the 'Return' series where we invite a key alum to talk about their experience to inspire other alumni. The Winton Society provides the opportunity for alumni to give back through inspiring and supporting the next generation of graduates through their expertise or financial support. The writing weekends I organize are an additional way of further engaging former students after graduation and giving them a bit of a 'safety-net' post-university, in that they are able to recreate and relive their experiences (at least to an extent). Says Clare Holman-Hobbs, a 2014 graduate and attendee of seven of our writing weekends:

> *My friends and I come from all corners of the country for the writing weekends and it's usually the only time I get to see other alumni from Winchester outside of my friend group. We also get the opportunity to meet writers from other academic years whom I wouldn't necessarily have met thanks to the Writing Weekend. But the important message is that it doesn't matter when you graduated or how often you write – everyone is welcome. I think one of the most important parts of the Writing Weekend is that it gives us a chance to step out of our busy, overworked lives and allows us to step into a comfortable, creative place that allows us to be curious and explorative, much like what the Creative Writing degree provided for us many years ago. We're able to regain a safe space that we no longer have access to thanks to our annual (occasionally bi-annual) meet ups. The Writing Weekend focuses on allowing us to reclaim a part of ourselves that we were allowed to let flourish whilst attending the University of Winchester. For me, the Writing Weekend reminds me that I'm not alone, that we are united, as writers, by our history, our creativity, our words, and our passion for our craft.*

Challenge #1: The importance of affordability

Arriving, faffing chatting, eating drinking talking
laughing singing, reading writing, attending and
writing again …

(Bristol Collaborative Writing Group, 2012: 429)

There are many writing weekends on the market at present, many of them coming with excellent reviews. Among them are Arvon, which 'for over fifty years […] has been the UK's home of creative writing [with its] three centres, in Devon, Shropshire and Yorkshire' (Arvon, 2022), and Writers Retreat UK whose retreats 'take place at lovely, quiet locations across the UK' (Writers Retreat UK).

But a four-day untutored retreat at Arvon costs £610 per person. And Writers' Retreat UK is upwards from £800 for three nights. The cost of our November 2022 retreat to Pagham from Friday to Monday is £20 per person. And, of course, the added benefit of being guaranteed to have something in common with every participant, what with everyone being a graduate of the Creative Writing degree at The University of Winchester. Yes, we could go to more glamorous and stately locations than the caravan parks we attend (in fact, my original idea back in 2012 was that we'd hold the weekends in suitably 'writerly' places like old gothic manor houses or crumbing castles). But to do so would be to drastically increase the cost, and to do *that* would be to exclude people who haven't got that kind of disposable income – especially recent graduates still looking for that well-paying job a few months after leaving university. And for these weekends to be successful, they need to be inclusive. Writing isn't just for those who have money; it's for everyone.

Challenge #2: Different people, different needs

The writing weekends have always necessitated delicate handling of different personality types, bringing together as it does those that could be classed as introverted and those who could be classed as more extroverted. My years of classroom management obviously comes in useful here, as does my existing knowledge of the students (the fact they need to be graduates to attend means I've known them for a minimum of three years prior to them coming to a writing weekend), but it's still a difficult balancing act. The online writing weekends, although introduced out of necessity rather than desire, actually made it much clearer as to how different personality types reacted to the environment. As Durak observes, '[I]ntroverted individuals tend to be more reflective and therefore may benefit more from online learning environments that are asynchronous, progress at an individual pace, and do not involve group work. Extroverted individuals, on the other hand, will experience social loneliness in online environments' (Durak, 2022). It was noticeable during the online weekends that graduates who had never shown any desire to join an in-person event suddenly registered and, what is more, thrived during the weekend, even when engaging with the more 'sociable' activities, such as quizzes and workshopping. The more extroverted individuals, however, were frustrated by the lack of face-to-face engagement. The online weekends showed me two things: (a) that there is definitely appetite to do things this way as well as with the traditional face-to-face weekends and (b) that the traditional weekends could be more accommodating for introverted personality types. Although the social aspect of the face-to-face writing weekends is a big part of the experience, the prospect of suddenly being in an environment with a lot of people (some of them inevitably strangers) can be overwhelming for introverted personality types. For the November 2022 weekend, therefore, I took the decision, for the first time, to allocate sleeping arrangements. We had three separate accommodations (all identical), so two weeks before the event, I split the graduates into three categories, which started off as Caravans A, B and C but, as the weekend progressed, they took on the names 'party caravan', 'puzzle caravan' and 'oldies caravan'. Although this last may seem to be a derogatory or mocking moniker, the name was actually coined by its own residents, which included me! The 'party group' consisted of those graduates I knew to be extroverted types who stayed up late, got up late and enjoyed the social aspects that come with a group of twenty-somethings reuniting (I believe 'Cornish Rattler' cider was the drink of choice). The puzzle caravan was inhabited by more introverted characters and those who were new (or newish) to the writing weekend experience. The 'puzzle group' was so coined (again, by themselves) due to their purchasing, and finishing of, a 1,000 piece puzzle from a charity shop on Saturday. Although I slept in the 'oldies group' section, I spent a great deal of time with this group, making sure they were OK and facilitating social interaction with the other groups should they wish to engage in that way. As it turned out, the aforementioned puzzle ended up attracting members of the other 'groups', so this ended up being quite the social hub. The 'oldies group' was so called because of the amount of writing weekends its members had attended and the age of some of us (by some, I mean me). As old hands in the writing weekend game, I often task some of these graduates with integrating new attendees so they don't feel like they are isolated in their own bubble, with me as the only common link. The group arrangements caused me some difficulties, as I was mindful that separating 'newcomers' from the 'oldies' and, indeed, 'party group' from both may cause immediate rifts. But my other options seemed too risky. There were five new or 'newish' attendees, so to split them across the three groups was already an impossibility due to the odd number. To put one in each group was a numerical impossibility, and not one I'd have wanted to explore anyway, seeing that to put a single person (especially an introverted one) into a group where everyone else knew each other would be a big mistake. Even if there were six of them, I decided it would still be a bad idea to split them into pairs across the three groups, as they would be inclined to segregate themselves from the rest of the group (who all knew each other) and simply pair together. As it was, as everyone arrived at different times anyway, we all began the weekend by congregating in 'the oldies group', where I could facilitate introductions and ice-breakers via 'fun packs'.

The 'fun pack'

Each attendee was given a 'fun pack' on arrival (the term being a nod to the handouts I give in classes, which I jokingly refer to as 'fun packs'). This included arrival and exit questionnaires, ice-breaker activities for those who were new, visual and written writing prompts to those who needed warm-up activities, or who wanted a leg-up for a new idea, and a workshopping feedback chart to maximize the usefulness of comments and encourage people to avoid the classic feedback no-nos of 'that was good', 'I liked it', or 'nice work', etc. Which any writer will tell you is utterly useless.

Arrival questionnaire

1.   Name:
2.   Graduating year:
3.   Writing aim for the weekend (in words, pages, or balled-up pieces of paper):
4.   Most looking forward to:
5.   Most concerned about:
6.   Project (if none as yet, please put 'TBC'):
7.   Will you be writing by hand, or on laptop (etc.)?
8.   First writing weekend? If 'yes', what made you come along? If 'no', what's made you return?

Exit questionnaire

1.   What and how much did you write?
2.   How did you feel about the 'communal writing' situation?
3.   Favourite part
4.   Least favourite part

A table of the answers to selected questions is included in Appendix A at the end of this chapter.

Ice-breakers

'Getting to know you' exercises. These were part my own, and part taken from Sharon Jones's *Burn After Reading*, which is great for exploring the writerly mind

Prompts

Ten Prompts

1. Describe the most gruesome or horrifying thing you've ever seen.
2. Think of a mistake you've made. Write a scene where you either repair it or, in a different reality, act differently.
3. Write about a break-up as if it's an instruction manual.
4. Write micro-stories about each room (including communal ones) in a ten-bed motel or B&B.
5. Go to a bench and imagine three different people who have sat on it before you.
6. Things that you've done today that *weren't* on your to-do list that replaced things that *were*.
7. Write a one-page whinge about something.
8. Write an explanation for 'the doorway effect' (when we enter another room and forget why we've gone in there).
9. The story behind the best photograph (a) you ever took, and (b) were in.
10. Someone you greatly dislike invites you out for drinks. And you accept.

Workshopping chart

	Needs improvement	OK	Good	Very good	Excellent
Opening (hook)					
Narrative voice					
Dialogue					
Showing, not telling					
Elements of style (humour, emotion, etc.)					
Technical accuracy					

Challenge #3: Where to write?

As well as working on the itinerary and the sleeping arrangements, I also wanted to dig a little deeper into the writing habits of the attendees to maximize the chances of them leaving the weekend with as much quality material as possible. So, a few weeks before the event, I sent this message to the attendees (excluding welcoming preamble) via the Facebook group:

'What I'm after is for you to conduct an experiment over the next two weeks with regard to your writing, whether it be fiction or non-fiction. Over that period, I'd like you to make notes on your writing habits based upon whether any of the following have an impact on the process:

– Time of day you write
– Location (including any differences between writing inside and out)
– Surrounding sound (ambient, music you've chosen/music you've had foisted upon you by someone else, etc.)
– Writing implements (inc. typed or handwritten, and if the latter, how different paper/stationery impacts the experience)
– Eating and drinking (before/during/after)

Obviously, in order to give a full picture of the experience, the process requires you to try different variations on the above, e.g. hand-writing indoors vs. hand-writing outdoors; typing indoors vs. typing outdoors; drinking while typing outdoors vs. not drinking while typing outdoors (caffeine or alcohol can be included in this as you wish!); listening to music while drinking and hand-writing outdoors vs. silent writing while typing and not drinking indoors; typing fiction indoors while listening to music and drinking vs. hand-writing non-fiction outdoors while silent and not drinking, etc.

If nothing else, hopefully this will get you all writing every day for the next fortnight!'

Five graduates responded to the request, which was a decent result given the amount of work involved. Here are the results:

Case study 1

I'm definitely most productive at my desk, but if I'm working on a specific project, then I'm better outside or in a cafe because then I feel the pressure from the outside world. I don't work well writing outside though, because I'm more likely to get distracted.

With drinks, I find that I absolutely can't write with alcohol, and I make too many errors. But I can drink coffee, especially in the morning, as it makes me more productive. I'm also most productive in the morning, which hurts because I enjoy my lie ins too much.

Then there's the music. If I need to get something done, then music is banned. If I want to chill and write, then music is okay, but it can't have lyrics or a catchy beat, or then I'll abandon the writing and just distract myself. I can also do writing well in the dead of night, but I think that's just because it's completely silent and I can't get distracted.

Essentially, I've learned I lied to myself about music helping me concentrate and that mornings are good.

Case study 2

Where do you work best, and under what conditions?

At my desk: very productive, arguably more distracted because of the knick knacks. Managed about 1,000 words. Probably my most productive, as it's my work space.

Outside: in the garden. Had to stop because my laptop got too hot in the heat. But under normal circumstances I imagine, I could've done a fair chunk Needed to up my brightness which was annoying

In bed: more comfortable, much more distracting and found myself wandering off a lot. Worst result probably, about 250 words.

In [coffee shop chain]: very productive. Talked a bit, but once got back into it, managed 1,250 or to that affect.

Case study 3

Location: Outdoor writing is good in small bursts, indoor is better for long stretches. Comfort played a big part there though.

Timings: Generally coffee helps more in the mornings, and moderate alcohol consumption in the evening is beneficial. If I haven't eaten a significant meal within two hours of writing, I find starting very difficult.

Sound: Ambient noise is better than silence for sure. But if music is an option, then I was much more productive with a cultivated selection than listening to a radio or random playlist. I was surprised that listening to music without lyrics was more productive but I couldn't say why. When writing outside though, conversely I found that ambient noise was better than music, cultivated or otherwise.

Implements: This came down to convenience. Outdoor-made tech-based writing is too hard. Notebook all the way. Indoor writing, I found I could do either as effectively. However I felt more productive when I typed instead of hand wrote. I do think this might be my own bias and reliance on an automated word count as a measure of progress though to be fair.

Time of Day: Evening and night are for sure better. Lunch times were productive but frustrating as I was working with a time limit due to the demands of the workplace.

Case study 4

Inside (office): The best for concentration, get a lot done but tend to be in shorter bursts.

Indoor (front room): Useless, too many distractions.

(Bedroom): Surprisingly good, before bed writing tends to be good for ideas, less good for content.

Outside: this may be skewed due to hot weather but I hate it, uncomfortable and sun gets in my eyes or on the screen of my iPad.

Time of day: Best times are mid-morning and evening. Mid-afternoon is the worst.

Case study 5

Inside: On lap with no music – word count fabulous, content ... not so much. Lots of editing required.

At 'official' desk – creativity stifled massively

Tried outdoors but the glare was annoying

Best result: in my room on my bed with music – felt liberated and a little bit naughty and music was the 'concentration' compilations Spotify generates. Music with words seems to impact my creativity, although if I'm in 'flow' then I guess I would probably tune it out anyway. As you might have guessed, I didn't achieve 'flow'!!

From these, I pulled out the following feedback that I felt I could influence the structure of the writing weekend. My thoughts on how to integrate them included in brackets:

'In [coffee shop chain]: very productive.' (Communal writing in a public place, with drinks available)

'On lap with no music – word count fabulous' (writing in accommodation).

'Best times are mid-morning and evening' (make sure there are writing times to accommodate different tastes/strengths).

'Essentially, I've learned that I lied to myself about music helping me concentrate and that mornings are good.' (ensure there are scheduled morning writing activities)

'Ambient noise is better than silence for sure. But if music is an option then I was much more productive with a cultivated selection than listening to a radio or random playlist.' (Ambient noise for those who want it, but also silent options need to be available for those who don't. Everyone always brings headphones, so music is an option at all times, but no 'communal' music.)

'If I haven't eaten a significant meal, within two hours of writing I find starting very difficult.' (Make sure writing activities outside the venue have affordable food options.)

A week before the event, I posted a 'suggested' itinerary on the Facebook group, stressing that engagement with it was completely optional (this wasn't uni, after all)! This included scheduled trips to a popular gastropub chain where ambient noise, coffee, food and communal writing opportunities were plentiful, scheduled writing time at the venue, scheduled workshopping time and social events for those who wanted them.

Below is my itinerary post as it was posted to the group, warts, idiosyncratic language and all.

Friday:

From 3: Get in, get settled, get to know those Winchies who weren't in your year

5–5:30 am: Overviews of the projects we'll be working on, and our target word or page counts.

5:30–7: Fast food run/other food arrangements/chatting/reading/having a good old-fashioned stare into space.

7–9: Writing/more discussions about ideas/collaborations.

Saturday:

7–10 am: Early birds getting various worms writing/breakfast/bottomless coffee session at xxxx

10:00–10:30: Discussing ideas/plans for the day

10:30–2 pm: Writing

2–2:30: Quiz #1

2:30–4:30: Writing

4:30–5:30: Mini golf/bowls/other potential delights

5:30: The food situation, etc.

7–9: Workshopping in small groups

9: Quiz #2

Sunday:

7–10 am: Early birds getting additional worms/breakfast/bottomless coffee session at xxxx

10:00–10:30: Meet up, chat about the day before, discuss biscuits, etc.

10:30–2 pm: Writing

2–2:30: Quiz #3

2:30–4:30: Writing

4:30–5:30: More mini golf or bowls?

5:30: Another food situation?

7–9: Workshopping in small groups

9 onwards: Smile at all the work you've done and all the fun you've had and count the hours until the next WW

Reflections

The coffee situation

According to Zabelina and colleagues, 'Caffeine is the most widely consumed psychotropic drug in the world [...] with 85% of adults in the US consuming at least one caffeinated beverage daily [...] In low to moderate doses, caffeine has been shown to increase people's alertness [...] improve vigilance and motor performance [...] enhance concentration and attentional focus [...] and elevate mood' (Zabelina et al., 2020: 3). Although cited here as a positive factor and indeed mirrored in the responses of some of the case study participants (and by writers in general, including myself), caffeine may not be as useful as we think for the *creative* process. Landrum and colleagues observe that 'data analyses revealed that caffeine consumption produced no significant effects on reading comprehension, writing rate, tapping rate, reaction time, or serial recall' (Landrum et al., 1985: 1), and, indeed, Zabelina and colleagues go on to say that although 'consuming 200 mg of caffeine (approximately equal to one 12 oz cup of coffee) in a laboratory session significantly enhanced convergent problem-solving ability, [... it] had no effect on divergent [creative] thinking or working memory' (Zabelina et al., 2020: 17). Caffeine is not necessarily good for the *creative* process of writing, therefore (although also not detrimental, either) but is good for the *analytical* side of writing (which, in fiction, would be the editing and proofreading process). The reliance on bottomless coffees for those of us attending the early morning writing sessions, therefore, may have been counter-productive, and going forward, it might be wise to abstain unless we are engaging in editing or proofreading activities.

Communal writing: The pros and cons

Writing is usually a solitary endeavour, but in those early stages of a project, especially if you're a little rusty or lacking in confidence, having fellow writers going through similar experiences beside you can really work. Smith observes that 'despite romantic notions of the lone scholar in the ivory tower, we don't actually do our best writing in isolation; writing is a communication process and thus a communal process' (Smith, 2019: 103), with Bishop and Starkey in agreement, saying: 'collaboration [… can] often prove both productive and fun for writers and can change their attitudes vis-à-vis a highly competitive and often discouraging publishing environment' (Bishop and Starkey, 2006: 36).

The collaborative writing experience was largely praised by the attendees, with the following comment from the 'exit questionnaires':

Respondent C: … 'having other people diligently working on stuff around makes you want to keep up with them.'

Respondent D: 'It was so helpful for the mindset. Just having people on hand to be like, "What's another word for … ?" Plus it's lovely to know the struggle to be creative in a world that lives off of it but doesn't support it is not just felt by me!'

Respondent E: 'If it wasn't for communal writing, I wouldn't have written the small amount I did, so very much in favour.'

But there needs to be more allocated time for those who *don't* want to engage in such a way, and perhaps the need to select a quieter place than our chosen gastro-pub, which did get progressively louder after about 10 am.

Respondent A noted that they 'really enjoy communal writing but I think I would have liked it to happen in a quieter place rather than [xxxx]'.

Respondent F said that they'd 'have preferred it if it was somewhere quieter' and Respondent I commented that it was 'too noisy in [xxxx] but in theory great idea'.

Respondent G observed that they think 'we need a little more structure and separation between those of us who are in the mood for writing/ workshopping and those who just want to hang out. Maybe a writing caravan might be good?'

This last comment is, perhaps, the one that needs to be thought of the longest. On past writing weekends (including this one), graduates have written in the caravans that they're sleeping in when not writing 'outside' the venue, but this doesn't necessarily allow a differentiation between those who want to deviate from the suggested itinerary and those who want to stick to the defined writing times. As such, I will certainly put Respondent G's suggestion into practice at future weekends, with a caravan always dedicated to writing during the day.

As well as holding both online and face-to-face events every year from now on, I am also exploring the possibility of writing *days* rather than entire weekends. I recently had a conversation with B.J. Hollars, Associate Professor at the University of Wisconsin Eau Claire, who is in the process of launching twelve-hour writers retreat. As he says:

> In the summer of 2022, the Chippewa Valley Writers Guild – a regional writers' organization that I direct – received the difficult news that our 3-day summer writers' retreat rental space was no longer available to us. As such, the board and I began brainstorming new retreat models.
>
> After receiving feedback from our members, it became clear that cost and time were the two major hurdles that often got in the way of their decision to participate. We decided to try to alleviate both problems by creating a more abbreviated (and cost-effective) model: the 12-Hour Writers Retreat.
>
> This morning-to-night writing experience is committed to supporting writers from idea to live reading. On January 14, from 9 am to 9 pm, I'll host our first attempt at this retreat model. To ensure individual instruction (and to keep our evening reading manageable), we'll cap participants at 20.
>
> The day will begin with guided writing exercises courtesy of the host, followed by free writing time, then an optional afternoon workshop, and finally, the live reading. Throughout the day we'll enjoy fellowship/networking by way of two meals, and plenty of coffee breaks.
>
> Our goal is always to create an inclusive space at an affordable rate. This retreat will cost 65.00. To keep costs low, we've received a sponsorship from the Wisconsin Writers Association and I'll volunteer my services. If the retreat is a success, we'll strive to create quarterly retreats in this model; each of which will specialize in a particular genre and will be hosted by an expert in that genre.

Final thoughts

Whatever form they take, be they online, in person, or condensed into a single day, I sincerely hope that our writing 'weekends' can continue long into the future and continue to attract new graduates with every passing year. As Respondent C said, 'It is the perfect scenario for meeting new people as you know immediately you have at least one thing in common and can bond regardless of what year you graduated.'

Appendix A

Participant	Graduated	Weekend aim	Looking forward to	Concerned about	First weekend? If 'no', why have you returned?	What and how much did you write?	How did you feel about the 'communal writing' situation?	Favourite part	Least favourite part
A	2019	To rekindle the writing spark! Haven't written creatively since graduating	Meeting likeminded people that will understand why I enjoy writing	Being shit ☺ e.g. someone workshopping with me and thinking it's rubbish	First writing weekend. Decided to come because I need something to motivate me	About 500 more words of diss, but it's given me the motivation I needed to carry on	I really enjoy communal writing but I think I would have liked it to happen in a quieter place	Meeting new people. Feeling inspired to write and improve	Not enough workshopping
B	2014	Re-connect with like-minded people and feel 'at one' with others who understand the creative process	Same	Nothing	No. Only time I can be around other writers who know the process of what it's like to be creative				

Participant	Graduated	Weekend aim	Looking forward to	Concerned about	First weekend? If 'no', why have you returned?	What and how much did you write?	How did you feel about the 'communal writing' situation?	Favourite part	Least favourite part
C	2017	Minimum of 500 words a day just to get back into a good habit	Meeting new people, seeing old friends and have a good catch-up/laugh	Amount of driving!	Third. Honestly, these have been highlights of the year for me. I always enjoy them and even if I don't get much writing done, I feel better in general for having gone	I managed a total of 600 words over the entire weekend. Not quite my target, nevertheless, I had a great time and the 600 words I did manage are better than anything I have written in the last 3 months	It was great to be able to write in a place where I wouldn't normally as it helps test my likes and dislikes for a writing situation. On top of this, having other people diligently working on stuff around makes you want to keep up with them	The people. It is the perfect scenario for meeting new people as you know immediately you have at least one thing in common and can bond of that regardless of what year you graduated	Having to leave

Participant	Graduated	Weekend aim	Looking forward to	Concerned about	First weekend? If 'no', why have you returned?	What and how much did you write?	How did you feel about the 'communal writing' situation?	Favourite part	Least favourite part
D	2021	To get back into the flow of writing and out of my block!	Being around other creative types	If the writing does not come	Yes! I was needing something like this to get my back into my brain and back to myself. Couldn't make the last one so was happy to come along	3,000 words of novel	It was so helpful for the mindset. Just having people on hand to be like "What's another word for..?" Plus it's lovely to know the struggle to be creative in a world that lives off of it but doesn't support it is not just felt by me!	Feeling understood and getting past writers block!	Being too tired to 'people' haha

Participant	Graduated	Weekend aim	Looking forward to	Concerned about	First weekend? If 'no', why have you returned?	What and how much did you write?	How did you feel about the 'communal writing' situation?	Favourite part	Least favourite part
E	2013	To be able to write *something*, first and foremost. More specifically to channel the autumnal atmosphere and location into something with a tinge of thriller about it	Being surrounded by other writers bashing away at their keyboards, which will hopefully trigger my own keyboard-bashing, like less problematic peer pressure	Meeting young people who still have hope in their eyes. Getting dragged into defensive conversations about how just because I don't do much actual writing anymore doesn't mean I'm not involved in other creative projects, thank you very much	No, a regular since the not quite earliest days. I come back because being around other writers is the thing that makes me most likely to write myself. It's also good to see old faces, and there is a pleasure in meeting new people	Wrote a paragraph of prose, realized it's been a decade since I wrote any prose, so wrote a few pages of radio script to get back into the rhythms of writing. Then never went back to either	If it wasn't for communal writing, I wouldn't have written the small amount I did, so very much in favour	Going to Wetherspoon on Saturday morning	Not going to Wetherspoon on Sunday morning

Participant	Graduated	Weekend aim	Looking forward to	Concerned about	First weekend? If 'no', why have you returned?	What and how much did you write?	How did you feel about the 'communal writing' situation?	Favourite part	Least favourite part
F	2014	Aiming to write 10k words	Mini-golf	Actually writing 10k words	No. Seeing everyone	2,500 words on my first short story plus a quiz	I'd have preferred it if it was somewhere quieter but fine with me	As always just being with friends	Lack of extra stuff e.g. bowls, mini golf
G	2020	To workshop my novel and get some ideas of how to move forward with the plot	Spending time with and getting to know my fellow writers	Having dedicated time to workshop	No – I enjoyed getting to know everyone and having fun together	Nothing – I couldn't access my novel as it's on OneDrive and there wasn't a good enough WiFi connection in our caravan!	I think we need a little more structure and separation between those of us who are in the mood for writing/workshopping and those who just want to hang out. Maybe a writing caravan might be good?	Getting to complete a 1,000 piece puzzle in just 2 days – an absolute achievement!	Poor wi-fi

Participant	Graduated	Weekend aim	Looking forward to	Concerned about	First weekend? If 'no', why have you returned?	What and how much did you write?	How did you feel about the 'communal writing' situation?	Favourite part	Least favourite part
H	2021	To write more than usual!	Doing writing exercises and the arcade	Not sleeping	Yes. Because I don't have many writer friends	Ideas	Nice. Maybe we need to be silent	Puzzle and friends	Rain ☺
I	2012	Short story	Dedicated space to write, with encouragement from like-minded people	Being in party caravan!	No, it's tradition	Worked on an existing short story and restructured it	Too noisy in [xxxx] but in theory great idea	Catching up with people	Party caravan!
J	2014	Hopefully 2,000 words on current novel 1st draft	Catching up with friends	Nothing	No. Enjoy catching up with friends, having a break, writing	Novel. Almost 3,000 words	It worked well	All good	The rain

Sources

Arvon (2022). https://www.arvon.org/about/arvon-home-of-creative-writing/ (accessed 14 November 2022).

Baxter-Wright, D. and Davies, M. (2019). 'Why is no one talking about post-university depression?'. https://www.cosmopolitan.com/uk/worklife/campus/a22575047/post-university-depression/ (accessed 14 November 2022).

Bishop, W. and Starkey, D. (2006). 'Collaboration', in *Keywords in Creative Writing*, 29–36. Colorado: University Press of Colorado. https://doi.org/10.2307/j.ctt4cgr61.11.

Bristol Collaborative Writing Group (2019). 'After writes: Some loosely threaded together writing about ending/not ending our time together in a collaborative writing group' (2012). *International Review of Qualitative Research*, 5 (4): 427–47. https://doi.org/10.1525/irqr.2012.5.4.427.

Delzell, E. (2022). 'Post-college depression: Why you feel lonely'. https://www.webmd.com/depression/features/post-college-depression (accessed 14 November 2022).

Durak, Y.H. (2022). 'Role of personality traits in collaborative group works at flipped classrooms', *Current Psychology*. https://doi.org/10.1007/s12144-022-02702-1 (accessed 19 November 2022).

Landrum, R.E. and Meliska, C.J. (1988). 'Caffeine use and extroversion', *Psychologia - An International Journal of Psychology in the Orient*, XXXI (2): 91–7.

Luxton, D. (2019). 'A fine meeting of minds – A look at graduate writing weekends.' https://www.winchester.ac.uk/accommodation-and-winchester-life/uwin-student-blog/blog-posts/a-fine-meeting-of-minds—a-look-at-graduate-writing-weekends-by-daniel-luxton.php (accessed 14 November 2022).

Smith, T.G. (2019). 'Writing is/as communal', in J.R. Gallagher and D.N. DeVoss (eds.), *Explanation Points: Publishing in Rhetoric and Composition*, 103–6. Utah: Utah State University Press.

Writers' Retreat UK (2022). https://writersretreatuk.co.uk/ (accessed 19 November 2022).

Wurdinger, S.D. and Carlson, J.A. (2009). *Teaching for Experiential Learning: Five Approaches That Work*. Ukraine: R&L Education.

Zabelina, D.L. and Silvia, P.J. (2020). 'Percolating ideas: The effects of caffeine on creative thinking and problem solving', *Consciousness and Cognition*, 79: 102899.

Conclusion: Improving Inclusivity through Creative Approaches to Learning, Teaching and Assessment

Cassie Violet Lowe

In the introduction to this book Glenn Fosbraey wrote, 'we need to keep evolving as people and as educators; we must listen to our students, observe our peers [...] and learn from their different styles; we must accept that each class will have a different dynamic with different personalities and be willing and able to be flexible'. This hunger for development and humbleness to continue to evolve flexibly is precisely what this edited collection seeks to inspire colleagues to do and be. It achieves its aim by providing an array of international perspectives and case study examples of creative approaches to teaching and assessment in the arts and humanities to inspire your own practice and invite you to explore new avenues for learning, teaching and assessment. It is through innovating teaching and assessment that we begin to break free from traditional didactic teaching methods and writing-based assessments as the only method and start to enhance student engagement and the overall experience of higher education (HE). This conclusion will draw upon the works of this collection to make the argument that these creative approaches do not only increase student engagement through active learning and authentic assessment but also work towards increasing the inclusivity of the learning environment and the accessibility of HE for a greater diversity of students.

Breaking with traditional assumptions of how students should be taught and assessed presents an exciting venture for the HE sector. Exploring creative teaching and assessment approaches, such as those practices outlined in this book, means that we must bravely enter into unknown territories and explore new ideas for how we can engage students in their learning experientially and assess this in new and, often, more authentic ways. In their chapter, Myers and Evert invited the reader to embark on the journey of developing creative approaches through reflection, delightfully referring to it as a journey to 'capture the mythical unicorn that is creativity'. The chapter provided a roadmap of sorts for this journey through posing several questions to inspire reflection and to challenge the reader to think differently, and importantly, personally, about their educational practice and their relationship to creativity, to be able to begin to push forward and innovate. Universities have for the most part sat comfortably within the bounds of traditional modes of teaching for hundreds of years, and the assessment methods have mirrored this slow response to change. However, much has evolved in contemporary education, and it is this innovation in teaching and assessment that paves the way forward for HE. Many colleagues across the sector have been inspired to be creative with their learning and teaching practices to design curricula in ways that break out of the box of tradition, and this book offers some of these practices for you to consider in your own contexts. Turner provided an excellent starting point in her chapter for considering practical strategies and activities to create effective learning experiences. She invited us to consider the many different types of learning environments and the varied learning experiences they can promote. The pandemic moved the vast majority of teaching in HE online, and, as Turner discussed, this invited colleagues to innovate and problem-solve, using their creative talents to find new ways to teach and assess.

This is not to set up such a clear-cut dichotomy between new and old with the latter, the traditional methods, being posed in this conclusion as the antithesis to 'good practice'. Nor is it to suggest that all traditional forms of education are to be thrown out to make way for completely radical practice in what could be a disorienting flurry of new educational techniques and assessment methods, as this, too, would be overwhelming for all and unproductive for students. Rather, it is to suggest that, where appropriate and in relation to the wider curricula students are experiencing, thinking outside of traditional boundaries with our learning, teaching and assessments can enable a greater diversity of students to succeed. It is at this point in particular that I wish to draw this edited collection to a close, to bring the chapters together and, through them, make a claim for creative approaches to learning and teaching as being intricately connected with inclusive pedagogical practice. As the HE sector strives to become a place of learning for a wider diversity of students, so, too, must the practices of learning and teaching evolve and innovate to reflect and be inclusive of the diversity of learners within the classroom. This means creative approaches to learning and teaching practice have become increasingly important as we aim to move forward as a sector with inclusivity at the heart of these developments.

Key to trying new ideas and practice, particularly if, for example, you are seeking to explore a new assessment method, is the implementation of the appropriate scaffolding to support the students in undertaking a new learning activity so that they feel they are working within more familiar territory. In the case of assessment, this might be supported through formative tasks that enable students to practise and receive constructive feedback on their work that can feed into their future summative work. Within this edited collection, Buchanan and colleagues provided a rich exploration of assessment practices within a spectrum of disciplines across teacher education – creative arts, English, humanities and science – to inspire development in your own assessments. The authors of the chapter explored their own practice in discussion with each other to learn from and challenge the approaches and underpinning philosophies of assessment practices outside of their disciplines. The chapter has highlighted that through humanizing assessment by making it diverse, providing opportunities for learner agency, and utilizing constructivist pedagogies, educators can enable a true sense of democratic learning through assessment. Buchanan and colleagues invited us in their chapter to resist hand-me-down formats of teaching and assessing and instead to take risks and be confident in building new futures for the student experience.

The shift away from traditional practice to more creative and innovative approaches is not without its challenges, as colleagues exploring such ventures within this book have testified, but it also provides an opportunity for new discoveries in improving student learning and the potential for a wider diversity of students to engage meaningfully. Inclusive practice works alongside and complements the exciting and creative approaches featured in this text, as both creative methods for teaching and inclusive pedagogies call for traditional practices to be challenged and developed beyond a 'one-size-fits-all' approach to education. Taking a more inclusive approach to learning and teaching is inherently a creative one, as we seek to find flexible ways for students to learn through multiple means of engagement and provide various forms through which students can demonstrate their understanding. It is this variety in pedagogical practice that enables a wider diversity of students to flourish. While traditional didactic modes of delivery and closed book examinations often testing rote learning suit a proportion of students and might be appropriate in certain disciplines and contexts for future employment, this limits the wider student body from achieving their potential. As we seek to diversify the students attending university, so too must we diversify our learning, teaching and assessment methods to incorporate a variety of approaches to engage the broadest spectrum of learners. Finding alternative means to achieve the learning objectives for the activity is where you will find yourself thinking creatively and, often, more inclusively.

To provide a concrete example of this in practice, rather than asking a question to the full lecture theatre of students, you might consider employing supporting learning technologies for questions and answers, so learners who find quick responses in front of large groups difficult or uncomfortable can participate in the activity without those pressures. Further examples of using technological solutions creatively to engage learners can be found within this book. The chapter by Luff and colleagues highlighted a range of excellent practice through multiple vignettes which explored using various digital platforms to enable deep and authentic learning. The authors shared four example case studies of their experiences engaging learners in technology-infused creative approaches to teaching, assessment and feedback practices, which are centred on their desire to design a digital and virtual environment that creates a sense of human connection and belonging for students. In Chapter 8, Houghton and colleagues also described their practice on the PGCert in Creative Education and the steps they take to foster meaningful engagement with the online programme. Built on the seven principles they outline as being core to their programme design (connecting, critical, creative co-constructed, inclusive, intercultural and research informed) and framed by theoretical works of Vygotsky, Rogers, Freire and Fung, they explored in their chapter the practical steps taken to foster a learning environment true to their principles and theoretical frames. With inclusive practice at the heart of the approach, particularly considering neurodivergent students, the authors noted that their creative use of the 'little and often' approach to the programme's online learning environment and assessments enabled a more equitable and effective approach to the design of the programme. This format requires engagement around more frequent activities but in shorter bursts, rather than the traditional patterns of lengthy assignments and longer lectures. This chapter showed that breaking away from traditional formats for the programme and assessment design, and creatively exploring different approaches simultaneously enables a wider variety of learners to engage with the course and all students to perform at their best. However, the chapter also provided an honest review of the time commitment such an approach requires in the longer term. Reflecting specifically on the wider issues of poor mental health in HE, they explored how the programme design is resource intensive and discussed the tensions between good pedagogical practice and the pressures on staff in a challenging HE climate. A challenge with which I am sure all readers can empathize.

Concerns for well-being of both staff and students have never been more important for creating an inclusive academic environment. Reflecting the growing concerns over mental health in HE, particularly when one considers the awarding gap for students with declared mental health conditions, Mills argued in his chapter for mental well-being pedagogies to be threaded throughout the course design. He put forward the argument that if one in four students is experiencing poor mental well-being then in order for them to be able to achieve their potential as learners this must be addressed within the course. In the chapter, Mills explored examples of how this can be successfully achieved in practice, from collaborative activities (student–student and student–staff) that foster a sense of belonging and deep learning to opportunities to learn outside of the classroom and many more implementable examples for readers to adapt to their contexts. The chapter also showed how well-being can move from pedagogical approaches to course content and provided three examples of how this is achieved in arts and humanities programmes. These tangible examples show how the educator is therefore tasked with being creative with their course content and design to embed well-being into practice and academic discussions. Bringing well-being front and centre to course creation and delivery is a challenge worth embarking upon in order to begin to tackle the inclusivity issues present within the HE system that students face regarding their well-being.

Taking a student-centred approach to developing our teaching and learning can also take the form of working directly with students. Shifting the focus towards students as co-constructors of knowledge can open up exciting opportunities to rediscover the teaching and learning experience anew, through perceiving it with new eyes and in a new light. Mounsey and Booth and Trelfa and colleagues have explored such practices in their respective chapters in challenging the traditional forms of delivery, in particular that of privileging the role of the tutor as the centre of knowledge production. The discoveries made through engaging students in the co-construction of knowledge can facilitate students to experience a more transformative and relational learning process. For Trelfa and colleagues, in the case study outlined in Chapter 3, this took the form of encouraging students to engage in a shared, creative process in the co-creation of curricula. In Chapter 5, Mounsey and Booth explored the teaching experiences of an English literature lecturer who lost his sight in 2010 and has to re-learn much of his practice as an educator, with the help of his assistant and colleague. Through this drastic change in the nature of his educational practice,

Mounsey and Booth identified how they have creatively adapted and, therefore, rediscovered the learning environment for both teacher and student alike. Throughout the chapter there are several examples of the transformative nature of learning when one recognizes and appreciates students as co-constructors of knowledge. Furthermore, through the dynamic created in teaching together, they also invite challenge from students by openly challenging each other live in the classroom, fostering a critical and independent thought from students. Mounsey and Booth demonstrated in this chapter how their creative approaches to learning, teaching and assessment in English Literature encourage relational, constructivist, and, importantly, transformative pedagogies. They outlined this approach in ten principles for effective practice in this mode of teaching, which guides any reader into a greater sense of understanding how to enact this effectively within their own practice. What both of these chapters have outlined is ultimately a more inclusive environment in which students can flourish to meet their own learning needs through co-constructing the learning experience.

Echoing this, the case study from Bernard also provided a great example of relational learning in practice in the form of students learning academic literacies. In this case study, students were tasked with deconstructing text and language and exploring the underpinning ideological assumptions behind them to develop in a way that values the students' perspectives, knowledge and languages. This case study offers a creative and more inclusive approach to destabilizing academic practice as a singular dominant discourse and brings to the fore issues of power and student senses of self. Stepping outside of traditional methods and creatively reimagining ways of teaching academic literacies has enabled the students in the case study to challenge any preconceived notions of an inherent and fixed academic authority and reposition the student and their experiences as valued sources of knowledge. Important work such as this in the case study highlighted here draws out the embodied experience of learning as being one that is shaped by students' previous experiences, their values, beliefs and motivations. In recognizing and understanding this as a key tenant of the learning process for students we, as educators, can appreciate more fully that learning is not a passive endeavour, but one that situates students at the heart of this process and that we must therefore provide opportunities to enable them to make the connections with their previous knowledge and experience to make sense of what they are learning. Deconstructing the notion of knowledge as being held solely by the centre, in this case the educator or institution, and valuing different perspectives and experiences are where the diversity of the student body can be better appreciated and practices can become more inclusive.

It is this variety of opportunities for students to engage and bring their knowledge to their learning that enables a wider diversity of students' needs to be met and therefore achieve their potential. Both Fosbraey and Wadsworth look to the future of such graduates and, in their respective chapters, offer creative opportunities to develop the students' employability. Wadsworth presented a call to arms for the development of creativity in students through their formal learning, teaching and assessment experiences. He put forward a strong case for the necessity of creativity in graduates entering the employment market beyond HE, which, as he highlights, is not a skillset employers feel graduates currently enter the workforce having honed through their HE. He situates this requirement in practicable terms and provides recommendations for colleagues for how to embed the development of creativity and creative thought processes into the student's learning experience more formally. Fosbraey has developed an altogether wholly different initiative for graduates of the Creative Writing programme at the University of Winchester. He described in his chapter a case study in which he has created space for alumni to come together and develop literary ideas and workshop their writing in the form of a 'writing retreat'. His chapter provided an example of how the learning and teaching spaces can continue postgraduation for students and, importantly, how the care for one's alumni can continue beyond the formal curriculum. Not only did this chapter provide an excellent case study of practice for engaging creative writing graduates in a somewhat structured retreat for writing – the practice is innovative in and of itself – it also importantly outlined how to take meaningful consideration for the varied personality types and learners present at the retreat, ensuring that one is responding inclusively to their needs. This chapter supports anyone interested in exploring a similar model and additionally provided the activity packs given to students to initiate a more friendly, inclusive and sociable setting – useful for any educational context. This edited collection invites you to step outside of the box – quite literally in Fosbraey's chapter as he leaves the formal HE setting of place and people behind – to enable a multiplicity of learning styles, and your own pedagogical creativity, to flourish.

As the external pressures placed upon HE institutions increase, it is understandable that colleagues might feel the need to hold firmly onto the familiar in learning and teaching practice. However, without colleagues venturing to develop education beyond that of the inherited practices and assumptions, HE will continue to remain for a privileged minority – open only to those that 'fit' with the traditional experience. As the sector looks to challenge such taken-for-granted practices in learning, teaching, assessment and curriculum design, this edited collection has invited us to consider how we might reimagine these structures and practices to develop educational provision for the future of our students. This book supports this through offering a selection of case studies as a foundation on which to build your own ideas and explore new avenues in your own contexts. In the introduction to this book, Glenn Fosbraey wrote, '[c]hange for change's sake is dangerous, but so is obstinately standing still and refusing to adapt simply because "this is what we've always done"'. I wholeheartedly agree with this summation, and in addition to this I hope that this conclusion chapter has also inspired you to explore creative approaches to your educational practice because, as highlighted throughout, it is through stepping outside of traditional methods of learning, teaching and assessing that we can promote a more inclusive environment for all of our students to thrive.

Index

360 degree video 66

abstract thinking 161
academic 77, 83, 84, 85
Action Learning Sets 42, 45, 46
applying 154, 155
arts based (subject domain) 157
assessment 74, 77–81, 83, 97, 98, 100, 102, 104, 106, 108, 110, 112, 115, 116
assessment criteria 99, 104, 105, 106
assessment practices 98, 115
assessment task/s 107, 108, 110, 116, 119
assigned values 164
Australian Curriculum 98, 99, 101, 114, 117
authentic assessment 110

belonging 53, 55, 84
benchmark 75, 78, 81, 82
blindness 72, 73, 82
business (case/concepts/school) 52, 53, 54, 55, 56, 59, 66

caffeine and creativity 178
challenges 100, 102, 104
choreographed teaching 38, 45, 46
clarifying 153, 155, 156, 157, 162
classroom 73, 76, 77, 79, 81, 82
collaborating 154, 157
collaboration 51, 53, 54, 55, 66
collaborative learning and teaching 36–8, 40–6
collaborative learning and teaching, and role of lecturers/teachers 41
collaborative learning and teaching: risks and challenges 38, 39–44
collaborative learning and teaching and lecturer/teacher concerns 38, 39, 41–4
collaborative learning and teaching and role of lecturers, as coaches 38, 41, 42
collaborative learning and teaching and student concerns 3–40, 42–4
communal writing 179–80

communicating with precision and clarity/ communicating clearly 102, 104, 107, 110, 111
communicators 21, 27
community 51, 52, 53
conceptualizing 153, 155
connection 51, 52, 55, 57, 59, 62, 67
constructivism 102
continuous learning 101, 102, 103, 114
core principles 153, 154
course design 123, 133, 143–7, 193
create, imagine and innovate 102, 103, 107, 111, 115
creating, imagining and innovating 113
creative 102, 104, 110, 113, 115, 116
creative and critical thinking 100, 105
creative arts 71
creative process 113
creative prompts 173
creativity 9, 40, 45, 46, 107, 111, 113
criteria 160, 161

deep learning 142, 144, 147, 193
democratic assessment 100
design thinking 44
designing 153, 154, 155, 157, 158, 160
disability 71, 74, 79, 80
discussion 71, 72, 76–8, 80, 83
dispositions 98, 99, 100, 114, 115, 117

eighteenth-century literature 74, 82
empathy 110
employability 151, 153, 154, 158, 159, 160, 161, 162, 163, 164, 165
employer satisfaction 152
engagement 60, 61, 62, 67
English 72, 74, 75, 81
essay 72, 73, 75, 78–9, 82
evaluating 154, 155, 157, 160
evidence-based assessment 98
experience 71, 73–7, 80–3, 97, 102, 104, 105, 110, 111, 113, 114, 115, 117

experimental 97, 105
experimentation 103, 105

facilitating situational factors 154, 157,
    159
feedback 55, 56, 57, 59, 60, 61, 62, 65, 66
flexible thinking 99, 107
formal assessment 102
future-focussed learning 101

gathering data through all the senses 99,
    104, 106, 112
genially 56, 57
Google form 66
graduate employers 151, 152, 153, 158, 159
graduate workforce 152
group work 52, 53, 54, 55, 59, 63, 65, 66

Habits of Mind (HoM) 97, 98, 99, 102, 103,
    104, 106, 109, 111, 112, 113, 115, 116
heutagogy 38, 44
HTML 5 Package 56, 57, 58, 66
humanistic approach 62, 67
humanization/humanizing 100, 102

ice-breakers 172–3
identity 9–11, 17, 21, 23, 25, 27–32
impairment 71, 72, 79, 80
incidental learning 16–17
individualised assessment 98
individualised learning 114
individualism 159, 163
Initial Teacher Education (ITE) 97, 98,
    100, 101, 111, 112, 114, 115
innovations/innovating/innovate 103, 105,
    107, 112, 115
intellectual behaviours 113
inter-disciplinarity 161
interactivity/interactive 51, 52, 53, 56, 57,
    65, 66, 67

language practices 22
learning environments (HE context) 12
learning environments (key factors) 13–14
learning environments (practical
    activities) 16
location and writing 174–7

mental health 132, 137–47, 168, 193
metalanguage 21, 24, 25

Microsoft Excel 55, 66
Microsoft Teams 53, 54
modality 23
motivation 14, 16, 62, 69, 111
multi-dimensional assessment
    framework 115

Office for Students 39, 45
one-size-fits-all 71, 72, 75
online delivery 10–1
open-ended assessment 105

Padlet 57, 65, 66
pedagogy 79, 81, 82, 84
peer critique 157, 162
peer to peer learning 53, 54, 59, 61, 62
Pencast 56, 57, 58
persist/persistence/persisting 102, 103,
    104, 107, 111, 113, 114, 115
personal agency 155, 159, 161, 163
personal characteristics 154, 155, 156, 157,
    159, 163
personal development 114
personal feelings 162
personal growth 102
personal skill 152
personality and interaction 170–1
plurality 155, 156, 157, 158, 159, 160, 161,
    162, 165
post-University transition 168–9
practical synthesis 160
practice 71, 73–6, 78, 82, 84
praxis 41, 46
problem-posing 110, 112
processing thoughts 153, 154, 157, 160,
    162, 163, 164
producing a valued entity 153, 154, 157
professional artistry 41
professional identity 11–2

reasonable risks 102, 103, 107, 111, 114
reflective practice 35, 41
research 71, 74, 77–8, 81–2
responsible risk-taking 99, 107, 112, 113
risk of failure 164

scholarship 79, 81, 84
science based (subject domain) 157
self-assessment 102
self-efficacy 98, 104, 113, 114, 117, 119

sexuality 74, 77, 81, 82
social science based (subject domain)
 157
standardized assessment 98, 114
standardized learning 115
student engagement 36, 37, 44
Student Relationship Engagement System
 60, 62, 63, 66
students-as-producers 37
surrounding factors 154
synthesising 154, 155, 160, 161

technology 72, 79
technology-enhanced learning (TEL) 51,
 52, 62, 67
thematic analysis 153

thinking about thinking 99, 102, 103, 111,
 112, 113
thinking interdependently 99, 102, 107,
 112, 113
transcend 161
tripartite perceptions 153
Triple P Learning Framework 43
tutorials 74, 78, 79

understanding the subject 154, 157

VariAbility 71

wellbeing 138–48
wonder and awe 106
wonderment 99, 112

9 781350 331488